Ranganathan Series in Library Science, 6

Madras Library Association Publication Series, 25

LIBRARY MANUAL

Library Manual

For School, College and Public Libraries

(With Revised Examples of Subject Classification)

S.R. Ranganathan

Published By:

Ess Ess Publications

For

Sarada Ranganathan Endowment for
Library Science
Bangalore

Published by:
ESS ESS PUBLICATIONS
4837/24, Ansari Road,
Darya Ganj,
New Delhi-110 002.
Tel.: 23260807, 41563444
Fax: 41563334
E-mail: info@essessreference.com
www.essessreference.com

For:
SARADA RANGANATHAN ENDOWMENT FOR LIBRARY SCIENCE
702, 'Upstairs', 42nd Cross, III Block,
Rajajinagar,
Bangalore-560 010.
Tel. : 080-23305109
E-mail: srels@dataone.in

Rs.825/-

First Published - 2008

ISBN: 81-7000-521-3 (10 Digit)
978-81-7000-521-6 (13 Digit)

Printed at Salasar Imaging Systems

PRINTED IN INDIA

CONTENTS

Part 4

Circulation Work

Part 5

Work behind the Screen

Part 6

Librachine

Part 7

Classification

Part 8

Cataloguing

The Five Laws of Library Science

1 Books are for use
2 Every reader his book
3 Every book its reader
4 Save the time of the reader
5 Library is a growing organization

ग्रन्थालयी सदासेवी पन्चसूत्रीपरायणः ।
ग्रन्था अध्येतुमेते च सर्वेभ्यः स्वंस्वमाप्नुयुः ॥
अध्येतुः समयं शेषेदालयो नित्यमेव च ।
वर्धिष्णुरेष त्रिन्मूर्तिः पन्चसूत्री सदा जयेत् ॥

Rendered into Sanskrit by the late Mahamahopadhyaya, Prof S Kuppuswami Sastriar.

CHAPTER 0

INTRODUCTION

01 New Life

India's community has been in a state of cultural exhaustion and sleep during the last few centuries. It began to recover and wake up about the turn of the present century. The process of waking up after long sleep took nearly half a century. During this period of morning slumber, Mahatma Gandhi appeared. He entered into full wakeful state earlier than the others. He harnessed the impulsive force of the patriotic emotions of the people. It stirred up more people. Ultimately, he brought India up to the eventful date of 15 August 1947. At its midnight, the British period ended and the Gandhian period began. The Indian community burst into the fullness of the new life, lingering long to come over it. The development of the library system of India has been steadily keeping steps with this new life.

02 University Library

During the last quarter century of the British period, the top-strata among the intellectuals got quickened into life. The universities were ashamed to continue as mere examining bodies. They wished to begin teaching and research. Formation of university libraries was the result. The first to reach maturity in finance, man-power, and service was the Madras University Library. The remaining three dozen university libraries are also fast entering the period of adolescence. The University Grants Commission has now begun to take care of their development. Its Chairman, Dr C D Deshmukh, is a bold free thinker. He is also a man of action. He appointed a Library Committee. He invited me to be its Chairman. Its recommendations are calculated to take the university and college libraries to the stage of maturity. Hereafter, it is up to the library profession to develop them to their fullness. Even here, Dr Deshmukh asked me to conduct a seminar on "From publisher to reader: Work flow in university and college libraries" [1]* to enable the university and college librarians to streamline their work.

* Figures in brackets refer to the Bibliography (p 397).

03 Madras Library Association

Within a few years of the organization of the Madras University Library, the Madras Library Association was founded. The two bodies worked hand in hand from 1928 to 1944. During this period, the rapid development of the University Library gave the benefit of an observatory. In keeping with university tradition, library work was taken to the scientific level. The normative principles of library science were formulated. The Madras Library Association published the result in the form of the book *Five laws of library science*[2]. The progress of the work in the Madras University Library till 1942 and the opportunity provided after 1947 by Sir Maurice Gwyer in the University of Delhi to devote all the time to think out the deeper problems fo Library Science led to the successive writing out of advanced treatises covering every aspect of library science and service [3-26]. Most of these treatises were published by the Madras Library Association. A few were published by other bodies. They made a profound impact on library thought in India and abroad. Reciprocally this impact continues to stimulate further thinking.

04 Research Library

In due course, one result of the co-operative effort of the Madras University Library and the Madras Library Association and of international contact was the development of documentation technique. This technique is essential in a research library. And the service of research library is essential for the industrial development of the country. And rapid industrial development and the stepping up of productivity are concomitants of the march of new life in the country. Some of the results on documentation technique have been given in the periodicals *Annals* of Indian Library Association and its current successor *Annals of library science*, and in books published by different agencies [27-31]. The INSDOC (Indian National Scientific Documentation Centre), founded in 1951, has taken over the *Annals of library science*. Its documentation activities are stimulating further work on documentation technique. Indeed it functions as a laboratory for the purpose. Thus there is ample provision for research and production of advanced treatises in Library Science.

05 School Library

Another sphere of co-operation of the Madras University Library and the Madras Library Association was the school library. Their joint effort culminated in a few annual courses of vacation lectures to headmasters and teachers, and regular lectures for some years to the teachers under training in the Teachers' College at Saidapet, on "Library work in schools". The Association eventually brought out the *School and college libraries* — a book based on the experience thus gained. A briefer version of this book has been brought out by the Oxford University Press in its Teaching in India Series.

But no state in India has yet begun to think seriously of energizing the few existing school libraries, or of co-ordinating their service on a rational basis. The work in school libraries has therefore to depend largely on the enthusiasm of individual teachers and headmasters. The two books mentioned in this section are helpful handbooks to such enthusiastic non-professionals [32-3].

06 Public Library System

061 South India

Another major sphere of work of the Madras Library Association was the public library system of the country. For twenty years, the Association engaged itself without respite in preparing the awakening public to sense their library rights. In 1948, the Government of Madras gave a lead in the development of the public library system of the country, by placing the Madras Public Libraries Act on the statute book. For the help of the State and Local Library Authorities, a handbook was published in 1953[34]. In 1954, this example stimulated the neighbouring State of Hyderabad to put its own Public Libraries Act on the statute book. As a result of the reorganization of the states of India in 1956, a Library Act is now in force in the whole of the Madras State and Andhra Pradesh. It is also in force in some of the districts of Kerala, Mysore State, and Bombay State, transferred to them from Madras, Andhra Pradesh and Hyderabad. There is every chance of all the states in South India soon having a comprehensive statutory public library system.

062 Other States in India

Apart from South India, thought has been devoted to the development of a statutory public library system in the other constituent states also. A master plan for the whole of India was worked out in a series of books. Further, a specific library development plan was worked out for each of the six states, Central Provinces, Cochin, Travancore, Bombay, Uttar Pradesh, and Bengal. The plans for the first three of these states were not published. They should be lying in their respective archives. The thought on the development of public library system has been recorded in a succession of books [35-42].

07 Man-Power for Public Libraries

071 Establishment of Library Schools

Another early step taken co-operatively by the Madras University Library and the Madras Library Association was the establishment of a library school to train library man-power. It began as a School of the Association in 1929. But it was transferred to the care of the University in 1931. The School has now got an endowed chair — the Sarada Ranganathan Professorship in Library Science. Today, there are post-graduate library schools in ten universities. The University Grants Commission has been advised by its Library Committee to provide for full-timed teachers in not less than six of these schools. In addition, several of the State Library Associations are giving short Certificate Courses in Library Science, to train semi-professionals.

072 Inadequacy of the Schools

But there is shortage in competent teachers of library science. Due to this, there is much deterioration in the standard reached by the schools. Even so, the supply of even nominally trained library man-power is far short of demand. There is another complicating factor. The libraries in universities, colleges, government departments, industrial houses, and documentation and bibliographical centres give a better salary scale than public libraries. Therefore, the public library system fails to attract or retain man-power with a sound training. At the same time, public libraries are increasing in number in response to the increasing book-hunger of the people. In the Madras State, for example, the shortage of trained man-power is as high as 98 per cent. In absolute figures, the public library system of the Madras State is in need of an addition of at least 500 trained librarians. This gap cannot be filled for many years.

073 Estimated Demand

We may take the experience of the Madras State as typical. On that basis, the following estimate may be made about the trained man-power required for the full-blown library system of our country.

Nature of the Library	*Estimated Number*	*Man-Power Needed*	
		Profes-sionals	*Semi-profes-sionals*
National Central Library	1	100	900
State Central Library	15	700	7,000
District Central Library	500	5,000	50,000
Branch Library	5,000	5,000	20,000
Librachine	15,000	15,000	15,000
Total (in round figures)		30,000	90,000

The above estimate is based on the assumption that, by the time the library personality of India grows to its fullness, library man-power will be conserved by centralized pre-natal classification and cataloguing, by the arrival of books in libraries with the class numbers printed in them, and the receipt of the catalogue cards along with the books. An earlier estimate was made in 1950 [43].

074 Anticipated Inadequacy

As this estimate is being realized in respect of the number of libraries, the inadequacy of trained library man-power will increase for some years. This will be due to several causes. As usual, with any new service, there is the initial wrong notion among the public, the Local Bodies, and the Governments that anybody can enliven a library — particularly even a person of too low an ability to make a living elsewhere. Those with a slightly greater sensitiveness damn the cause by faintly conceding that sub-normals can be rigged up for library service by the ritual of a short course of two or three months. The result is the starting of library schools without competent teachers and without any respect for the standard to be reached. Even then the half-baked library man-power will continue to be too inadequate to meet the demand.

075 Transitory Arrangement

In spite of the delay in the creation of competent library man-power, the size of our public library system will keep on increasing. Money will be increasingly sunk in books and library buildings. An increasing number of people will resort to public libraries. Some transitory arrangement will have, therefore, to be made to transform the book-fund into real book service. This arrangement will depend on division of labour. The Central Library should have their full quota of professionals and semi-professionals. It should take full charge of book order work, periodicals work, accession work, catalogue and process work, accounts, budget, etc. In a branch library, the remaining routine work, such as circulation work, maintenance work, and other work behind the screen will have to be left to the care of semi-professionals. The essential service — viz reference service — will have to be left to the care of honorary workers drawn from among the retired persons and other leisured people in the respective localities. This should be done also in respect of the librachines.

076 Genesis

The standard of the treatises will be too severe for the semi-professionals. It is neither necessary nor proper to expect the honorary workers to get into the full swing of the treatises in the different branches of library science. There is therefore need for a simple single manual to help the semi-professionals and the honorary workers to do their respective items of work satisfactorily. This is the genesis of this book. The semi-professionals need help in respect of the routine of circulation work, maintenance work, and administrative work. The honorary workers need the help of correct orientation in respect of the social implications of library service, the laws of library science, public relation work, and reference service. Both classes of workers will need help in appreciating the significance and the use of class numbers and catalogue entries.

077 Aim of the Book

The aim of this book is to serve as such a manual for the semi-professionals and the honorary workers. It is a popular epitome of the essence of most of the treatises enumerated as the first 26 items in the bibliography at the end of this book. The parts 1, 2 and 6 — on the Laws of Library Science, Public Relation, and Rural Library Service — are also intended to give a helpful orientation to the members of the Local Library Authorities — that is, those in the top-management of the District Central Libraries and the Advisory Committees of the branch libraries and of the service stations of the librachines. The book as a whole can form the basis of the training to be given to semi-professionals. In fact, in the short period of training extending only to about six months, the best that can be done will be to train the candidates in effectively using this book in their day-to-day work in their libraries, with a proper sense of perspective. Thus, this manual has been designed to be a book for the work-table. The instruction in the course for the semi-professionals may also aim at appetizing the trainees to look up some of the basic treatises epitomized in this book. Perhaps, a perusal of the first three parts may induce the top-management and the honorary workers also to make a study of the *Five laws of library science* and the *Reference service*, of which parts 1, 2, 3 and 6 are a rapid summary. Parts 2 and 6 have been newly added and parts 1 and 3 have been expanded and completely re-written in this edition, to meet the needs of members of Library Authorities and other honorary workers.

078 Translation

This English edition may be used as the basis for the translation or free rendering into the important regional languages of India. Our languages are now without a proper terminology for most of the current ideas that have taken shape during the last one hundred years. And Library Science is practically a creation of this period. It will be helpful if all our languages use the same Sanskrit radicals in evolving technical terminology. The glossary at the end gives the Sanskrit terms evolved till now. If the translators could use terms of their own languages which are cognate to these Sanskrit terms, they will be helping the formation of a uniform library terminology for all the libraries in India. In this matter, the Canons of Terminology [44] may be borne in mind. Applications for translating this book may be made to the author through the Asia Publishing House.

08 Conspectus

Edition 1 of this book has been used widely. When it was written, the necessity to bring in honorary workers into branch libraries and travelling libraries had not been realized. Its focus was therefore on library technique. The chapters on orientation and reference service were brief. The experience gained in the working of the Library Act in South India has brought the need for making the book tri-focal, as pointed out in sections 06 and 07. Therefore equal emphasis is laid in this edition on the broad human side for orientation purposes and on the side of technique for administrative purposes.

Part 1 begins with a brief exposition of the Five Laws of Library Science. It has new chapters on open access and on the sociology of the wearing out and some loss of books in an open access library geared to an active promotion of the use of books by one and all. The attention of members of the Local Library Authorities and of the Department of Library Service is specially invited to this part.

Part 2 is on the need for and modes of public relation work in order to make every citizen go to the library and accept library service. It also explains the deep interest of the State in a democracy to make everybody accept library service. Besides being of orientation value to Local Library Authorities and the Department of Library Service, the chapters on the methods of public relation and library extension service are of practical value to librarians.

Part 3 is on the vital importance and the methods of reference service. It also describes the joy of reference service and recommends to the retired leisured people of each locality the helping of readers in the local public library and thus at once find joyful occupation for their leisure and help the public to make a purposeful use of the public library.

Parts 4 and 5 are respectively on the library routine of circulation work and of the administrative work behind the screen involved in selecting, buying, accessioning, processing, maintaining the library accounts, and the looking after of the buildings and the stores.

Part 6 is on the extension of library service to the rural areas. It brings out the futility of developing small independent libraries. It recommends the formation of a District Central Library for the towns, villages and hamlets. It discusses the first and the ultimate phases of the transport of books to and from service points and the routine connected with them. Finally, it shows the harm being done by the merging of city library service and rural library service under the Madras Public Libraries Act.

Part 7 is on classification. It gives a brief schedule of class numbers by Colon Classification and Decimal Classification.

Part 8 is on cataloguing. It explains the structure and function of different kinds of catalogue entries. It also extracts a few essential rules from the Classified Catalogue Code. It gives 36 examples of catalogue entries.

Part 1

LAWS OF LIBRARY SCIENCE

CHAPTER 10

INTRODUCTION

101 Library as a Social Institution

A Library is a social institution. As such, it has to serve several purposes :

1 It should help the life-long self-education of one and all ;

2 It should furnish up-to-date facts and information on all subjects to one and all ;

3 It should distribute, in an unbiased and balanced way, all shades of recorded views and thought to one and all, as a help in the discharge of their political functions in respect of local, national, and international affairs ;

4 It should contribute to productivity-drive by informing top-managements of the latest trends in diverse enterprises, by ploughing back into the minds of researchers, designers, and technologists every piece of relevant new thought, promptly and pin-pointedly;

5 It should provide to one and all a harmless and elevating use of leisure ;

6 It should preserve the literary remains of humanity for posterity, as vehicles of culture and as source materials for antiquarian research ; and in general

7 It should work for continued social well-being, as the agency in charge of all socialised recorded thought.

Thus a library has educational, informational, political, economic, industrial, cultural, and antiquarian functions.

102 Division of Functions

The diversification of the functions of the library is a result of social pressure. Democracy makes the library serve one and all. It should serve not merely the aristocracy of birth, wealth, power, or intellect. On the other hand, it should serve every citizen — high or humble by birth, rich or poor, powerful or meek, each in the measure of his intelligence quotient and field of interest. There is a division of functions among libraries, in order to increase the total efficiency of the library system of a nation.

103 Special Library

Some libraries are organized to serve the needs of specialist readers of different kinds. Such a library is called a Special Library. In a special library, the readers are restricted in quality and number. The reading materials too are restricted in subject-coverage, standard, and number. The mode of service also is specialized in its nature. It is essentially a Service Library.

104 Storage Library

Function 6—preserving literary remains for posterity and for antiquarian research all through time—is no longer made the responsibility of every library in a country. This responsibility is given to one National Central Library in a country of small area. It may also be given to a few additional Regional Libraries in a country of larger area. In a federal State, each constituent state also maintains a State Central Library to look after a similar responsibility within the State. A library of this kind is called a Storage Library or a Dormitory Library. The term does not imply the absence of service-function. It merely emphasizes storage to be the distinctive function of such a library.

105 Public Library

A library is now-a-days expected to be organized in each locality to serve the general public. Every locality with a population of between 5,000 and 35,000 is given a stationary library. It has a building of its own. It is usually a small library. It has a permanent collection of books of its own. It has, in addition, books sent to it in circulation periodically from a reservoir central library. It has also a permanent staff of its own. A locality with such a small library of its own may be a town or a division of a city. Every locality with a population below 5,000 is served by a travelling library. I call it a Librachine. It carries an assorted collection of about 2,000 books taken out from a Central Library. It distributes them among the villages periodically. It also takes back the used books from the villages. This is really a small library on wheels. Any such small library or any reservoir District or City Central Library feeding it is denoted by the generic term Public Library. This term connotes that:

1 It serves the general public of its locality ;
2 It is financed with public funds ;
3 It gives free service ; and
4 It is essentially a Service Library.

106 Mortal Books and Immortal Works

From the point of view of a service library, every book is a mortal. Its physical body will perish by use, or by mere efflux of time and ageing even when locked up against use. This does not mean that the work embodied in a book is necessarily a mortal. The work may be immortal. Examples are the Vedas, the Talmud, the Bible, the Koran, the Gita , the poems, the dramas, and the stories handed down through ages, and the seminal books in any subject. Such immortal works get embodied repeatedly in new editions, translations, and versions. It is called a Classic. Each particular embodiment of a classic is mortal. But the work contained in it transmigrates from one body to another. It is like the immortal soul in a mortal body.

107 Power Station

A service library does not worry itself too much by the harm done to a book, by the wear and tear of use. It can stop worrying itself about this. Because a sound copy of each book will be found in the storage library of the country or the constituent state. This division of function between Service Libraries and Storage Libraries is a major contribution of the Modern Theory of Library Organization. The management of a Public Library can therefore concentrate totally on service of books. The management should look upon a book as a dry cell, containing thought-energy transformed into a portable material. It should regard itself as in charge of a power-station with a battery of such dry cells. Its duty should be to help the re-transformation of books into thought. This thought may be merely absorbed by many for their own immediate benefit. It may also lead to the creation of new thought by some, for the use of humanity at large. Library work is the sum-total of all the work needed to effect such a re-transformation.

108 Five Fundamental Laws

A wide and intensive observation of such a re-transformation in

Europe in 1924-25 led to the formulation of the normative principles of library work. These principles were formulated in 1928 as the Five Laws of Library Science. After exposition before several audiences, they were published in a book in 1931 [44]. Here are the Five Laws:

1 Books are for use.
2 Every reader his book.
3 Every book its reader.
4 Save the time of the reader.
5 Library is a growing organism.

My revered friend, the late Mahamahopadhyaya Prof S Kuppuswami Sastriar, clothed these five laws in Sanskrit verse. Here is its latest version:

कोशवान् हि सदाचार्यः पञ्च-सूत्री-परायणः ।
पुस्तानि पठितुं तानि सर्वेभ्यः स्वं स्वं आप्नुयुः ॥
पठन्तं समयं तस्य शेषेत् कोशः सदापि च ।
वर्धमानः स चिन्मूर्तिः पञ्चसूत्री विदन्तु इमाम् ॥

CHAPTER 11

FIRST LAW

111 Enunciation

Books are for use. They are to be used for their thought-content. A library authority should countenance no factor likely to obstruct or minimize the use of books. It should interpret all codes and regulations in a liberal spirit so as to maximize the use of books. It should nip in the bud even the slightest inroad of the spirit of bureaucracy into any affair connected with the use of the library. It should always bear in mind that the library socializes the use of books. A library is made big not by the number of its books, but by its use [46]. A few books kept continuously in active use form a bigger library than miles of books kept largely locked in the cupboards of a monumental building. Here follow some of the implications of the First Law.

112 Library Building

The exterior of a library building should be inviting. It should have a glass-front all along the road faced by it, so as to disclose to the passers-by the busy readers using its collections in full freedom. The inside colour-scheme should be soothing and subdued. The vacant wall-spaces should be treated with significant murals. The building should be functional. The circulation counter, the reading room, the stack-room, the administrative room, and the staff-room should be well-articulated. There should be an open-air reading room for the cooler hours of the day. There should also be space for lectures, seminars, reading circles, and every other form of extension service. Above all, the building should be located in an easily and readily accessible part of the locality.

113 Fittings and Furniture

The book-racks should be short enough for the top-most shelf to be reached standing on the floor. The tables in the reading rooms should be smart. The chairs should be comfortable. It should be possible for all the readers to be so seated as not to face the traffic within the library. The colour-scheme of the fittings and furniture should harmonize with that of the walls.

114 Gangways

The gangways between rows of book-stacks should be generous. So also should be the gangways between reading tables.

115 Lighting

The colour-scheme should smoothen the glare of the natural light. The artificial light for the darker hours should be least tiring to the eyes.

116 Ventilation

The reading room and the stack-room should have the benefit of natural ventilation. The incidence of solar heat should be eliminated. The well-known indigenous method of using wet *kuss kuss* for cooling should be used ungrudgingly during the hot season.

117 Library Staff

An earnest appeal of the First Law to the library authorities is in regard to the library staff. Geniality, scholarship, and professional competence should be the first consideration in the recruitment of the staff. The salary scale should be able to attract and retain men and women endowed with personality and initiative. These should be given full responsibility to promote the use of books. There should be no soul-killing interference, either in a formal or an informal way. In their turn, the staff should remember that library service is social service. Their joy should be derived from the joy blossoming on the faces of readers served to their satisfaction.

118 Book Selection

A public library should not waste its money on book curios or on costly books in infrequent demand. The responsibility to acquire them should be left to the National and the State Central Libraries. Again, the appearance of the books should invite people to pick them up. The size, the shape, and the weight should make a book easy to handle. The style of printing should make it easy to read. The First Law would urge the library profession to act collectively for the promotion of the production of beautiful books on all subjects and in all styles suited to the different intellectual strata. This message of the First Law is fully expounded elsewhere [47]. The books should be kept clean and in good repair, consistent with wide use. Worn-out and out-of-date books should be weeded out without hesitation. In fact, the First Law will not allow in a service library any ugly and repulsive book. Nor will it care for a handsome book to be kept merely for show. It will allow only books to be continuously read, enjoyed, understood, and acted upon by readers.

CHAPTER 12

SECOND LAW

121 Enunciation

Books for all. Every reader his book. These two alternative forms of the Second Law emphasize in greater detail the implications of the First Law, as viewed from the side of readers. They expect the public library to take into consideration every kind of reader, whatever the age, the sex, the vocation, the capacity for self-help, and the willingness to read.

122 Book Selection: Subject-Scatter

The Second Law indicates the subjects to be covered in book selection. It expects the library to inform itself of the subject-interests of its readers. It should select books on all the major occupations of its actual and potential readers. These are likely to cover many arts and crafts, the basic sciences, and the commonly recognized professional or applied fields. The curiosity and the interest of the people of a locality may be widely varied. They are likely to call for biographies and travel-books of all kinds. A public library should also go beyond books of current information. It should select light literature for relaxation *cum* elevation. A public library should also provide profound books to satisfy the inner urge towards whatsoever is elevated, enlightening, and sublime. These will be books in Fine Arts, Literature, Religion, and Philosophy. The subject-scatter of book-selection should thus be closely correlated to the needs of all the readers of the locality in all their moods.

123 Book-Selection: Style-Scatter

According to the Second Law, book selection should be closely correlated, with equal thoroughness, to the language and style of exposition suited to all the intellectual strata. It should care as much for the needs of the neo-literates at the one extreme, as to the seasoned scholars at the other. The whole spectrum between these two extreme standards should be covered, in the measure of its reflection in the reading capacity of the people of the locality.

124 Book-Selection: Physical Make-up

In book-selection, attention should be paid to the physical make-up necessary for the comfort of old people at the one extreme down to that of children at the other. The old and the children may require large types, large paper, and ample margin and space between lines. The neo-literates need special attention. We are not now having a sufficient variety of books to suit them. A detailed study of the standard of book-production needed for neo-literates will be found in a book forming the proceedings of a Seminar on the subject conducted by the Indian Adult Education Association at Okla in 1953 [48].

125 Inter-Library Loan

Even the richest of libraries cannot find finance to buy books in occasional demand. It is still more so with a small public library. The Second Law, therefore, recommends all the libraries of a land forming a single system, with inter-library loan facilities. The entire book-resources of a country should be regarded as a single pool. A book lying idle on the shelf of any library should be made available to any reader whatever be his own service-library.

126 Viable Unit

Even a more pressing corollary from the Second Law concerns the viability of a library area. The Second Law is against every locality having an independent library. A city with a population of not less than 100,000 may be tolerably viable. All the smaller localities in a district should be taken together to form a single library-unit. Each district should have a District Central Library. This Library should purchase the books for the whole district. It should also keep the books circulated continuously among the hamlets, the villages, and the towns in its area.

127 Catalogue: Analytical Entries

Another indication of the Second Law concerns the catalogue. Many books are of a composite nature. Neither the title nor the main entry of a composite book may disclose fully all its contents. The hidden contents should be brought out by cross-reference entries — that is, subject-analytical entries — in the library catalogue. Otherwise, every reader may not get his material, in spite of its lying inside the pages of some of the books standing on the shelves of the library.

128 Open Access

Above all, the Second Law pleads for Open Access. In open access, books are kept on open shelves; and any reader can handle them directly. A reader browsing amidst books will find his books much better than one working only through a catalogue. Many a reader is unable to enunciate his requirements in exact terms. We are often unable to state precisely the clothing, the shoes, or the furniture we want. But placed amidst an assortment of clothes, shoes, and furniture, of every variety, we are able to decide what we want. So it is in the choice of books for study. Open access is common in shops and restaurants. Enterprising book-shops practise it. Libraries too should practise open access without hesitation. For, it will increase the chance for every reader to get his book.

CHAPTER 13

THIRD LAW

131 Enunciation

Every book its reader. This emphasizes in greater detail the implications of the First Law as viewed from the side of the book. It takes the First Law to mean that "the destiny of the book is reader's hands". According to it, the book pleads with the librarian as follows: "I am inert. Of my own accord, I am unable to leap into my reader's hands. My voice is not audible to him. I depend on you for my being taken to my reader or my reader to be taken to me." Every book left for long on the shelf pining away for its reader, covered with dust, and untouched by readers, would leave a curse on the librarian. It will leave a curse on the library authority too, if it does not provide librarians, adequate in quality and sufficient in number, to find readers for every book.

132 Book Selection

The Third Law would give some negative counsel on book selection. "Do not select books in languages not commonly read in the locality. Do not select books of a standard not suited to the majority of the readers in the locality. Do not select books on subject-fields — on the vocations, technologies, and sciences — with few practitioners in the locality. Depend on inter-library loan for books in occasional demand."

133 Classified Arrangement

The Third Law pleads for the arrangement of books in a classified sequence based on their contents. Such a classified arrangement will present subjects in a filiatory sequence. The subject-interests of a reader follow such a filiatory sequence. Therefore, the attention of a reader coming for books on a particular subject will be attracted, in this arrangement, to the books in the neighbouring subjects also. Thus the chance for these neighbouring books getting their readers will increase.

134 Re-Arrangement

"Novelty" in shelf-arrangement is another means, not infrequently adopted, to attract the attention of the visitors to books that need help in finding their readers. An occasional redistribution of the contents of shelves may help in establishing fresh contacts between men and books.

135 Show-Case

Another usual device employed in this connection is the location of small attractive show-cases with books in strategic positions of the reading-room and the stack-room, labelled with catching legends like "Books Worth Looking Into", "Books of the Hour", "Interesting Books Recently Unearthed", "Long-Forgotten But Useful Books" and so on. Even a label like "Do Not Read These Books" may prove effective!

136 Accessibility

Another important factor in shelf-arrangement which has a decided effect on the chance of a book to get its reader is its easy accessibility or otherwise. Books within the comfortable reach of a reader of average height are much better used. I have experimented with an assorted set of books by placing them for a few weeks on the top-most shelf, which is 6½ feet from the ground, on the bottom-most shelf, which is only 6 inches from the ground, and on the intermediate shelves. The books found readers more frequently while on the intermediate shelves than while on the others. Shelves at a height greater than 6½ feet are a standing defiance of the Third Law. The Third Law would insist that the top-most shelf of a book-rack should be within the easy reach of a man of average height standing on the floor. Similarly, shelves broader than what is necessary to hold one row of books are great sources of temptation for the library staff to arrange two rows on them — one behind the other; with the result, the books of the hind row are denied the chance to get their readers. Moral: Do not have more than one row of books on a shelf.

137 Catalogue: Subject-Analyticals

Subject-analyticals in the catalogue form a favourite of the Third Law. For such entries are of help in finding readers for a book. For example, a subject-analytical for the excellent essay entitled *Pragmatism of William James* got a stream of readers to the composite book *Shelbourne essays* of More. A cross-reference card with the heading "Coffee" inviting attention to pages 615 to 660 of the fifth volume of the *Complete works* of Rumford made all the difference in the chance for that book getting its readers. The cross-reference entry brought out the enticing title *Of the excellent qualities of coffee and the art of making it in the highest perfection.* Thereafter, instead of being an inert victim to the ravages of silverfish, the volume began its unending series of triumphant marches to the house of one reader after another.

138 **Open Access**

Open access is another favourite of the Third Law. Some years ago, I watched a library change from "Closed" to "Open Access". I could then see the powerful service of the open access system to the Third Law. It is a matter of common experience that the change increases manifold the number of volumes drawn for use. More important than that is the frequency with which readers "make discoveries." Not a day passes without some reader exclaiming with an agreeable surprise, "I didn't know that you had this book!"

CHAPTER 14

FOURTH LAW

141 Enunciation

Save the time of the reader. Save the tempo of the reader. The second of the above is a corollary from the first. Physical hunger for food is compelling. Physical thirst for water is inexorable. Neither will extinguish itself by its not being attended to. Each will persist through time till satisfied. But mental hunger for books is not compelling in the case of most people. Mental thirst for information is not inexorable in the case of most people. Both of them are fleeting in their nature. They both die out, unless satisfied immediately on their taking shape. No time-lag should come between demand and supply. The tempo for reading is often momentary. It should be harnessed at the very moment. That is the message of the Fourth Law.

1411 Subjective *vs* Objective Time

The Fourth Law distinguishes between subjective time and objective time. When we wait at the airport expecting a dear one from a far-off land, every minute looks like an hour to us. When we are losing ourselves in enjoying something, even an hour runs out as quickly as a minute. If time is hanging on us, each second strikes our consciousness; we become impatient, sour at heart, and restless. If we are kept busily absorbed in some work or thought, time races; but we are composed; we are even surprised that a long period slips out without our realizing it. This difference is due to the difference between objective and subjective time. The Fourth Law asks us to save objective time as well as subjective time.

142 Classified Arrangement

Classified arrangement of books in the stack-room saves the objective time of the reader. In such an arrangement, a reader finds all his books arranged together consecutively. Therefore, he need not examine all the shelves to find his requirements. Suppose the books are arranged alphabetically. Let us take Physics to be the subject of interest to the reader. Alphabetically, the authors of the book in Physics may range from Abraham to Yogeshwar. To examine the books in Physics, the reader will have to walk down all the gangways in the entire stack-room. With classified arrangement, he may have to walk down only one or two gangways. A similar thing happens also with the library catalogue. In a classified arrangement of entries, the reader will find all the cards in Physics within a single catalogue tray. In the alphabetical arrangement of entries, the reader will have to turn through all the cards in all the trays of all the catalogue cabinets. Therefore, the Fourth Law calls for classified arrangement of the books in the stack-room and of the cards in the catalogue cabinets.

143 Catalogue

1431 Subject-Analyticals

Classified arrangement is not, by itself, sufficient to save objective time. This is due to books being composite. A book may have within its covers some pages devoted to one subject and some other pages devoted to another subject. But the book itself can be put only in one place, as if it were devoted to one and only one subject. Therefore, to get all his reading materials, a reader is obliged to go beyond the books classified as belonging to his subject of pursuit. He is obliged to examine many, many other books, placed in subjects other than his own in order to find out if any pages of them are on his subject of pursuit. This examination of the many, many other books calls for much time. This time can be saved by the catalogue putting in an analytical entry for every book, partially dealing with subjects other than its main one, under each one of those other subjects. This is now commonly done in every library catalogue.

1432 Bipartite Catalogue

The Fourth Law is aware of the diverse approaches of readers to books. Some make a subject approach. Others make an author approach, title approach, collaborator approach, or series approach. The time of the reader should be saved whatever be his approach. The Fourth Law recommends a bipartite catalogue for this purpose. In one part, the entries are all arranged in one alphabetical sequence, by the name of each subject, author, title (if equivalent to a proper noun), collaborator, and series. It is the Alphabetical Part. In the other part, the entries are arranged in the filiatory sequence of their subjects. To mechanize this filiatory sequence, each subject is represented by an ordinal number. It is its Class Number. This part is the Classified Part of the catalogue.

1433 Use of the Alphabetical Part

If the reader's quest is for a particular book by a particular author or in a particular series, the Alphabetical Part is sufficient by itself to satisfy his want. But if it is interest in a subject by itself that takes him to the Library, his wants will be better served by a catalogue, spreading before him a full, connected, panorama of all the materials on his specific subject, all its sub-divisions, and all broader subjects of which it is itself a sub-division. Moreover, few readers are able to name their specific subjects exactly. It is a broader subject that is usually thought of or mentioned or looked up in the catalogue. However wide of the mark the subject mentioned by the reader is, the Class Index Entry in the Alphabetical Part directs him to look up the entries in the Classified Part under the Class Number representing it.

1434 Use of the Classified Part

The function of the class number is exhausted as soon as the reader enters the region indicated by it. Thereafter, the class number does not occupy his thought or distract him. His mind is fully occupied with the helpful filiatory way in which the names of his books follow one after another. He is delighted. This delight is at bottom due to the satisfaction of unexpressed wants and to the getting of something which he did not know how to ask for. This represents a deeper function to be performed by the library catalogue. It is the duty of the library to meet such unexpressed wants, particularly because an ordinary reader does not know how to give shape to them and state them.

144 Reference Service

A good classified arrangement and a good bipartite catalogue with subject-analyticals are not by themselves sufficient to save the time of the reader. In addition to these, the library authorities should also provide for adequate personal help to readers. Such personal help is called Reference Service. A reference librarian should, with a cheerful face, welcome and receive every visitor to the library. He should, in a friendly and pleasant way, help each visitor to enunciate his reading requirements — the exact topic on which he seeks information, or the knowledge he wants, or the particular emotional appeal needed to soothe him. He should thereafter put him alongside the books and the periodicals which can meet his requirements. He should indeed work with the reader in his hunt for information, knowledge, or entertainment.

145 Standardization

The Fourth Law contains another implication. We have seen so far that in order to save the time of the reader, the library staff should find time to attend to each reader individually. This implies no doubt, more staff than is easily seen to be necessary by library authorities. It also implies saving the time of the staff itself in getting through the routine work involved in the administration of the library. To save the time of routine, full advantage must be taken of standardization and simplification of materials, specifications, and procedures. This is briefly indicated in Part 6. Full details can be found in *Library administration* [49]. The card system of records and the system of vertical filing may well be claimed as contributions of the library profession to the other professions and trades. These systems were evolved under the pressure of the Fourth Law. It may be stated here that standardization does not imply freezing originality. It does not prevent change for improvement. It does not curb creative re-thinking about the standards.

146 Centralization

Centralization of impersonal processes, such as classification and cataloguing, is another suggestion of the Fourth Law to release more of the staff of a library for the human and personal purpose of Reference Service. It pleads: What is it that is gained by copies of the self-same book being classified and catalogued by a thousand different persons in a thousand different libraries in the land? Will not the same result of classification and cataloguing be achieved with greater uniformity and consistency if each book is classified at the State or the National Central Library, as the case may be, and its catalogue cards printed by the same central body and supplied to each of the thousand libraries? For every two thousand books added to a library in a year, such a centralization will release one member of the library staff; and the library can get a better return for his time by turning him on to reference service. It has been shown that 79 per cent of the staff now doing the work of classification and cataloguing can be diverted to reference service [50].

1461 Pre-Natal Classification and Cataloguing

An interval of about two weeks now lapses between the receipt of a book and its release for readers. This time is taken up in classifying and cataloguing it. This also is a violation of the Fourth Law. To eliminate this time-lag, each book can be classified and catalogued by the State or the National Central Library even at proof-stage. The book will then have its Call Number printed in it. The catalogue cards can also be printed and released simultaneously with the release of the book. In my lecture at the Whitall Pavilion of the Library of Congress in Washington in August 1948, I called this Pre-Natal Classification and Cataloguing. This suggestion is now being approximated to by the British National Bibliography. In the USA also, a movement to implement this has been set up since 1958 by the Foundation called Council on Library Resources.

1462 India's Opportunity

India should take advantage of her starting library service virtually from scratch in this late hour, when rational planning with the nation as the unit has come into vogue. It should straightway commence with centralized classification and cataloguing. Let not her librarians be confused by the misgivings of countries which have drifted into their present library position, which, advanced though it be in many respects, has to allow many wasteful practices to continue, as they have entrenched themselves behind prestige. Mr. Edward J. Carter, the then Head of the Libraries Section of Unesco, for example, endorsed my view with these words in 1948: "I am impressed by your remark that it is too late now for India to develop its library services in a casual and *laissez faire* manner — you must jump several steps and by so doing, it is quite possible that you will jump ahead of countries whose development has been gradual."

147 Issue Method

The Two-Ticket method of issue virtually eliminates wastage of objective time. It is described in Chapters 42 and 43. In this method, the reader does not spend any time in writing out an application slip for the book to be borrowed. Nor has the circulation librarian to write anything. Issue work can be done with comfort at the rate of 10 books per minute.

148 Open Access

Open Access alone can save the subjective time of the reader. However much the issue method eliminates wastage of objective time, it can do little to the reader's sense of loss of time in waiting for a book to be brought out by a member of the staff. The following anecdote illustrates it. In 1925, I was studying the working of the Mitchel Library — the big Central Library of the City of Glasgow. It was found that the application slip for every book was stamped with a time-piece with its dial and the minute and hour hands in rubber. The dial had to be inked and the time-piece had to be banged with force on every application slip. One can imagine how short-lived the time-piece would have been and how much money that library should have been spending on the frequent replacing of this special make of time-piece. The librarian was asked why they were indulging in this expensive luxury. The following scene which was witnessed some time later demonstrated that it was not a luxury. It was a necessity in order to help the psychological tempo of the reader by making him see the illusion which his subjective sense of time had produced in him. He asserted that he had "waited for ages" to get his book; he was fretting and fuming; he was swearing that he would not any more come to that library as it was wasting his time. The librarian approached him and asked gently how long he had waited. He said that he had waited at least for a quarter of an hour. The book arrived. The reader was asked to note the time of his receiving the book and he was told that he had waited only for five minutes. "How do you know ?" he asked, and added "I know I have waited for more than fifteen minutes." He was then shown the rubber stamp of the face of the time-piece on his application slip. This convinced him that he was under an illusion caused by waiting in idleness and he promised to continue to be a patron of the library.

CHAPTER 15

FIFTH LAW

151 Enunciation

A Library is a growing organism. This is the Fifth Law. This is different in nature from the other four laws. These may sometimes lead to over-enthusiasm and excesses. The Fifth Law acts as a corrective to it. The other laws view as a whole the trinity in a library — the reader, the book, and the staff. But the Fifth Law concerns itself with the growth of each of them severally. Of course, it also considers the repercussions of the growth of any one upon that of any other.

152 Organic Growth

Before examining these, we must recognize at the outset the nature of organic growth. Organic growth can be one of two kinds — growth as of the body of the child and growth as of the body of an adult.

1521 Adult Growth: Service Library

The body of a child grows steadily in size and weight. So also, a newly started library grows steadily in the number of its readers, books, and staff. But, there is an upper limit to the possible size and weight of a child. This upper limit is reached when adulthood is reached. Thereafter, growth consists only of a continuous replacement of cells and tissues. So it is with a Service Library. After some time, there can be no increase in the number of readers or books or staff of a Service Library. Thereafter, its growth consists only of a new generation of readers replacing the old continuously, of a new set of books replacing the old continuously, and of a new staff replacing the old continuously.

1522 Child-Growth: Storage Library

On the other hand, a Storage Library continues to have child-growth for ever. It has such a growth in respect of books and of staff. That is, there can be no limit to the size of its book-collection or of its staff. It may attain the stage of adult-growth only in respect of readers. In the past, it was the practice to allow a Service Library to grow without limit in respect of books — without weeding out worn-out and out-moded books. This practice has now been given up.

1523 Toddler Stage

In India today, hardly any service library has reached the stage of adulthood. Most of them are only in the toddler stage. Many are yet to be born. Most of the present generation will have, therefore, to spend their life-time only with service libraries with child-growth. Perhaps, they will reach the stage of adult-growth in about a generation or two. In the countries where the libraries developed during the last one century, this early feature of a service library contributed to failure in distinguishing consciously between the problem of service library and storage library. But we can learn from the experience of the others. Though our service libraries have to grow like a child for the time being, we can organize them with a full knowledge of the limit to their size.

153 Library Building

The building of a storage library — say a State Central Library or the National Central Library — should be capable of indefinite growth. The site chosen for it should be very large indeed. Its building — particularly the stack-room — will have to be extended in a number of successive phases. On the other hand, the building of a service library need not grow beyond a certain size. A branch library in a town, or in a division of a city, need not grow beyond the capacity to hold about 50,000 volumes, and to accommodate about 100 readers at a time. The site chosen for it can be a relatively small one. Perhaps, the building can be erected to its maximum size in not more than two or three phases. The building of a City or a District Central Library also can be erected to its maximum size in not more than three or four phases. The overall lay-out for a service library should be so designed as to admit of completion of the building in two to four phases.

154 Growth in Readers

Every service library of India today should expect a steady growth in the number of readers. For it takes more than one generation to make all the public of a locality come to the library and accept library service. Till all the public of the locality become library-goers, the service library cannot reach the adult stage of growth in respect of readers. This has been the experience of the West, which started public library service many years before us. Even in cities which have had compulsory education and a well-conducted library system for nearly 75 years, the percentage of the population which has begun to use public libraries has not yet reached 30. Assuming that 30 per cent of a community will always be unfit to use a library on account of age or other handicaps, it can be seen that 40 per cent of those that can use the library are still staying out. This shows that the libraries of those cities have not yet reached the adult-stage growth in respect of the number of readers. The situation is much worse in rural library systems.

155 Growth in Staff

The effect of the Fifth Law on the staff-requirement of a service library in the stage of pre-adult growth is seldom realized. It invariably leads to vexatious situations, if the staff has sufficient enthusiasm to make the library grow. The authorities seldom realize how quickly the sanctioned staff is outnumbered. They complain of frequent applications for increase of staff and turn them down. Even with the best of effort, the inadequate staff is unable to render even half the service which they announce and aspire to render. Publicity brings in more readers than can be served and more books than can be organized. The result is complaint and disappointment from all quarters and ridicule and underwriting by a handful of cynics whose voice drowns the voice of others. Most librarians feel frustrated. They begin to drift along at the risk of the library repelling readers. I have seen this phenomenon recur in library after library in the East and the West alike. Till recently, I had taken this to be as providential and inexorable as an earthquake. Of late, I am able to see some light. Some means can be found to avert this form of frustration of the growth of a young library and of the spirit of hard-working, enthusiastic, pioneering staff who put service before self-interest. The means I recommend is that library authorities should once for all agree to a mathematical formula for the staff of a library in terms of work-load. Once this formula is accepted, the alteration in the strength of the staff would become automatic and impersonal. There need not be recurring opportunity for the play of cynicism and vexation. The full staff-formula is given in the *Library administration* [51].

1551 Substance of the Staff-Formula

A statement of the staff-requirements for a public library is given below in simple terms. The strength of the staff for the different sections of a library may be determined on that basis.

1 *Book-section.* One person for every 6,000 volumes added in a year.

2 *Periodical-publication section.* 1 person for every 1,000 periodicals currently taken.

3 *Classification and cataloguing section.* 1 person for every 2,000 volumes added in a year.

4 *Maintenance section.* 1 person for every 2,000 volumes added in a year and 1 person for every 50,000 volumes in the library.

5 *Publicity section.* Minimum 1 artist.

6 *Administrative section.* Minimum 1 library accountant, 1 steno-typist, and 1 correspondence clerk.

7 *Reference section.* 1 person for every 50 readers using the library in a day of the year.

8 *Circulation section.* 1 person for every 1,500 hours for which one wicket-gate of the library has to be kept open in a year.

9 *Supervisory section.* 1 librarian and 1 deputy librarian.

1552 Branch Library

In a branch library, the full quota of staff is not necessary. It need not have a book section, classification and cataloguing section, and administrative section. The work of these sections will all be done by the Central Library. Thus, the only sections to be maintained are the maintenance section *cum* publicity section, the reference section, the circulation section, and the supervisory section. Even here, the smallness of the collection of the library and of the clientele may call for only one member in each of these four sections. The ideal is for the branch library to work two shifts on all the days of the year. In that case, the strength of the staff of the reference section, the circulation section, and the supervisory section should be multiplied by $2\frac{2}{8}$. Thus the total staff will have to be 9 instead of 4. The librarian and the reference librarians should be professionals. The circulation librarian and the maintenance librarian may be semi-professionals.

1553 Librachine

Each librachine — travelling library in the form of a motor-van or book-mobile as it is called — should have a librarian (professional) and a circulation librarian (a semi-professional). This staff will go out in the librachine five days in the week. They will work at the headquarters one day in the week, charging and discharging the books of the librachine. They will of course have the seventh day as their weekly holiday. In some places, one of these members of the staff drives the librachine. In other places, there is a separate driver. Probably we may have to go in for a separate driver — at least in the earlier years. The driver should engage himself on the sixth day at the headquarters in servicing the librachine and assisting the other staff in the charging and discharging work.

156 Classification

The universe of knowledge is evergrowing. From time to time, it puts forth new subjects. Books appear in these new subjects. With the formation of new subjects, the old subjects sometimes stand in need of re-evaluation in respect of their filiation. The Fifth Law asks us to remember this growth in the universe of knowledge. It therefore invites our attention to an important policy in regard to classification. It is necessary to adopt an established, published scheme of classification. Some library authorities fail to realize this. Some librarians too, with little experience, fail to realize this. The library improvises its own scheme. It is often designed in a rule-of-thumb manner; and it is found to break down in a short time. This is a common feature in some libraries today. The classification has thus to be started again. Another equally objectionable policy is adopting a published scheme either partially or in a modified way. This also leads to breakdown. "Our library is very small. We do not want any elaborate scheme. A simple numbering will do", is an argument which one often hears. The Fifth Law of Library Science protests against this. I should like to add that a good scheme of classification will give only simple numbers for the simple books found in a small public library. In fact no book can take a more elaborate number for itself than what its specific subject demands, simply because the scheme of classification in use has provision for elaborate numbers to individualize specific subjects of any degree of intension and with any number of facets.

157 Cataloguing

The Fifth Law has a similar warning about cataloguing. The cataloguing elements in the title-page of a book change with time. For example, symposium with a number of authors mentioned on the title-page has now become frequent; some symposia have only the name of an editor on the title-page. Nowadays, some books have to be entered together or linked up by entries as they are related to one another. To meet such new factors, a catalogue code should have already some potential capacity. It must take new rules without disturbing the existing rules. Therefore, failure to follow a rigid catalogue code leads to making the catalogue a hotch-potch. Here again people falsely argue: "My library is a simple one. I want only a simple set of cataloguing rules which can be understood by a cataloguer of average ability, though without training." Here again, as the library grows, who can say that it will not add books which bring cataloguing difficulties? The Fifth Law would insist that wisdom lies in adopting a published catalogue code in full without modification.

1571 Physical Form of the Catalogue

Books will be added to a library from time to time. Therefore, new catalogue entries will be added to the library catalogue from time to time. These entries will have to be interpolated among the already existing ones. The Fifth Law, therefore, asks us to choose the physical form of the catalogue with care. The chief possible physical forms are:

1 Hand-written card catalogue;
2 Typed card catalogue;
3 Hand-written bound book catalogue;
4 Printed catalogue in book-form.

1572 Card *vs* Bound-Book

In the bound-book form, it is not easy to interpolate new entries from time to time. Even if we leave space between one entry and another, this space is all soon choked up in many cases. Then we have to begin all over again. This is wasteful. Therefore, the Fifth Law recommends the card catalogue. Here each card has only one entry. Therefore, any number of entries can be interpolated at any point at any time.

1573 Printed Book-Form

It is a criminal waste to spend a part of the all-too-small library fund in printing the catalogue of a growing library. By the time the catalogue comes out of press, it will be out of date by several months. And the books of the greatest interest are the latest books. Because it is a printed book, no interpolation will be possible. Perhaps, one copy may be bound interleaved for additional entries. This can be of use only to the library — but not to every reader. Moreover, the cost of printing the catalogue cannot be justified by any means. When libraries are unable to provide sufficient staff to help readers by reference service, there is no point at all in turning the staff-time on to preparing the press-copy of the catalogue, reading proofs, maintaining the stock of the printed catalogue, and selling them. Hardly any reader will care to buy this out-of-date stuff. Therefore, no catalogue in printed book form is required in any growing service-library.

CHAPTER 16

OPEN ACCESS

161 Pressure of the Laws

Practically every Law of Library Science presses the case for Open Access. Open access increases the use of books according to the First Law. In the Madras University Library, open access was quietly introduced in 1925. By the end of 1926, the number of volumes used by readers increased ten-fold. For, few readers know their book-needs. In the physical presence of the books in the stack-room, they find out their book-needs with ease. This has been explained in section 128. The Third Law too pleads for open access. According to it, readers frequently "discover" books if allowed to walk amidst them in the stack-room. This has been explained in section 138. The Fourth Law stresses that the subjective loss of time is more painful than its objective loss. According to it, open access allows readers to adventure among books. In this adventure, they do not feel the flight of time. This makes them love going to the library again and again. The pressure of the Fifth Law grows out of considerations of economy. In open access, there is no need to have a special staff — book-lifters, as they are called in North India — to take out and bring the books needed by readers. For, the readers take them out themselves. Even the staff for replacing books can be reduced considerably. For, in the open access system, all books returned by readers are kept temporarily in special book-racks near the entrance. They are kept in them in a roughly classified sequence. These are the books much in demand for the time being. All readers, therefore, go to these book-racks first. As a result, most of the returned books are taken away by readers. They go back into circulation without the need to be replaced in their respective places in the stack-room. Nearly three-fourths of the returned books go back into circulation in this way. Thus, the staff-time for replacing is reduced by more than half.

162 Essence of Open Access

The essence of open access consists of:

1 Putting the books in open book-racks free from doors and locks;
2 Admitting the reader inside the stack-room;
3 Freedom for readers to walk amidst the books in the open shelves;
4 Browsing by readers without let or hindrance;
5 Guidance to readers by the reference librarian, both in anticipation and on demand; and
6 Right of readers to take away any book to the reading room for study or to circulation counter to get it issued for study at home.

163 Counter Set-up, Controlled Wicket-Gate

Open access has come to stay in all modern service libraries. Open access, no doubt, carries with it a certain risk of loss. The loss likely to occur in an open access library should be minimized by the very design of the building. All entrance and exit to and from the library are to be only through controlled wicket-gates. All the other doors and windows are to be made book-proof. They should be fitted with mesh-shutters. These are provided for in the modern specification for the library building. A possible design of a small library is shown in the opposite page.

164 Denial of Open Access

Even then, there will be some risk. To minimize the damage due to this risk, rare and costly books, pamphlets and under-size books, books with too many plates and other weakly built books, are not to be given open access. They are to be kept locked in closed shelves and issued only against formal application. This class of books is permanently denied open access. They are kept in "closed access". Each library will know from experience the other books to be so denied open access. Sex-books usually need this treatment. In certain periods — e g, the season for examination in the local schools and colleges — there will be a great run on certain books. During this period, these books may have to be denied open access, as a temporary measure.

165 Replacement of Books

There is another policy to be followed in open access system.

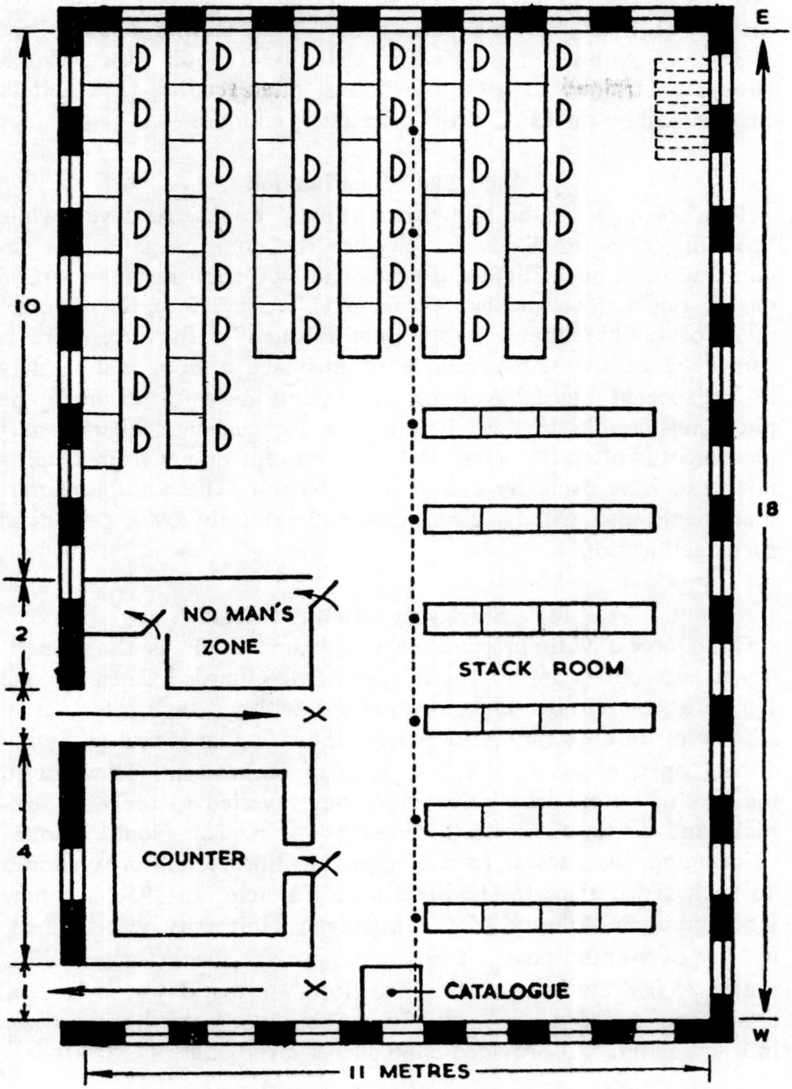

BRANCH LIBRARY

No reader should be allowed to replace in the stack-room the books taken out of the stack-room. Otherwise, books will be misplaced. A book misplaced is virtually a book lost. Readers should be trained to leave the books, after reading them, either on the reading tables or at the circulation counter.

166 Shelf-Rectification

Readers may not be allowed to replace books. And yet, while browsing, they are likely to misplace the books slightly. An accumulation of such slight misplacements will soon result in virtual chaos. For many a mickle makes a muckle. Therefore, the derangement of books should be set right frequently. Further, there is some chance for selfish people to misplace a book deliberately in unexpected places. A book in Physics may, for example, be put amidst books in Law. The motive for such a deliberate misplacement is often the selfish desire to prevent others from reading it and to have exclusive use of it for oneself. These criminal misplacements also will be discovered and set right by a periodical shelf-rectification.

167 Safe-Guarded Open Access

Open access with precautionary measures such as those mentioned in sections 163 to 166 is called Safe-Guarded Open Access. No library should introduce open access without such safe-guards. I know of libraries failing to provide the safe-guards and yet introducing open access in the first flush of enthusiasm. They found the loss of books prohibitive; and they reverted to locked book-racks and denial of access to the stack-room. This would amount to bringing open access to contempt. No library authority should do such a disservice to the open access system. In 1958, the new Undergraduate Library of the Michigan University was opened. In its over-enthusiasm, it did not provide wicket-gates. With nearly 15,000 students visiting the library every day, the loss of books was found to be prohibitive. This made the library wise. In a few months, it provided controlled wicket gates.

1671 Human Safe-Guard

The provision of ample reference service is the best human safe-guard. The kind personal service will wean away many, who are not confirmed criminals, from stealing, mutilating, or hiding books. Apart from this, the constant movement of the reference staff in the stack-room provides incidentally some vigilance service.

168 Kaleidoscope

To get the full benefit of the open access system for the Third Law, the sequence of the subjects in the stack-room should be changed at convenient intervals. The continuation of the same sequence of subjects for a long time is likely to tempt readers to go straight to their shelves, as if they were in blinkers. This will take away from the full benefit of open access. Change in the arrangement of books will evoke new curiosity even as the shaking of a kaleidoscope. The Third Law will bless the librarian for this.

CHAPTER 17

SOCIOLOGY OF LOSS OF BOOKS

171 Inevitable Loss

Even with the best of safe-guards, the most human treatment possible, and vigilance of a high order, there will be some loss. The authorities of the library should be prepared for it. In British libraries loss of one book for an issue of 1,000 books is now considered tolerable. About ten years ago, Mr W C Berwick Sayers of Croydon Public Libraries wrote to me as follows on this question:

> One book for an issue of a thousand volumes is probably a tolerable loss. (I have just discovered by a count of our shelves that in sixty years we have lost 37,000 volumes. In this time we have issued 56 million books.) I should say this was about as low a loss as one could expect in a well-managed library, and that in a library where there are students who very much covet certain books some moral questions may be involved. But I like your idea of the library as a social institution in which the risk of loss should be undertaken if thereby the "first law" of library science can be completely realised.

It must be remembered in this connection that during a large part of the 60 years which had been taken into account by Mr Sayers the library had been without open access. The fact is that loss due to miscreants will take place and does take place even in libraries which have no open access. The American Libraries are prepared to face even a higher percentage of loss.

172 Mutilation

Mutilation is sometimes mentioned as a ground against open access. Let us examine this. One could mutilate a book only in privacy. Privacy, every reader gets when he is reading the library book either in the reading room or in his home. Even within a reading room, it is impossible to have a close watch over every reader. Open access does not add much to the opportunity to mutilate books. It would be particularly so, if there is adequate reference staff who personally help each reader and incidentally deny privacy to the reader when he is in the stack-room. It is a matter of experience that mutilation in open access system is not of a higher order than in closed system. This means that denying open access is by no means a method of minimizing mutilation. The only method, to be adopted to minimize it, is to turn public opinion on the problem by contacting the clientele individually, and occasionally collectively. This method is no doubt slow in results. It requires persistence; but it is the only practicable method. At any rate mutilation cannot be used as an argument against open access.

173 Modern Library Policy

Modern Library Policy in respect of open access and the inevitable risk of loss is based on the following consideration:

1 Some loss is considered as a fair price for the enormous increase in the use of books, which open access invariably stimulates.

2 Even on socio-legal grounds, it is considered unjust to penalize the honest folk of the community and deny them the immense benefit of open access, simply because there are a few criminals in the community who could neither be detected nor prevented from doing mischief.

3 On purely sociological grounds, it is considered that the patrons of a library are only a random sample of the community. Until the community as a whole is absolutely purified, the community will have to face the consequences of its possessing criminal-minded members. It does so in all spheres of activities. It cannot hold a contrary attitude in the sphere of library service.

4 If we remember that safe-guarded open access system will not give open access to rare and valuable an irreplaceable books, loss will be most incident only in the case of ordinary books. These books are not eternal entities by any means. Hardly any of these books will be physically fit for use after being circulated about 500 times, which means for a few years. By that time many books may also be outmoded in their thought-content. If a book has served well at least for a few years, it becomes fit for withdrawal from circulation. The old Victorian notion, that every scrap of paper once accessioned in a library should be preserved permanently and for ever, is derived from a sense of property

in books which originated in the medieval age when a book often meant a unique manuscript of considerable money-value also. Today the printed books do not have that money value; they are not unique; in fact they grow out of date in their thought-content and are replaced by more up-to-date books from time to time. It is wrong to continue in these days of cheap, rapid and plentiful printing, attitudes that were formed in the centuries prior to the invention of printing.

5 Another ground on which open access is practised in Western libraries and in some of the libraries of India also, is based on the view that the library is a social institution. It is indeed a kind of social power-station where the minds of the members of the community are energized. The thought-energy which lies locked up in a potential state in books is transformed by libraries into a kinetic state, in which it can stimulate the mind of a reader into helpful activity. Thus a library represents transformation of energy. There is a well-known law in Thermodynamics that it is not possible to transform energy to an easily available state with cent per cent efficiency — i e, without some dissipation and loss. The library cannot escape this inexorable law of nature; if books are to do their job for the community, we must be prepared for loss due to wear and tear, and to some extent due also to uncivic propensity in some of our brethren. Viewed also in the larger context of ultimate national economy — economy due to the enormous saving in men-hours which open access will effect in the getting of light and relaxation by the people — the risk of loss involved in open access is negligible.

174 Write It Off

The cost of books inevitably lost in an open access library should be written off. If the proportion of loss to the annual issue exceeds 3 to 1,000, the matter should be investigated and the causes for the loss should be found out and removed. This does not mean a premium for unwariness on the part of the staff; nor does this imply that we want to free librarians from any responsibility whatever. If there is reason to suspect the *bona fides* of the staff they should certainly be sent out. If there is reasonable ground to believe that the librarian is likely to thieve, there is no objection to his being treated as a thief.

175 Anachronism

It is as much an anachronism today to charge the librarian for inevitable loss, as it is to deny open access and to make the reader wait on the other side of the barrier till the book could be found by an attendant and handed over to him. With or without open access, books are liable to be mutilated and lost. Even if left free from mutilation and loss, they soon cease to have value or use in a service library. It is therefore improper to follow the Victorian tradition of being penny-wise and pound-foolish in public administration. Sometimes, an unscrupulous person in the top-management of a library uses the inevitable loss of books in a library as a stick to beat the librarian against whom he has developed a grudge for some reason or other. In some libraries, such a top-management man even deliberately concocts false loss to wreak his vengeance on the librarian. These anti-social persons are a menace to society. Public opinion should grow strong enough to eliminate such persons from positions of power.

176 Effect of Predatories

A worse thing happens occasionally. A misfit and predatory in the profession seeks to propitiate his little ego and to advance himself by creating a scare among library authorities about open access. He advises them to have the books checked volume by volume on the basis of the vouchers dating from the foundation of the library! He even recommends the collation of each volume!! "A Daniel come to judgment," some library authorities feel. They ask the Daniel himself to do the work. Some library authorities have spent almost one year's budget on such a maddening pursuit. During the process, which takes a long time, the service to readers is neglected if not abandoned. This absurdity should be stopped.

177 Humanism and Open Access

Humanism would ask for the abandonment of all such inhuman policies and practices, in the light of the sociology of open access. According to humanism, open access blesseth him who gives and him who takes. The joy of a librarian reaches its maximum only in an open access library — only when the right reader and the right book choose each other in the *swayam-vara* set-up of open access. Apart from overall cultural, economical, political and educational value, open access conserves and enhances the self-respect and personal dignity of the reader. The self-confidence, and the self-help inherent in open access in a service library will have an invaluable human influence. It will chasten and stabilize many millions of people. It will release the blossoming of the personality of the reader. It will go a long way in adjusting him to the tremendous social changes characterizing society today. According to humanism, such is the benefit of open access falling to the share of the reader.

178 Time Factor

Experience all the world over shows the survival of the open access system, in spite of the Victorian outlook, predatories among the library staff, and anti-social power-mad element in the top-management. Indeed, the pioneer generation of librarians introducing open access should proceed doggedly with faith. It should be prepared to face the inevitable teething trouble and perhaps even to face some humiliating treatment. Time will heal all these. The appeal goes in equal measure to our library authorities. India is rather late in developing its public library service. India should learn from the experience of other countries. Her library authorities should heartily introduce open access.

CHAPTER 18

CONCLUSION

181 Overall Test

Every element in the organization of a library and every routine in the daily working of the library, should be watched with vigilance. It should be continuously re-designed to increase conformity to the Laws of Library Science. These Laws have certain ways of testing the loyalty of a library to them.

182 Location

They examine the location of the library. Is it located in the community centre of the locality ? Is it centrally situated ? Then, the Laws of Library Science are satisfied. Is the library located in the outskirts of the locality ? Then they protest. Thirty years ago, I was called by the Municipal Chairman of Dindukkal for consultation about its proposed library. The lawyers of the locality were dominant there. The law court was outside the town. Their recreation club also was there. The lawyers wished to have the public library also near the court outside the town. But the Laws of Library Science had to protest against this. For the proposed site was beyond the reach of the majority of the residents of the town.

183 Buildings and Furniture

The Laws of Library Science look at the library building, and its fittings and furniture. Is it an old, ugly, dingy building ? Do the chairs have hard wooden seats ? Are they rickety and half-broken ? Are the tables huge and dirty ? Then, the Laws protest. On the other hand, is the building smart and functional ? Are the walls painted with a soothing colour ? Is there an overall harmony of colour among the walls, the furniture, and the hangings ? Are there flower-pots ? Are the seats comfortable ? Is there ample table-space for each reader ? Is there ample light ? Is there good ventilation ? Is the floor sound-proof ? Then the Laws are satisfied.

184 Stack-Room

They walk into the stack-room. They feel fulfilled if the gangways are wide, if the books are in open shelves, if the top-most shelf of each book-rack is within reach, if there are good guides for every tier, gangway, bay, and shelf-plank, and if the readers walk alongside the shelves and handle them without any restriction.

185 Extension Activity

The Laws of Library Science walk into the library during hours of relaxation. They feel happy if reading circles are busy, if there are group-discussions, if there are cinema-shows, if there are public lectures and story-hours, and if there is activity everywhere as in a bee-hive. If books are taken out for service in prisons and hospitals, the Laws bless the library.

186 Library Hours

The Laws of Library Science ask about the library hours. Is the library closed on some days ? Is it kept open only for a few hours in a day ? Does the library authority direct it to be closed now and then in order to use the staff for other purposes or to use the reading room for a dinner party or to let it out for other purposes ? Then the Laws condemn the library. Is the library kept open all the 365 days in the year ? Is it kept open for at least 14 hours each day ? Then the Laws praise the library.

187 Reference Service

Are the readers left to themselves without any help ? Is there nobody in the staff to receive them and guide them ? Then, the Laws curse the library authorities. On the other hand, is every reader welcomed with a genial smile ? Is he taken to the catalogue and to the stack-room by a reference librarian ? Is he helped in the choice of his books ? Is he shown the latest books with enthusiasm ? Then the Laws bless the library authorities and the library staff alike.

188 Service to Country-side

The Laws of Library Science ride into the country-side. They visit villages and hamlets. They find books in active use among the rural folk — among the farmers, the shepherds, the masons, the weavers, the carpenters, and the blacksmiths. Occasionally, they find a libracnine plying along the highways and the village roads. They find a librachine pulled up in a village. The villagers throng into it. The travelling librarian gives them a talk, introduces books to them and shows them pictures. Men, women, and children walk home in joy with new books in their hands. The Laws of Library Science feel assured that the masses will pull up in no time and they will ever be in a high level of awareness and enlightenment.

Part 2

PUBLIC RELATION

CHAPTER 21

CREATING THE CLIMATE

211 Command of the Laws

The Laws of Library Science command the library authorities and the librarians to work actively to transform the library fund into actual book service to the people. The command of the First Law is unequivocal. It calls for the promotion of a wide use of books. The Fourth Law asks for the location of the library amidst the very people to be served by the library. Alternatively, it asks the library to take its books periodically to the houses of the people to be served by it. The Third Law too emphasizes use in another way. It wants the library to find a reader for every book. The chance to realize this increases with the increase in the number of people made to accept the service of the library.

212 Change in Outlook

The command of the Laws of Library Science amounts to a change in the outlook of libraries. It implies an alteration of their very character and function. The libraries should bring about an adequate understanding of this change among the people. For some the library is still medieval. To others it is principally a purveyor of entertaining novels. Surprise is continually expressed when the public discover the extent of its service and the catholicity of its interests. "I didn't know that you had Music books ?" "Are you open on holidays ? I didn't know that." "I didn't know that your catalogue is so analytical." Such expressions as these, no doubt, interest and please the librarian; but they are also a disquieting indication that a knowledge of the service he offers has not yet permeated among the entire public. They make it evident that well-considered publicity is as necessary for the public library as for a commercial firm, in order that the public may know of its existence and of its varied services. Stated generally, a new climate should be created in favour of the recognition and of the acceptance of the service of the library by one and all.

213 Value of Publicity

In a paper on *Library publicity methods,* Miss Wildred Othmer

Peterson, Director of Publicity of Des Moines Public Library, says:

> Publicity, the art of influencing Public Opinion, in all its varied forms, holds a large place in the world of men to-day. It has proved its value to the business world; for, had it not, certain firms in this country, would not spend as much as a million dollars a year for publicity. If publicity is important to them, is it not also important to libraries ? The only differences, however, are that librarians, in a great many cases, need to be educated to the importance of publicity and that libraries do not have the millions to spend. Every library now directs much time and thought towards publicity. The press lends its powerful aid and even such agencies as moving pictures and radio are enlisted [52].

Broadly speaking, library publicity falls into two classes — general publicity and individual publicity.

214 General Publicity

General publicity is of the type "Eat more fruits" and "Buy more *khadar*" without mentioning any special fruit-merchant or khadar-merchant. Such general publicity in the library sphere may try to emphasize [53]:

1 The value of books and reading; the superiority of the books as a source of opinion, information, inspiration and education, over other forms of communication;

2 The library as a public institution, publicly supported and administered;

3 The all-round service of a live library, emphasizing information service, adult education, and, other less known aspects;

4 Some accepted library standards, as book circulation per capita and book ownership per capita;

5 Comparative figures of the use of library in different states and countries; and

6 Library anecdotes of librarians, library promoters, and library users.

215 Agency and Medium for Publicity

Some general publicity falls within the sphere of central organizations such as State and National Library Associations and the State Department of Library Service. This form of publicity should be organized with care. It should be properly timed. But it should be a continuing matter. It can be carried on through the daily press, popular periodicals, radio talks, demonstration tours, attractive posters and sign-boards displayed at vantage points within residential areas and in public highways, periodical and itinerant fairs and exhibitions, celebration of library week, and free distribution of attractive folders, leaflets, and bulletins — all organized country-wide by central agencies. The objective is to create in the community a climate favourable to make people go to the library.

216 Library Civics

Library civics does not sprout of its own accord. It has to be deliberately developed among the people. Laws and regulations may be necessary, but seldom prove sufficient in this matter. Penal clauses will defeat the very purpose of the Laws of Library Science. Persistent, persuasive public relation work is necessary to develop library civics. The factors needing it are illustrated in Chapters 26 and 27. This too falls partly in the sphere of general publicity.

CHAPTER 22

WORK AMONG THE PEOPLE

221 Local Publicity

Individual libraries should see that their service is constantly brought to the notice of the public in an effective way. It is worth while for large libraries to have a special public relations officer. It should be his business or of the librarian himself, if he does not exist, to adopt all the recognized methods of attracting the public to the library, so that every potential reader may be converted into an actual one, thereby increasing the chances for the fulfilment of the Third Law. In organizing its publicity campaign, a library should bear in mind the general principles of publicity, such as continuity, variety, novelty, clarity and personal appeal.

222 Local Press

Perhaps the cheapest and the most easily available medium for library publicity is the local Press. The library should keep itself in touch with the local newspapers. The newspapers would generally be willing to allow some space in the general columns and the local news column for information about the library. I approached the local Dailies of Madras in this matter in 1925. They readily responded. It is gratifying to find that they have since extended the privilege to the other big libraries in the state. Delhi too imitated this for some time. To preserve this privilege, a library should be regular in its announcements and respect the agreed time-table. It is desirable that the librarian or the public relations officer should frequently consult the editors and try to conform to their instructions in the matter of style, length, periodicity, and other details, so that the matter sent by the library can be directly passed on to the compositors, with the least editorial labour possible. It may be useful to publish certain types of information such as recent additions, statistics of readers, monthly issues, and similar data on definite days of the week or dates of the month, so that the public may know when to look for them. They will act as systematic reminders to the public. It is not uncommon that the number of visitors to the library is slightly greater on the second or the third of each month, as a result of the monthly statistics appearing in the local news column on the evening of the first. In addition to such systematic statements, the library should seek to appear in the press at odd intervals, whenever an opportunity offers itself for announcement such as, changes in the issue method, changes in the arrangement of books, changes in the hours, receipt of free gifts or special collections, improvement in the amenities to the public, participation of the library in exhibitions and conferences, and occurrence of events about which special bibliographies may be prepared. The library staff may also be encouraged to contribute occasionally readable articles bearing on the humorous side of library experiences. It may be desirable to send to the newspapers occasional reports or extracts about the outstanding events in the libraries of other lands. Such publications sometimes rouse the curiosity of the public and induce them to take greater interest in their own libraries.

223 **News-Sheet**

Next to the local Press, mention may be made of the issue of printed or typed hand-bills and news-sheets. A good duplicating machine is a great necessity for libraries to use this form of publicity. It would be cheaper to use such a machine than to print. Recent additions, special bibliographies, notifications about change of methods, descriptive notes about the personal service offered by the Reference Staff, and several such announcements can be issued in this manner both to those who are already on the members' list and to those who are yet to be attracted to the library. Although a little more costly, unlike the Press method of publicity, this form does not depend on the co-operation of outside agencies. It would also give ample scope for the resourcefulness of the library staff. It would be an advantage to keep a chronological and a classified file of such materials for future guidance. The library artist can make such news-sheets particularly attractive. A librarian with artistic skill is an asset from this point of view.

224 **Library Bulletin**

A more costly mode of publicity adopted by some libraries is that of publishing a printed periodical, e g *Readers' index* of the Croydon Public Library; *Bulletin* of the New York Public Library;

Harvard library notes of the Harvard University Library; *Bulletin* of the John Rylands Library, Manchester. Such library periodicals seek [54]:

1 to interest the public in the library as an institution;

2 to keep the public informed of all the library's activities and facilities;

3 to relate books to the existing tastes and interests of the public;

4 to relate fresh topics to those about which borrowers already read;

5 to arouse fresh interests;

6 to keep the reader in touch with methods that can be followed up in books; and

7 generally to stimulate — in an attractive "gentle" way — education, vocational, and other interests and culture.

These periodicals usually contain an annotated list of recent additions as well as books of topical interest, special articles dealing with the varying forms of the activities of the library and illustrated accounts of matters of local interest capable of being connected with the library. Such periodicals have usually to be distributed free, if they are to serve their purpose. The cost and labour involved are generally prohibitive, unless it is possible to secure a sufficient number of advertisements.

225 Library Poster

A library may advertise its services by means of posters. This will need a library artist. The Laws of Library Science plead with library authorities that the maintenance of a library artist on the staff is a legitimate and worth while charge on the library fund. Here is an account of the ingenious and extreme form of advertisement which has the flavour of the marketing methods of a business concern.

> During the annual fair which lasts for eight or ten days . . . to give publicity to the California county library system, the large electrically lighted county library map of California and Sacramento county used at the A L A Conference in Phila-

delphia is maintained in a prominent place in the Agriculture Building. To emphasize this publicity the county libraries financed the making of thousands of county library fans bearing on one side the county library sign and on the other information regarding California county libraries. Each day a county librarian and State Library Staff member passed out fans to multitudes of adults. The fans served to suggest many questions by the visitors and gave an opportunity to explain the county library system and to illustrate from the electrically lighted map points that needed clarifying visually. People from the counties of California which are without any county library . . . were among the interested recipients of this novel bit of publicity [55].

There can be no end to the methods which the public relations officer of the library authority can invent to attract the attention of the people to the services of the library.

226 House-to-House Survey

Another possible form of establishing public relations is to organize a house-to-house survey. In this, the library may enlist volunteers for work. A card may be maintained for each house to record the findings of the survey. It may mention the number of persons in the house, their respective occupations, their respective reading interests, and the names of those not enrolled as library members. A cabinet of these survey cards gives a useful picture of the locality's acceptance of library service and of the book-needs of the locality. It is the business of the library staff to spot out potential readers from the cards and to convert them into actual readers by personal visits.

227 Personal Talk

By far the most effective means of public relations is personal in its nature. A direct personal talk is also the least expensive method. This method can convert many persons into regular readers, if the library has on its staff one or two members with the necessary personality and power of speech to address gatherings of probable readers. It has been found from experience that if such addresses are to be effective, too much time should not be spent on vague and general subjects like the benefits of reading or the services of a library in general. After a very short preliminary reference to topics of such a nature, one should rapidly descend to particulars and dwell in detail upon the specific services that the library in question can render to the members of the gathering. It may be serviceable to present comparative statistics of membership and book-issues. At the same time, one should not be carried away by enthusiasm to promise to serve more than what the limitations of staff and stock would permit. The reactions of such unfulfilled promises will do more harm than good.

228 **Demonstration**

The accompanying table and the graph showing the growth of issue in the Madras University Library illustrate the result of such personal appeals.

Year	*Number of Vol*	*Year*	*Number of Vol*	*Year*	*Number of Vol*
1914	5,100	1920	22,236	1926	42,336
1915	11,600	1921	27,920	1927	70,914
1916	11,600	1922	24,975	1928	79,756
1917	14,000	1923	22,339	1929	99,600
1918	15,000	1924	20,075	1930	1,13,321
1919	15,300	1925	27,629		

In the year 1927, several visits were made to students' hostels, and small groups of undergraduates were addressed whenever an opportunity occurred. Professors of colleges who took interest in the matter were requested to mention in their lecture-hours the services offered by the library. That these quiet personal appeals had the desired effect may be seen from the steep ascent of the graph during the year 1927.

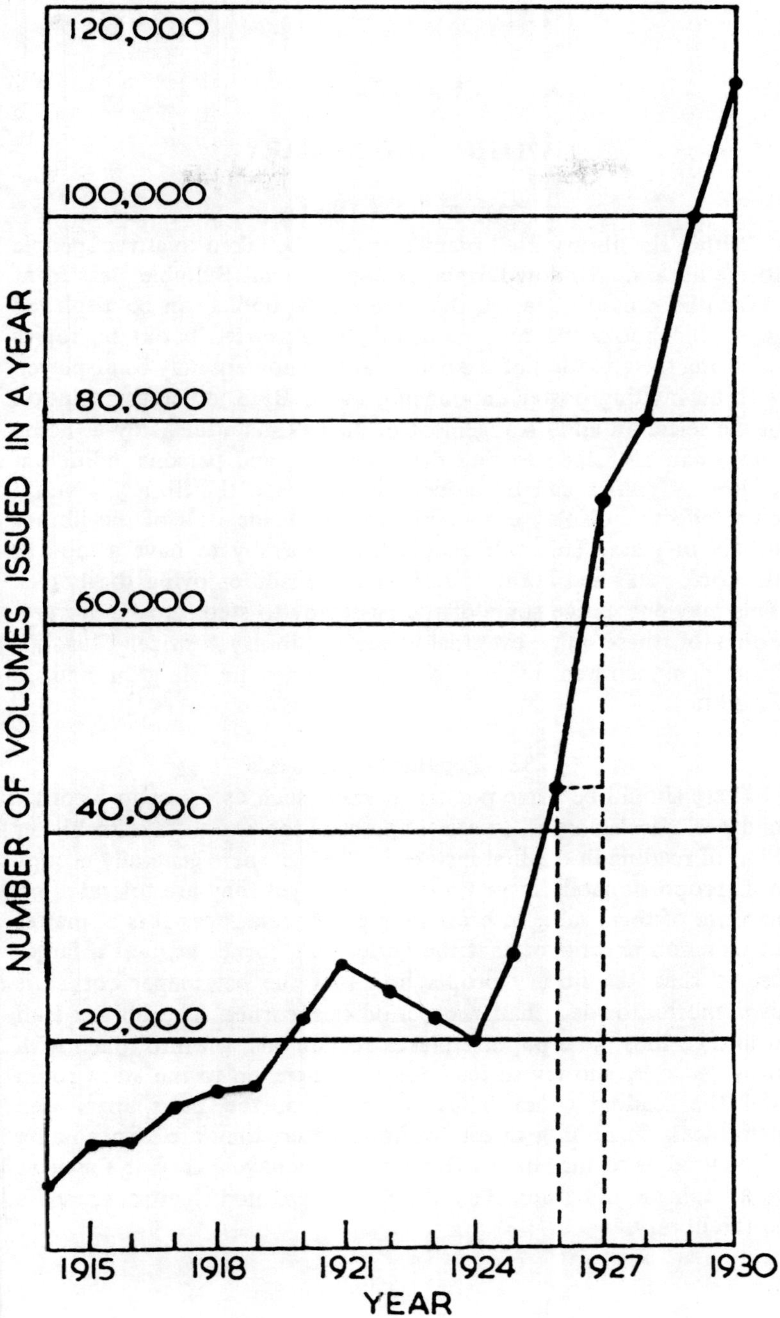

120,000
100,000
80,000
60,000
40,000
20,000
NUMBER OF VOLUMES ISSUED IN A YEAR
1915
1918
1921
1924
1927
1930
YEAR

CHAPTER 23

WITHIN THE LIBRARY

231 Window Display

Within the library itself many steps can be taken to attract people to the library. Window Display is one of them. Suitable glass-front should be provided, facing the street. New books can be displayed in it. Old books too may be displayed. Assorted books on topics engaging the attention of the people at the moment may be displayed with an inviting poster announcing them. By a judicious variation in the selection and arrangement of display materials, stay-at-home books can be helped to find their readers ; and persons indifferent to library service can be induced to step into the library. Even a more effective display is to make the road-side wall of the library totally of glass. This will enable the passersby to have a look at the book-racks and at the readers amidst them, enjoying the books. This may encourage some of the passersby to step into the library. Some of these may eventually accept library service. This has been demonstrated by one of the libraries in Islington and in Frankfurt.

232 Popular Departments

There should be some popular corners such as newspaper corner and periodicals corner, to attract persons too shy to take to higher kind of reading in the first instance. These corners generally occupy a disproportionately large floor area and yet they are tolerated on account of their value in promoting public relations. It is a matter of common experience that the periodicals corner attracts a larger crowd than the library proper and that the newspaper corner is even more crowded than the periodicals corner. The library staff would go into these popular places at intervals, get into touch with their patrons, and try to lead some of them on to the stack-room and the reading room. Thus, apart from the newspapers and periodicals furnishing direct reading matter, they are also coming to be used as regular baits. Humanity does have a craving for news of an ephemeral nature. This should be exploited to attract readers to the library.

233 Non-Conventional Collections

It is possible to make the library a centre of attraction by building collections of certain kinds of non-conventional materials. These are not strict reading materials. And yet libraries are now stocking them and serving them. Sound-records of music, photographs, and framed pictures belong to this category. All these may be issued for use within the library. They can also be lent out. Sound-record plates and talkie reels need special receptacles for their being carried home by the members of the library. Photographs bearing on particular themes may be lent to institutions for exhibition as well as projection with an epedioscope. Framed pictures may be given on long-period loan to individual members. Such non-conventional materials form important aids in attracting people to the library.

234 Comfort and Composure

Every attempt should be made to retain the custom of every citizen of the locality coming into the library. To this end, he must be welcomed with geniality. His comfort should be attended to. A sense of composure should pervade him. The liveliness of the library should charm him. Its silence, in spite of its being busy, should impress him. He must feel a sense of freedom. Nothing should be forbidding. Nothing should scare him. The kindness of the staff should make him love to come again and again to the library.

235 Guides and Attractions

There should be helpful guides to enable him to make his way to the reading materials satisfying his interests. Charts and pictures should rouse his curiosity and engage his attention. Every week he should find something new to attract him. It may be a display of a special assortment of books. It may be an exhibition of pictures, rare books, or manuscripts. All these should be well-guided.

236 Relaxation and Refreshment

The library should also provide relaxation corners with comfortable chairs for use of readers in between hours of serious work. A distribution of fresh flowers in vases in the different parts of the library will add a charm of its own. There should be a supply of clean drinking water. In larger libraries, there should be a quiet place for taking light refreshment and beverage. Of course, there should be good sanitary arrangements. There should also be open-air reading rooms for use during cooler hours.

CHAPTER 24

LIBRARY EXTENSION SERVICE

241 Meaning of the Term

Apart from such methods of pure publicity, libraries are nowadays developing certain new types of work. In addition to their being directly educative or recreational, they also lead to good public relations as an important secondary product. Such new lines of activity may be referred to as the "extension service" of libraries. The object of extension service may be said to be to turn the library into a social centre with the encouragement of reading as its ultimate objective. Its aim is to make readers of non-readers, to create and stimulate the desire for good reading, and to bring book and reader together. Libraries, under the influence of the Third Law, value these aims highly and take to extension service with great zeal.

242 Reading to Illiterates

One form of extension service is very urgent in our libraries of today. It is the institution of the "reading system". As a result of high percentage of illiteracy the present generation of illiterate adults can be made to have the benefits of library service only by arranging to have books read to them at stated hours either by paid readers, or by honorary readers who are actuated by a spirit of social service. About 1930, this system was experimented upon in some of the towns in the neighbourhood of the City of Madras, at the suggestion of the Madras Library Association. For several years, the Association arranged for books to be read to the illiterate patients in the hospitals of Madras [56]. This "reading system", coupled with the formation of clubs for the liquidation of illiteracy, has even converted many an illiterate adult into eager literate readers in post-revolution Russia. There is no reason why libraries, with this extension side properly developed, may not provide a sure solution of a similar problem in Adult Education in India as well.

2421 Reading Manuscripts

Owing to the present paucity of books on current thought in the modern Indian Languages, this form of extension service may have to be carried even further. To induce and maintain the interests of the illiterate people in books and in hearing books read out, it would be necessary to read to them, not only books of a religious or recreational nature, but also books of useful knowledge dealing with their daily avocations and leading to increased efficiency in their work. In the absence of such books in the mother tongue and in the absence of any prospect of such books being printed immediately, the only practicable course would be for the library to prepare a manuscript translation of suitable books from English and have the manuscripts read to them. It must be possible to find, among the English knowing local residents, persons willing to do the translation as a piece of social service. If each library in a district undertakes the translation of one or two books in a year and all such manuscript books are systematically exchanged between the different libraries, an appreciable region of knowledge can be provided with such improvised reading materials, in a reasonable time. If no competent non-commercial agency like the State or the Universities would undertake the initial supply of such books on useful knowledge, this seems to me to be the only practical way of cutting the vicious circle of the law of supply and demand. But this extreme phase of extension service is only a strictly temporary expedient, for which there will be no need as soon as a market is created for the publishers to step in.

243 Reading Circle

A third form of extension work for the libraries to pursue is that of organizing reading circles. Persons pursuing a particular subject for profit or pleasure may be brought together by the libraries, so as to form a reading circle. Each such circle may have a leader and not less than two and not more than five other members. The library may give special facilities for each reading circle in the matter of books, periodicals, and meeting places. For this purpose a library should have a suitable suite of small rooms. Such reading circles are usually effective agencies in thoroughly exploiting the resources of the library in their respective subjects of study. Therefore, their formation gives unusual satisfaction to the Third Law.

244 Intellectual Centre

One of the necessary conditions for social service institutions, such as the library, becoming popular is the fostering of a feeling of mutual cordiality and helpfulness between those who offer service and those who are served, together with a disposition to self-sacrifice. To this end, the library should strive to reduce formality to a minimum and make everyone feel at home. As a natural extension of this attitude, a modern library even goes so far in its effort as to make personal and social contacts and not infrequently offers meeting place for local learned organizations in an attempt to make them, as constituent parts of the general public, feel that it desires to function as an intellectual centre for the locality. Such meetings offer opportunities for the fulfilment of the Third Law.

2441 Example

The possibilities of this form of extension service can be inferred from the folllowing statement by a small English town library, of the societies meeting there regularly — The British Legion, Cage Birds' Society, Chess Club, Draughts Club, Church Lads' Brigade, Church Mothers' Meeting, Church of England Men's Society, Folk Dance Society, two or three Friendly Societies, Free Church Mothers' Meeting, Gardeners' Society, Grocers' Society, Farmers' Union, National Union of Teachers, Radio Society, Women's Institute, and Workers' Educational Association [57].

245 Library Talk

Another common form of extension service is that of arranging for public lectures in the premises of the library. For this purpose, all modern library buildings are provided with spacious lecture halls, fitted with a stage, a magic lantern, a cinema apparatus, and other related appliances. In our country, we may have open-air meetings and theatres. In addition to the local associations being invited to hold their public lectures in the library's lecture hall or open-air space for the purpose, the library may frequently arrange for special library talks either by the members of its staff or by outside experts. One special feature of such library talks is the announcement of a select list of books on the subject-matter of the talk, available for the library for loan or consultation. The subjects chosen for such library talks are usually of local or topical interest. Scientific subjects also come in for a good share. Such talks ought not to be exclusively confined to topics of a religious, philosophical, or Puranic nature. But care should be taken to widen the range of subjects and give a chance for every phase of current thought. Whenever possible, it would be an advantage to illustrate the talks with lantern slides and moving pictures.

246 Story Hour

Similar to the library talks for adults, libraries arrange also for story hours, lantern talks, dramatizations and other attractive forms of extension service and similar privilege issues, to establish contact with the children of the locality. Again it is not unusual for the library to arrange occasionally for dramatic performances by amateuring troupes. But in all such cases the performances do not form an end in themselves ; but they are all made to serve as aids to the ultimate satisfaction of the exacting Third Law.

247 Kalakshepam and Music

The unique Indian Institution of *Kalakshepam* or *Katha* with its happy blend of music and talk, presents enormous potentialities as an instrument of this form of extension service. But due care should be taken, in this case also, to lift the *Kalakshepam* or the *Katha* from the narrow rut of traditional subjects. In Western countries where this institution is unknown, the lecture hall is used for musical concerts. This enables the Third Law to find readers for the comparatively large quantity of printed music usually available in those libraries.

248 Festivals and Fairs

Another form of extension service is the celebration of local festivals and special days of the year dedicated to particular persons or ideas, and participation in local fairs. Here again the demand of the Third Law is always kept in the forefront. In our own country, where such celebrations are still attracting large crowds of people, this form of extension service is full of great potentiality to serve the Third Law. Examples are New Year Day, Rama Navami, Diwali, Holi, Independence Day, Gandhi Jayanthi, Moharram, Nanak's Day. These are all national days. There will also be local days. In addition to the celebrations, books on these days may be exhibited. A list of them may be distributed.

CHAPTER 25

TAPPING THE COMMUNITY POTENTIAL

251 Religion as Activating Force

As shown in the earlier chapters of this part, the primary aim of good and persistent public relation is to bring more readers into the Library. But it can also release the social qualities lying deep in the recesses of personality. In the distant past, loyalty to the temple activated community-potential into public service. Years ago, I went to a small town in Malayalam to meet a friend. I went without notice. His house was locked. Most of the houses in the street were locked. I wondered what had happened. A farmer passing by smelt a stranger in me. He said, "They are all in the *Sasta* Temple." It was 11 A M. I found my way to the temple. I saw my friend — a learned professor in the local college — perched up on the top of a gabled roof being put up for a festival. He was engaged in fixing up a row of plaited coconut leaves. I looked for another colleague. He was in the kitchen, dressing vegetables. They were enjoying this way of community life and service. This is possible even in towns, not grown too big to preserve group-life.

252 Personality as Activating Force

Loyalty to a powerful personality can also activate community-potential into public service. We are witnessing it today in the "walking mission" of Vinobha Bhave. We saw the height reached by it during Mahatma Gandhi's days. I saw it recently in the camp of Sri Sankaracharya, the head of the Kanchipuram Mutt. The newly formed university at Vallabha Vidyanagar near Anand is another demonstration of the activation of community-potential by the force of the personality of a leader.

253 Service Library as Activating Force

Library service is public service. It can activate community-potential into public service. Here is an example from USA. It was June 1953. There was a lady in Louisville, Kentucky, with leisure and with some experience in social work. The State University of Kentucky held its annual function to award its

Medallion to the State's "outstanding citizen of the year". The recipient was that lady. Her merit was that she used her leisure in a public cause. The public cause was the promotion of library service to the rural folk of the State.

2531 The Trigger

She was drawn to it in 1947. She happened to glance through a statement that 80 per cent of the people of the State lived in rural districts and they had no public library service whatever. This acted as the trigger. This made her feel, "I have leisure. If I can find someone to work with, who knows more than I do about libraries, perhaps I can help her." She started visiting nearby places and towns ; she studied the situation ; she got some ideas. The Kentucky Library Association was working hard to get legislation for State aid to libraries. But it was facing much opposition. She decided that a demonstration was necessary. An organization called Friends of Kentucky Libraries was formed. Then she said to herself, "I want some one to work with, who is or has been a librarian. He must be a sincere, far-sighted, and public-spirited person. He must be willing to take any help provided by the Friends of Libraries and use it right away without waiting for the State aid. If that person is in one of the State agencies, I can make a worth-while public-private co-operation."

2532 Public Servant and Private People

She soon found such an in-service person, working in the State Library at Frankfurt. That person satisfied herself that there was nothing in the law of the State preventing her from co-operating with private persons and agencies for public benefit. She had had some experience with the working of librachines — motor-vans used as travelling libraries. She spotted out a second-hand van for sale. The Friends bought it. The Friends also built a book-dump mostly by collection and partly by purchase. The dissymmetry of the collection was revealed by the work done by the assistants of the in-service lady sorting them out and roughly classifying and listing them during their out-of-office hours. The State Library lent a few books to correct the dissymmetry. In her off-days, the in-service lady drove the librachine herself from one village to another. Soon, some private people began to emulate her and relieved her from the task of driving. She could devote her spare time fully in organizing the book-dump. This also made the librachine go out more often. Thus, the leisure of private persons and public servants were jointly turned on the promotion of library service.

2533 Specialist in Promotion Work

This demonstrated the keenness of the rural people to read and to keep knowing. This also attracted more leisured people to work for the cause. A specialist in Promotion Work soon joined the Friends of Libraries. He drew up a scheme for 100 librachines to cover the whole State. Each librachine was estimated to cost Rs 12,000. A special donation campaign started to raise Rs 12,00,000 for the purpose, from industrial corporations and private people. Each district was promised a librachine, if it pledged itself to vote annually a sum of Rs 12,000 to pay the library staff and maintain the librachine. The Government of the State was persuaded to pay an equal amount, and to strengthen its own staff to administer the programme ; it needed only three additional hands.

2534 Specialist in Public Relations Work

A specialist in Public Relations Work felt attracted by this venture. He arranged for a film to be prepared. It showed the librachine doing its rounds, with a sound commentary — arrival at the village school, the children running with smiling faces and fleeting feet to get their books exchanged, the librarian-driver telling them stories ; the men in the fields and the women in the homes getting intimate reference help and walking away with books in their hands and delight in their faces, books being taken to the home of a person lying in bed with paralysis and depending on reading as the only relief from boredom.

2535 Panel of Speakers

A State Speakers Panel was formed. They were all drawn from those filled with faith that book-service is indispensable at the stage society has reached today, and for the democratic form of government to succeed in building a welfare state. Each was willing to give a few days once in three months to go long distances in the librachine to address and enthuse the village folk to accept the book service brought to their very doors. Sympathetic co-operation soon came from everywhere. The press and the radio gave a helping hand. The farmers' groups and the women's groups were eager to give their platforms to the visiting speaker or the librarian. The regional fairs in the district were never missed by the librachine.

2536 Literacy Level

In six years of the leisured lady looking round for an ally in the library profession, half of the districts in the State had established active library service. Six years earlier, 50 per cent of the rural folk were illiterate. In the district which started working the librachine first, illiteracy had already come down to less than 20 per cent.

254 A Madras Example

The community-potential is not yet totally extinguished in the heart of our people. It can be tapped by a service-library owned by the public for the public. Here is a recent example. It is an extract from the report furnished by the Local Library Authority of Coimbatore — a district in the Madras State.

> We had almost fixed a building for the Branch Library at Lakshminaickenpalayam and we were waiting for our bus. Then an elderly gentleman came towards us and some time later we were busily engaged in talking various things which touched also on the purpose of our visit. On hearing the purpose of our visit, the elderly gentleman took us back to Lakshminaickenpalayam proper and earnestly requested us to see a particular building. We were very satisfied about its suitability for the Branch Library. Then when we began to discuss the financial matters, he put a full stop to the talk, saying that he with all his heart wished to give the building to switch the library free of cost [57].

255 Lead by Librarians

The library staff can give a lead in activating community-potential. Here is an example from USA. It may look strange, and perhaps undignified to see two librarians swaying on eight-foot ladders and painting high above the doors. Or another bending double over a design low on a bookcase. Or still another balanced precariously on a seven-foot bookcase painting on window frames ; or all of them ranged on chairs on top of tables, while they did the design on the centre beam in the ceiling. Was the library closed while this work was going on ? Oh no ! There was "business as usual". Whoever was lowest on the ladder or nearest the desk, took care of the readers who came in. Every one was tolerant. In fact some readers were so interested that they volunteered to help. Before long the decorating work became a community project. Here, in a small way, is a sample of what can be done in a community, where there is an idea fired by enthusiasm and willingness to work, and backed by the co-operation of all the people concerned with the objectives. This is what happened in a public library at Wisconsin. On hearing the word "Wisconsin", the cynic may dispose it off saying, "It is America. In our country, you can't expect that kind of public co-operation." Is it ? Is human nature so different in India ? Let me describe what happened 25 years ago in Madras City.

256 Madras Example

2561 Start from Library Staff

It was September 1936. The new University Library Building was getting ready for occupation. The making of bundles of books began. The statistics of issue during the preceding ten years and the memory of the reference and circulation librarians decided the sequence in which the books should be bundled up. Each bundle had its inclusive class number. The technical and administrative staff took up the task of bundling. This made it possible for the library to function without interruption. Occasionally, the Maxwell's ghost of decimal one per cent probability prompted a reader to ask for an out-of-the-way book bundled some days earlier. But the staff was not frightend by the ghost. Sundaram, the indefatigable chief of reference staff, would look up the chart, go straight to the bundle, unbundle it, pull out the wanted book, and rebundle the rest. Each book so pulled out would go into a separate bundle. Thus the Method of Osmosis kept the ghost at bay. In the meantime, the new book-racks were put in position in the stack-room of the new building. Each gangway, bay, and plank received its number. A chart was prepared establishing One — One correspondence between the bundle numbers and the shelf numbers. The bundles with little chance of being called for within a month were transferred to the stack-room and put in their correct position. Then its string was pulled off and used to bundle up other books.

2562 Stimulus to Readers

The readers got interested to know how we managed to serve them in spite of the tremendous bundling work going on. Those that were more than curious were explained the objective and the plan. They were taken to the stack-room in the new building. One of them asked, "How can you find where each book is ? In the basement of the Senate House you had bay-guides. But you are now spreading out the books. Those guides will not serve here." "No", they were told, "Instead of the three-hundred old bay-guides, we should have 1,200 here in the new building." "How are you going to make them ? It will take a month at least. Are you going to close the library ?", they asked. "No", they were told, "With four hands working on them, it will take a month. But with forty, we can finish the work in three days." One of the readers asked, "Will you mind if some of us come and help you ? We can give two hours each evening." The offer was accepted. About 100 readers came for a few evenings and finished the work. They also helped in fixing them. Thus, the community-potential was tapped and the work was completed without much ado.

2563 The Result of Readers' Help

The library had to be formally closed only for three days to give the final check ; and yet, all serious students and research workers were informally informed that they could have their urgent needs looked after. Every such person who came for a book or a periodical invariably gave us at least one man-hour to do some work or other for us. An old student of the University had just then returned from abroad. He wanted to look up some reference, just during these three days. He felt disappointed that the library was not functioning. However, he had the pluck to catch me in the second tier of the new stack-room with my fingers jammed between two book-racks ! He was easily given access to his periodical. He said, "It seems you are closing the library only for three days. Even then you allow some of us to use it. Is this sufficient time for you to transfer the library to here ? In the university abroad, where I was working since I left Madras, they closed the library absolutely for

45 days. Even after that, open access was not given because the bay-guides were not yet put up." I replied with joy, "It is all due to the community-potential of your student successors here."

257 Immediate Application

We are now experiencing a sudden expansion in our public library system. Let us illustrate from the Madras State. About ten years ago, there were only about a dozen free public libraries in the whole State. In 1958, each of its 13 old districts had a District Central Library under the Public Libraries Act. Its new District of Kanyakumari will also have one soon. In 1958 the 14 districts taken together had 486 Branch Libraries. In 1958, the skilled staff of these 500 stationary libraries was not more than 503. Of these, only 11 were professional librarians with a Diploma in Library Science ; and only 8 were semi-professionals with a Certificate in Library Science [59]. The remaining 484 employees should have been doing merely the routine work of maintaining the issue register and safe-guarding the collection and the buildings ! They could not establish any public relation. Nor could they do any reference service. Here is a splendid opportunity for tapping the community-potential in each locality. It should be found from among the educated retired residents of the locality. A person with a good pension, keeping him above want, can be persuaded to give to the public library of his locality his part-time honorary service. A person with a meagre pension may be given an honorarium in return for a similar service. By doing so, our new libraries can be made to function up. This may have to be continued for some years. For, the State of Madras will take at least 20 years to train the necessary number of professionals to man all its public libraries.

CHAPTER 26

BUILDING CIVIC RESPONSIBILITY

261 New Civics

Formerly "civics" meant the study of civil government. Now it means a study of the development of the procedure and process which make for the greatest good of the greatest number in the governmental and group relations of all social units. It embraces much more than a study of structures and function. It includes public-mindedness ; the creation of right attitudes towards public duties; the formation of habits of helpful, constructive, participating citizenship. This new view of civics appeared during the closing years of the nineteenth century and it became very pronounced during the second decade of the present century. The new civics places emphasis upon behaviour rather than upon knowledge. It stresses the activities of the individual as a member of a social group. It embraces all the important factors of citizenship which vitally affect the life of the individual and society — essential facts concerning sanitation ; personal and community hygiene ; fire prevention ; care of the water supply ; respect for the rule of the road ; respect for the rule of the queue. In short all that affects the well-being of social units is considered a part of civics. As the library is a social institution which is guided by the most democratic principle — every reader his or her appropriate book ; every book its apropriate reader ; and save the time of the reader — life in a library itself implies a civics of its own. It presents all the important factors of citizenship which have been enumerated in elucidating the connotation of the term New Civics. Hence, the library forms a very effective laboratory for practical training in citizenship. Here comes the opportunity for productive public relation.

262 **Public Property**

The training of the people in civic responsibility is an essential item in the work of a library. This has to be done largely through the medium of public relation. Let us take the development of respect to public property. A public library socializes books. The books in it form public property. The fact that it is public property for the use of every member of the present generation as well as the future generation takes a long time to dawn upon the minds of the people. It takes even longer for the realization of the full implication of these facts. What is worse, even when the implications are intellectually perceived, it appears to be almost impossible to implement them in practice, if they are pursued for the first time in adulthood.

263 Mal-handling of Books

Within living memory, many communities have introduced a public library system for the first time. The fate of the books in those libraries makes sad reading. They suffered at every stage. The tops of their backs were broken while being pulled out of the shelf. The stitches, holding the gatherings, gave way when the books were opened. Many of the leaves had their top corners folded and eventually broken in the forced labour they had to do in serving as book marks. The book as a whole had not infrequently to serve not only against the sun but also against the rain. There was no limit to the load of dirt it had to carry silently. No wonder that many a book met with premature disablement, if not death.

2631 Spectacular Methods

India is now having its public libraries established. Its first generation of librarians has a great responsibility in curtailing this civic pathology. All kinds of methods should be adopted in public relations work. Leaflets should be distributed. Talks should be given. Pictorial appeals should be made. The theatre should be pressed into service. Dramas should be put up with books as characters, narrating their woes. In one country, they even went to the desperate length of making a spectacular demonstration, like conducting a public funeral of a murdered book ! The funeral orator bemoaned its premature death and condoled with the people for the cruel and thoughtless way in which they had been deprived of the long long service which the murdered book had intended to render them.

264 Misplacement of Books

One of the unintended difficulties brought about by readers in an open access library is the misplacement of books. A misplacement within the same shelf plank may be unavoidable. But the placing of a book into a wrong shelf or bay or tier should be avoided. If the readers realize that a book misplaced is a book lost — not only to others but perhaps also to themselves — readers will certainly respect the request of the library that they should not replace the books on the shelf, if they had taken them away even some small distance only from their places. Readers should not insist that because they have the freedom to pick out books from the shelf, they should also be allowed to replace them as they liked. Several readers pick up a quarrel with the library staff on this point, which would not happen if correct public relation methods are adopted.

2641 Deliberate Misplacement

But a more serious anti-social tendency is visible in just a few readers. While the born criminals cannot be dealt with in the mild way suggested nere, it is our belief that if public relation uses its opportunity to induce a high civic sense in the readers, those who are not born criminals may be saved from the temptation to hide books in unexpected parts of the stack-room with the sole object of depriving the fellow readers of the use of those books. It is a sad fact that this anti-social tendency is to be found most among the pick of our students, appearing for competitive examinations and aspiring for a place in the highest civil service in the land. No theoretical instruction can perhaps purge our bright young men of this unfortunate selfishness; it is only a healthy life in a free open access library with good public relation work, which can prevent the setting in of such selfish tendencies in the best of our men. The important civic rule of "the greatest good for the greatest number" can get woven into the texture of the moral personality of our readers only by making them live that principle actually in common community institutions like the public library. A reader takes away the periodical from the proper place and hides it in some unexpected place. Due to this propensity, economic periodicals are caught up among zoological periodicals, until the very hands which hid them there come to their rescue. It is difficult to detect such mal-practices on the spot and set them right immediately. Nor is it proper to deny the readers all the freedom that the Laws of Library Science expect us to give. The only means of getting over this difficulty is through proper public relation work pursued patientlv.

265 Mutilation

2651 Periodical

One comes across the display of criminal habits in the periodicals room. If any periodical contains a good exposition of any topic of the day, the article vanishes in a mysterious way in a couple of days.

2652 Reference Books

Another type of vandalism is even more deliberate. It concerns reference books such as encyclopedias, dictionaries, and directories. By their very nature, these books are of large size and are heavy. They are also costly. They are generally in use all through the day. The absence of a properly developed civic responsibility makes some readers so unscrupulous as to mutilate the costly reference books. Here is an extreme example of this anti-social propensity. Some years ago, the article on "ethics" in the *Encyclopedia Britannica* of a big Madras library was lost! Surely the book-vandal responsible for this would not have gained any special advantage in having committed that atrocity. It is only his failure to recognize that there were also others to benefit by that article that should have been responsible for his act. The sense of "the greatest good for the greatest number" had not developed in him. I have seen some libraries in the West employing detectives to catch such vandals. But a confirmed criminal of this kind is seldom caught by the detective. The only hope is to wean away the others by the promotion of public opinion through good and persistent public relation work.

2563 Pictures

In several other cases the books are relieved of the burden of the loaded art paper which contain pictures. We wonder what lasting use people can make of such stolen plates. Surely, their life would become much shortened when taken away from the book. Why should not the adult readers realize that these pictures will be available to them quite readily whenever they want them, if they are left undisturbed inside the books. How little do they realize how much the value of the book is diminished if it is deprived of its plates ?

266 Disfigurement

A more widely spread vandalism is with regard to the plates and pictures of the books. Mohammedan faces are given Hindu caste marks Clean shaven faces are fitted with ugly beards and European heads are fitted with the cap of the crescent. Margins are taken as free spaces to write upon. Line after line is underlined, as if it had only one reader to serve. I have come across an interesting case of disfigurement. Every line of some costly medical books was found underlined in the Madras University Library. This was a problem for us. A new medical book had arrived. It was put on the recent additions shelf. Everybody was on the alert about it. Its inside was examined quite frequently. Its pages were quite clean at 12 noon. At about 1.30 a reader replaced it on the shelf. The book was promptly examined. The lines in about 20 pages were found underlined. The colour of the ink was just the one used by that reader in signing the gate register. He was a rich doctor with wide practice in the City. He was one respected by all. I showed him this new book. He was not conscious of having underlined in it. But he recognized the colour of his ink. Then, the old underlined books were all shown to him. He felt his mistake. He said that it was probabiy his unconscious habit. He further offered not to come to the library any longer. On hearing this, the first three Laws of Library Science frowned at me. I requested him, therefore, not to take that extreme step. I suggested his surrendering the pen to the circulation librarian before entering the reading room. He tried it. But his ill-luck was that without the pen he could not read at all. Then, we decided to give him a small pen-like stick with which he could go on underlining without leaving any impression ! Good public relation can avert many cases of disfigurement of books.

CHAPTER 27

LIBRARY ETHICS AND HYGIENE

271 Respect for Library Rules

Conformity to rules by readers is not easy to secure. Readers have to be constantly educated in this matter by good public relation. One usual rule objected to is the one of fixing an upper limit to the number of volumes that can be taken home at a time. Readers have to be educated to see that this rule is necessary in public libraries, as its books have to be shared by all. The rule regarding the period of loan is another vexatious one. Experience all the world over has taught the Library Authorities that this rule cannot be enforced without a monetary sanction in the form of an overdue charge at so much per volume per day. Public relation work should convince readers that this monetary sanction is not intended to be a source of revenue. One way of getting the co-operation of the reader is to help him in every possible way to avoid paying the overdue charge. The stamping of the due date on the special date slip attached to the first page of the book is one form of public relation work in this matter. Sending a reminder on the very first day of a book becoming due is another form. An unreasonable reader may regard the overdue charge as a charge for the privilege of keeping a book longer. This is as bad as it would be if a motorist should take with him extra money for fines to be able to pay for the privilege of rash driving. Reference books form a source of irritation. Readers want to take them home. They have to be educated that they are not books to be read through, that they have to be looked up only for a few minutes at a time, and that they are frequently wanted in the library by other readers.

272 Respect for the Queue

The Library offers an excellent opportunity to train our citizens in respect for the queue. The very counter set-up mechanically enforces the queue. However, some people resent it. A considerable tact is necessary to persuade people to respect the queue. Two anecdotes will make this clear. The new building of the Madras University Library was opened in September 1937. There was an unusual rush. I posted myself at the entrance gate to persuade the people to observe the queue. It was then something unknown to most people. A knighted gentleman passed alongside the long file in the queue and reached the entrance wicket-gate. When I requested him to take his place in the queue, he asked for the meaning of the word and later for its spelling. But a more serious situation arose later. An elderly gentleman was exasperated beyond control, when requested to fall into the line and await his turn to enter. However mildly and however distantly he was requested to do so, he got exasperated and bowled out, "We are not school children to stand in a line. I am not going to enter this library so long as we are asked to stand in a line like labourers and sepoys." So saying he went away. The Laws of Library Science frowned at me. Later in the evening, I went to his home. This cooled him down. I could then explain to him the rule of the queue. A tragic fact is that some members of the top-management of the library lend their ears to people of this sort and harass the librarian.

273 Hygiene of the Catalogue

The catalogue of a modern library is in cards. The cards are filed in cabinets. They are permanent records. Their handling should be such that they last longest, undisfigured, and undirtied. This implies that the readers should make their hands clean and dry before touching the edges of the cards. They should on no account wet their fingers with the tips of their tongue to facilitate turning the cards. Nothing but persistent persuasion, standing by the side of the catalogue cabinet can bring readers to observe the hygiene of the catalogue.

274 Stack-Room Ethics

The stack-room is a place for browsing and selecting books only. The place for study is in the adjoining reading room. Readers are frequently to be reminded of this in as polite a manner as possible. They do not easily realize the obstruction they cause to others by settling down to read in the stack-room.

275 Reading Room Ethics

A reading room has to accommodate many readers for study. Here, not infrequently we come across all imaginable forms of ugly habits. We find a reader with his feet shot up high in the air, the table acting as a prop. We find another reader leisurely dressing his long hair, and now and then dropping down tiny rolls of black stuff, quite unmindful of the disgust that such an activity should produce in the minds of the other readers. Sleeping, to the point of snoring, is not uncommon in the reading room. Only good public relation work can induce respect for reading room ethics and minimize such ugly happenings.

276 Temple of Silence

A reading room should be a temple of silence. It is a place where many people do serious intellectual work. Silence is often disturbed by the shoes of the readers. This can be obviated by sound-proof floor or by a sound-proof covering of the floor. Disturbance of the silence by conversation among readers can be minimized only by public relation work. But it is not difficult. By paying thought to it, the library staff can easily bring about an atmosphere of serenity and calm in the reading room — too powerful to allow people to make noise. Putting up placards with the legend "Silence Please" is seldom effective. It is only by personal persuasion that proper results can be obtained in this matter.

277 Scraps of Paper

Waste paper baskets are provided in reading rooms almost at every turn. In spite of it, scraps of paper are littered about on the floor of the reading room. This is not due to unwillingness to put them into the waste paper basket. It is due only to their not being habituated to it while young. Preaching about this is not an effective form of public relation. I found one method fairly successful. As a reader throws waste paper on the floor, I would pick it up and put it into the waste paper basket before his very eyes. On seeing this, his facial disfiguration would show that he was feeling for it. This method had to be adopted persistently for several days before the very atmosphere of the reading room could persuade people to use the waste paper baskets.

278 Reading Room Hygiene

The reading room is naturally the place where most of the readers stay longest. Hence the hygienic and sanitary responsibilities of the readers are high while in that room. And yet, the ugly habit of spitting on the floor and at the windows with the least sensitiveness to the sense of disgust in others, can be eliminated from our reading room only by a long process of training. Unfortunately the tobacco-cum-betel habit of many of our people often leaves a permanent pink mark on the window sills, floors, and the walls of the open space adjoining the reading room. We should not take these as if they are irremediable. Persistent public relation work in this matter is necessary. It will also prove sufficient in the long run. A milder form of disfigurement is the spilling of ink on the table, floor, books, and so on indiscriminately. None of these is due to wilfulness. It is due to lack of preparation while young and lack of thought. It can be set right by public relation work.

CHAPTER 28

THE STATE WANTS IT ALL

280 Not by Law

A modern State finds it impracticable and unwise to invoke laws and sanctions as the sole means of making citizens do their civic duties. It finds it necessary to invoke the aid of social institutions such as the library to achieve that purpose. The library has, therefore, to be an indirect medium for the development of correct civic sense and habit in the country. This view has been gaining in weight with the increase in the functions of the State.

281 Sphere of Government Action

From the very earliest time Government has had some preventive functions : to prevent private violence, interference with life and property, and aggression by foreigners. In due course, it began to assume responsibility for positive functions needed to facilitate the realization of desires deemed to be common to the great majority of citizens. The positive functions are being enormously enlarged in recent years. One of them is education, consisting not only of scholastic attainments by a few, not only of the liquidation of illiteracy at the other extreme, but also the perpetual self-unfoldment of one and all by intellectual means.

282 Educational Function

2821 Scholastic Education

Of these three elements in the educational function of the Government, the first appeared very early — even in the days of personal rule, divine right of kings, and court life. India has never been lacking till recently in the provision for scholastic attainment by the few.

2822 Liquidation of Illiteracy

Liquidation of illiteracy appeared as a positive function only after the democratic form of government came into vogue. It appeared first in some of the countries of the West in the second half of the nineteenth century. It took various shapes, the chief of which was compulsory and free elementary education provided as a public project on a legislative basis. India has yet to reach the world-standard in this. It is behind the world-standard by a hundred years.

2823 Perpetual Self-Education

The provision for the perpetual self-unfoldment of every citizen by intellectual means is beginning to be recognized as one of the positive functions of the Government only in our own days. No country has had too great a start than India in this matter. In every country where this function has been assumed by the Government, the organization set up for its discharge is the library. This does not imply that a library is an organization newly created for this purpose. It had existed ever since writing came into vogue. It had been set up long ago mostly for preserving written or printed reading materials and to make them available for use on demand by the few who were after scholastic attainment. The Government now seized its potentiality for the perpetual mental advancement of one and all. It was first put to the use of leisure hours for mental recreation. Later it was developed also as a store-house of reference books for furnishing information on demand. It was thus made to function as "externalized memory". It is now used also as a means for the sharpening of intellect and the sublimation of emotions. In short, it is now being fully exploited for the perpetual self-education or self-unfoldment of each citizen.

283 Library Function

Library Service is thus brought into the list of the positive functions of the Government, because the success of the Government has now come to depend on the state of enlightenment of the several people in the nation, their individual skill in some job — whether manual or clean-collared — and their mental agility to adopt new points of view and new methods of work. To make the State efficient, certain mental dynamism has to be maintained by feeding the mind of all the citizens with new and nascent thought. Library function is indeed a part of its major educational function. The well-being of a State demands, it is now realized, not only physical hygiene, but also mental hygiene. To secure this, the Government of a State has to maintain not only a public health service but also a public educational service. Just as public health service includes child-welfare work, public educational service includes child education and adolescent education, i e, elementary and secondary education — general as well as vocational — in short what is known as formal education. But public health service is not exhausted by child-welfare work ; so also public education service is not exhausted by formal education of the children and the youth. A kind of inversion has occurred in the development of these services. Public health service first seized general service in which the adult population was more in mind and it is only later that it extended its organization to provide distinctive service to children. On the contrary, public education service first seized specific formal education in which the immature population was more in mind and it is only later that it came to be extended to cover the perpetual self-educational needs of the adult population.

284 Mental Hygiene

It is being increasingly realized in most of the developed countries of the world that mental hygiene demands not only on elementary and secondary education but also on adult education — in the sense of perpetual self-education of all the members of the nation, of the ultra-normal as much as the infra-normal. The provision for universal adult education demands the supply of books — gratuitous supply of books — as a public project. The obligatory function of the Government in the field of education thus brings into the sphere of Government action the promotion of library service and the maintenance of a net-work of public libraries throughout the land. To make them achieve the intended objectives, active public relation is necessary on the part of libraries.

285 Fundamental Right

This demand on the Government has the backing of the Sankey Declaration of Fundamental Rights. These include :

"Every man is the joint inheritor of the powers, inventions, and possibilities accumulated by our forerunners. He is entitled to mental development from birth to death.

"It is the duty of the community to equip every man with sufficient education to enable him to be as useful and interested a citizen as his capacity allows. Furthermore it is the duty of the community to render all knowledge available to him. He shall have easy and prompt access to all information necessary for him."

This is equivalent to saying that Library Service is one of the fundamental rights of citizens.

286 State and Leisure

Arrangement and enjoyment of leisure is an art which needs careful thought and preparation. The art of life, indeed, consists largely in the capacity to spend wisely and happily the moments in which we are most free — free from the demands and behests of others, free from the demands of relaxation and hygiene, free to plan our activities in and at our own time. To waste these moments is to waste something extraordinarily precious. One of the most horrible and insensate forms of cruelty is "killing time". It is a most vital concern for organized society — the State — that the leisure of its citizens shall be wisely spent. Change the character of a nation's leisure and a corresponding change in its efficiency and culture is bound to follow. Thus, use of leisure leading to the enrichment of adult life is no light activity. It is no peripheral problem. Nor is it an incidental task. It is rather a fundamental problem affecting the welfare of society and its prosperity. As such, the State calls for a major consideration to it.

2861 Out-moded Utilization

A very efficient mode of utilizing leisure, which centuries of folk ways had established, has now been rendered unavailable. This outmoded utilization was of the group variety. As those were days of mass illiteracy, the leisure was transformed by some folk-institutions, not demanding literacy, into periods of intellectual, social, and spiritual enrichment. The holy-days were days of religious, social, and family festivals. They did not connote days of inaction. They were filled in an organic way. As the whole community had leisure at the same time, it was spent in the re-winding of the individuals and the community as a pleasurable group-project. Such modes of using leisure are dying out with the impact of industrialization and urbanization. Another efficient and stable way of utilizing leisure has to be evolved. Western countries in which this phase began about a century ago have been experimenting in various ways. India, which is just entering this phase in the present generation, can put their experience to use and shorten her own period of transition.

2862 New Mode of Utilization

The new mode of utilizing leisure is through Library Service. The mere putting in juxtaposition of the books of the library and the people during leisure time, does not lead to the occupation of leisure by reading for relaxation or inspiration or information. The affinity between books and men is weak. It needs the catalytic action of library staff to get activated. The demand of this new way of using leisure for the benefit of the individual and society is one of the factors which has led to the emergence of library service, backed by active public relation.

2863 Example from Sweden

During the state of illiteracy, people had been depending on group-activities for utilization of leisure. Such people were more community-minded than individualistic in their ways and outlook. This indicates that library service for the newly-literate should lean more upon group activities like film-shows, exhibitions, talks, reading circles, and discussions. The spontaneous organization of reading circles with a small library as the nucleus, among the labourers of Sweden during the last ten years, acts as a pointer. No less than 20,000 such reading circles have come into being in this short interval. In them, we find the maximum possible activation of a small but purposive collection of books. To my mind these little reading circles represent a well-balanced state of a library and library service. It was while visiting them that I was able to visualize what the ideal library would be like if it satisfied all the Laws of Library Science. The development of local reading circles and the provision of a small library for each circle has been the charge of the Department of Libraries of the Swedish Government. The library is only transitory. Here public relation functions at its best.

287 World Context

Humanity has now to work for its vital, mental, and spiritual sufficiency in a world-trend, which had long ago transcended the closed systems of village life and of provincial or regional life and is struggling to replace even closed national systems by a world-system. However much national barriers persist in matters material, they have been nearly washed out in matters mental. Occurrences, utterances, and additions to knowledge of all kinds in any corner of the world get reported in print and relayed everywhere. All thinking has now to be in a world-context of facts and figures. Even the most encyclopaedic memory will fail in these circumstances. The only memory that can function is what I call "externalized memory". A library is really "socialized externalized memory". The State wants that the library should induce all to use it. This can be done only by public relation work.

288 World Peace

The State is interested in world peace. Without world peace, no nation can thrive hereafter. But world peace is being constantly threatened by the spirit of aggression. Spirit of aggression is but the next cousin of cold war and of war-like preparation for defence. This is because of mutual suspicion among the nations. The suspicion is born out of mutual ignorance. The State wants this mutual ignorance to be replaced by mutual understanding. The State looks upon the library as one of its agents to promote mutual understanding among nations. For this purpose the library should make all the people accept its service. For this purpose, the library should promote public relation in all possible ways.

PART 3

REFERENCE SERVICE

CHAPTER 31

DOWERING BOOKS WITH PERSONALITY

311 Mechanization

Attractive library building, comfortable furniture, classified arrangement of books, multi-purpose catalogue, open access, guides of the right kind in the right places, time-saving issue system, serene silence, pictures, flowers, composing atmosphere — all these are necessary to facilitate contact between reader and book. But they are not sufficient. For, most of the above amount but to mechanical aids. Mechanization is now being carried even to further stages of efficiency. We even hear of Press-Button Library [60]. Rider has described it. The living quality is usually disregarded if not destroyed by mechanization. We therefore speak of mechanical things as "dead".

312 Animation of Mechanism

Anyhow, mechanized things are dependent things. They no doubt exist for use. But they are dependent upon use for beauty. A turbine at work is a thing of wonder and of beauty. But out of use, it is as dead as it was before its elements were taken from the earth. Because of this need for redeeming use, the multitude of mechanisms with which we are surrounded may justly be regarded as appealing objects making persistent demand upon us — as things, which, because of their inanimation, threaten us with the sense of death unless they are continuously dowered with our own life-energy. This pressing demand made by the mechanisms and techniques amidst which we live compels from us a question of momentous importance, "How much have we the desire and strength to animate them before they become burdensome ?" When the material, technical, and red-tape activity of conducting a library begins to take precedence over the experience of living, sooner or later we shall have to pay in ennui and decadence [61]. Hence the need for introducing a human agency — a "someone" — to redeem everything else by putting them to active use. When the reader comes amidst the library, there must be "someone" to say,

Take my hand ;
For I have passed this way,
And know the truth. [62]

313 Artificiality of Books

In addition to these general reasons, there are special reasons for providing that "someone". First, books are after all artificial entities. It is not natural to pick up ideas and information through recorded phonetic symbols. There are books of a variety of standards on one and the same subject. There are also books within books. These are elaborately illustrated in *Reference service and bibliography* [63]. As a result of such qualities of books, appreciation of their value does not come naturally. It has to be induced deliberately. This cannot be done except by intimate personal methods.

314 Conventions of Cataloguing

In the catalogue which lists the artificial entities called books, we reach a higher order of artificiality. We call it by the dignified name "conventions". The cataloguing conventions are on the surface so contrary to what Mr Everybody is familiar with, that he needs personal initiation. Entering "Bernard Shaw" under "Shaw" is a baffling convention. The convention reaches a higher degree in the choice and rendering of the headings under which governmental books are entered in the catalogue. The *see* and the *see also* entries form another puzzle to readers. Personal help is necessary to get over these puzzles.

315 Classified Sequence

Every Law of Library Science points to the need for arranging books on the shelves in a classified sequence by subjects. The maintenance of this sequence has to be mechanized with call numbers. These call numbers are too artificial not to be a distraction to the unaided reader. They form no doubt, a necessary evil. The readers can, however, be helped to appreciate their helpfulness by a helper in the library.

316 Tempo of the Reader

The psychological tempo of Mr Everybody is such that we cannot retain his custom unless he is given prompt and exact service in a personal way. He is human; and a human personality alone can keep him in good humour, make the appreciation of the value of books blossom in him, and transform him into a willing beneficiary of the library. To make him love to come back to the library quite often, he must be attended to by a library "hostess".

317 Human Converters

If such a human personality is not provided, the potentially great plenty in the holdings of the libraries of today will be nothing but a mockery. Indeed the problem in libraries is no longer one of scarcity in any sense, except that of scarcity in the human converters of the potential energy, stored in books mouldering on shelves, into the kinetic energy of use by readers. This in its turn is due only to absence of initiative and of understanding generally in high places. It is painful to find that, in India today, even well placed members of the library profession show a similar lack of understanding.

3171 Definition

Reference Service, let it be asserted, is the essential process in a library of establishing contact between the right reader and the right book by personal service. Reference service is essentially individual in its nature. Its character varies with every reader-book context. But in all contexts, reference service amounts to dowering books with living energy and personality.

3172 Change in Social Concept

So long as knowledge is taken to be hereditary or intuitive, the need for reference service could not be seen. But today, knowledge and information are taken to be communicable to anybody whatever. There is also the present insistence of democracy on equality of opportunity for all to have help in getting at knowledge and information. This change in social concept makes us go to the length of saying this. A library exists only at the moment when the three members of its trinity — the reader, the books, and the staff — are in purposive contact with one another. The old concept, that a mere collection of books is a library, is as wrong as holding that a mere group of readers or a mere squad of staff can constitute a library. In the night, for example, when there are no readers and staff, there is only a collection of books and not a library. Even when all the three exist without relation to one another, there is no library. On the contrary, even a single book in the hands of a librarian being introduced to a reader is a library. Reference service is therefore the paramount duty of a library.

318 Ultimate Fulfilment

Every other work in the library is itself fulfilled ultimately only through reference service. To collect books, to organize them, and to go through all the endless routine prescribed in Parts 4, 5, 7 and 8 — book selection, book-order, periodicals work, classification, cataloguing, accessioning, organization and display of books, and charging and discharging them — will become fruitless unless proper reference service is done. Indeed reference service alone can lead to the ultimate fulfilment of a service-library and of the Laws of Library Science. Let us therefore examine how it should be done.

CHAPTER 32

WORK WITH BOOKS

321 New Books

Reference service requires patient and arduous preparation with books. Every new book, coming into the library, should be rapidly perused. The perusal will no doubt be guided and made efficient by the class number of the book. While perusing, the reference librarian should be having a split mind as it were. While one part of it is glancing through the pages, the other part should be sweeping the world of readers and locating the readers with whom it should be brought into contact. It is not only the subject-matter but also its standard of exposition, the style of the language, and the extent of illustrations, and other auxiliaries, which would determine the possible readers. It is not the mere title that can determine it. This purposive perusal should be made not only of new books but also of new editions of books, new issues of annuals, and all the current issues of periodicals, arriving in the library from time to time. For example, the 1947 volume of the *Proceedings* of the Aristotlean Society arrived in the library. A glance through the pages revealed an article on Existence Philosophy. This set up associative memory into action. It was recalled that Mr G had asked for information on this subject some weeks earlier. A note was sent inviting him to the library. But before it could reach him, he was met on the road and personally informed about the article. He walked along immediately to the library with joy ; and the *Proceedings* blessed the librarian, along with the Third Law for his so promptly securing a reader for it.

322 Old Books

Old books, too, will have to be re-perused from time to time. Old books, which do not leave the shelves, should be perused to find out what information or what features contained in them could be brought, by special effort, to the notice of probable readers. Old books may also have to be perused so as to bring them in relation to the new books added from time to time. In this way some books, which could not find a reader till then, can be impregnated with new values by being put in relation to some new arrivals. The *Proceedings* of the Aristotlean Society referred to in section 321 gave a number of references. Some of these were located in the library. These, in their turn, led to parts of other books. All these had been lying on the shelves untouched by human hand for many months; they were naturally glum and depressed, and had covered themselves with dust. When they were pulled out, cleaned, and put into the hands of Mr G, they burst into joy and thanked the *Proceedings* as their redeemer and the librarian too received his own share of thanks. It must be emphasized that when such a relation is being established by one part of the mind, the other part should be on the look out for probable readers.

323 **Books with Intangible Qualities**

Certain intangible qualities are possible in books. A reader cannot by himself easily spot out the books with these qualities. These qualities transcend the capacity of classification as well as cataloguing. They are of the nature of a flavour. No mechanical or objective norm can size them up. In this matter, the general reader has to lean on the reference staff far more than on any other. He has to seek their help in choosing the book of the right flavour. Three kinds of flavour figure frequently in requests. The reference staff can recognize them, both from their own experience and from the unique opportunity they have to pool together the experiences of readers. They may gather the necessary help even from the frequency of demand and from the quarter from which it comes. A resourceful and genial reference librarian will get it reinforced by judicious participation in discussing the books with the users. In any case, the reference staff should devote all free time to shelf-study to capture such books.

324 **Books with a Message**

The first intangible quality needing exploration is the possession of a message by the books. Generally speaking, the main classes Literature and Religion (the sacred books mostly) abound in books with a message. Not that every book in those classes possesses one. But the density of message is greatest in these classes. Ordinarily the general reader is not able to discard from these classes the books without a message. Books with a message are not so abundant in the other subjects. Not that they are totally absent. That is impossible; because there is progress in those subjects and progress implies the existence of books with a message. But the ordinary pedestrian books, simply transmitting information, are so many in those subjects that the few germinal books are virtually lost among them. The general reader usually lacks the flair to spot them out readily. No doubt he may hit on them by chance. But on account of their relative scarcity, the odds are very much against him. Of course, he can arrive at them by the laborious process of trial and error. But it is seldom that the necessary patience and perseverance go with the general reader. Hence there is the danger of his going without the book and the book lying neglected on the shelves longer than it deserves. The business of the reference staff includes averting such miscarriages.

325 Books with Flair

Another class of books for which the general reader depends largely on the help of the reference librarian is books rich in flair. Such books are personal in their method. They display much judgment in the selection of details. Their style is racy. Once we begin them, we are led from page to page; we don't like to be disturbed; they have an aroma of their own; they are alluring; our curiosity never wanes; on the other hand, it ever grows; we want to finish them at the very sitting—even though it takes us late into the night. Turning their pages is like turning the pages of life itself. They are illuminating books. Such books make reading popular. The reference staff should give them a central place in their memory. They should be their pets. They should virtually hawk them about.

326 Orientation Books

Then we pass on to the third intangible quality in books. It is a quality much sought by readers with a catholic taste. Books, possessing it, may be called orientation books. They owe their value to the way in which specialization gets intensified nowadays, while at the same time there is urge in the man of culture to know the inter-relation of the various branches of knowledge. It is hardly possible for him to sense this inter-relation merely by reading the specialized books ; and they are myriads. It has been estimated that about 300,000 books are published each year. This makes one believe with Pope that

> When so much is said,
> One half will never be believed,
> The other never read.

And so the man of culture wants to have books that will explicitly show him the moorings of the present-day progress in knowledge. The library stands to gain generally by finding such books for those who want them. The gain is so much that they should also find readers for such books. For, they are the books that widen the interests of those who are, by nature, conservative in their field of study. Once their curiosity is stimulated by orientation books, it can be kept up and even sublimated by feeding them with the books with flair.

327 Seminal Works

Lastly come the seminal works. These can act as a lever to lift the universe of knowledge. They open up horizons even wider than their ostensible subjects. They stir the imagination over the whole broad scope of life. They skirt the deep ineffable impulse of religion. They stimulate the flow of life itself. The ultimate consummation of the purpose of a library lies in finding currency for such seminal works. They are charged with the personality of their authors. They are immortal. New editions of them continue to come for ever. New books on them continue to come for ever. Their flavour is unmistakable.

328 Examples

Here are three sets of four books each. Each set belongs to a different subject. In each set, the first is a book with a message; the second is a book with flair; the third is an orientation book ; and the fourth is a prosaic pedestrian book.

3281 Mathematics

11 Russel (Bertrand). Introduction to mathematical philosophy;
12 Hogbern (L). Mathematics for the million;
13 Place of mathematics in modern education (forming the

eleventh yearbook of the National Council of Teachers of Mathematics of the United States, 1936); and

14 BOWLEY (Arthur). General course of pure mathematics from indices to solid geometry.

3282 NATURAL SCIENCE

21 CRILLE (George). Phenomena of life ;

22 WELLS (H G), etc. Science of life;

23 THOMSON (J Arthur). Introduction to science; and

24 SCOTT (George G). Science of biology.

3283 ECONOMICS

31 STEINER (Rudolf). Problems of world economy;

32 COLE (G D H). Intelligent man's guide to the world chaos;

33 KIRKPATRICK (E A). Sciences of man in the making;

34 THOMAS (S Evelyn). Elements of economics.

3284 SEMINAL BOOKS

NEWTON'S Principia and DARWIN'S Origin of species are seminal books.

CHAPTER 33

KNOWING THE READER

331 Meek Reader

Some readers are meek. They are too shy to ask the library staff for help. They fumble with the catalogue. They are afraid of going to the shelves. Their eyes tell their tale. The reference librarian should put them at ease by voluntarily welcoming them. He should behave like Rama. He should speak first. He should not wait to be asked to give help. On the other hand we must remember that it is only during recent years that the general public have begun to get rid of the fear of the printed word and of the place housing it. The public are only now looking upon libraries as places that they have the right to explore.

332 Inferiority Complex

Some readers are afraid of being misunderstood, of being treated in an off-hand manner, or even of being made to show their ignorance. That is the mentality which we are constantly meeting ; and it is the stuff of which many a difficult reader is made. Obviously the attitude, if not indeed, the duty of the reference staff should be to inspire confidence and to give satisfaction to such people. A shy research student asks in low tone for the book "*ibid*", whose pages are referred to so often in his book ! The reference librarian should quietly explain what "*ibid*" means, without betraying any sign of ridicule, surprise, or superiority. Do that and even the slight disappointment in the reader's mind will be erased and he will respect you, because he realizes you are doing your best. Several such incidents will occur to all. One day by a fluke perhaps, we clear up some tangle or dispel a mist in a reader's mind and we have made a friendly patron for life. This winning of readers has to go on every day to satisfy the Laws of Library Science.

333 Superiority Complex

The floor of a library is always believed to be a place of great equality. There we meet at the democratic level of the world of thought and its records. But some readers set this at naught. Our courage in such situations should be drawn from the words of our national poet : "Come friend, come my hero, give us courage to serve man even while bearing the brand of infamy from him"[64]. The moral is "no pestering". Some one has said, "you must beware of bludgeoning the mind into sensibility". That is advice worth remembering.

334 Book Thief

At the other end of the scale there is the doubtful reader. He not only shows great familiarity with the library and sends you away, but peels off the stiff covers of the books to facilitate smuggling — he steals ! The vigilance required to watch in an open-access stack-room is most trying. This is the type of difficult reader abhorred by the reference librarian. He is most unscrupulous. Any precautionary action taken makes him simulate righteous indignation and make a scene to the chagrin of the library staff. He is so dangerous!

335 Selfish Reader

Perhaps a more numerous species is the fraud. He would abuse the freedom given to him by hiding away books. Whenever the reference librarian comes to him, he pretends intense seriousness which seems to say, "Don't disturb me". He skulks and loiters in the stack-room with all cunningness until he gets his opportunity to remove the book in great demand, which has just chanced to come back, and insert it or hide it some thousands of feet away in some other region of the stack-room, because he has not brought his ticket.

336 Difficult Readers

Such is the variety of difficult readers. These are the persons for whom all our routine is built up. They are the chaps that keep us up to scratch. We must think particularly about each of them. We should get at the back of his mind. We should examine and organize reference service from his point of view. A beginner in reference service will do well to maintain a case-book in cards. They may contain records of situations, events, and all varieties of readers.

337 Normal Readers

But the majority of readers are normal. They are not under the spell of any complex. They ask what they want. They take help easily. It is a joy to work with them. But the privacy possible in the stack-room may tempt them to deviate from normalcy. It is therefore wise to rescue them from possible aberration by exercising unobserved vigilance. For this purpose, a reference librarian should keep moving constantly to all the gangways containing readers — especially containing a solitary reader.

CHAPTER 34

WHAT ABOUT US ?

341 Coming to Terms with Readers

While admitting that there are meek readers, ignorant readers, loiterers and wasters of time, and that unreasonable, irritating, pompous, insulting readers drift into the stack-room, we must also agree that we too are sometimes tarred with the same brush. As individuals we each fancy ourselves as "easy to get on with". We go on thinking so, quite simply and sincerely until one day a good friend, perhaps the wife, says, "You know you are a difficult person at times, perhaps just a wee bit selfish." Then we shed our self-complacency and realize all of a sudden that our self-satisfaction is largely based on the fact that we usually get a good deal of our own way. If we can, by seeing the faces of readers, gauge the depths of their experience, let us not forget that our face too speaks volumes to them. How quick we are to see the weaknesses and the faults of others; how blind we are to our own !

342 Inexperienced Librarians

The readers could tell a tale of their difficulties with reference librarians. That might stagger us. How often a stammerer voluntarily banishes himself from the library, because an inexperienced reference assistant burst into laughter. As for the long-suffering unemployed visitors, what could they not say of the minor rebuffs and little discourtesies encountered in their search for solace from libraries. Perhaps the reference librarian's superior familiarity with books blinds some of us to the difficulties and to the points of view of the readers. To know, or try to know, the facts relating to readers would make a sensible difference in our attitude. Pugnacity, that prolific source of all kinds of warfare, would give place to geniality. Let us admit it. We too are difficult. Bricks of fair size could be exchanged in a battle of complaints, and one day it may be worth while staging a show of the kind.

343 Good Temper for Two

Even experienced men lose their temper when over-worked and

exhausted. As reference service is a new idea, the amount of physical and mental strain it involves is not yet realized by those in power. Explosion between reader and librarian develops occasionally. And the recipe for such miscarriages; is there one? One really can't say, because we all go on doing our job to the best of our ability learning from actual experience — and then find our knowledge has come a trifle late for practice. Life batters us into shape; we are examples and spectacles to the young at our heels. There is a modern craze for sharing. May be the sharing out of good temper — witness Henry James's four words "Good temper for two" — would help to solve the problem of facing readers. Let us try.

344 Square Man in Round Hole

Knocks received from the public may by degrees batter up an otherwise competent reference librarian into a shape that will not allow overwork or exhaustion to betray him into bad temper. But the situation is quite different if the initial recruitment itself is faulty. There are moments in the history of any society when a false philosophy guides recruitment. About a century ago, for example, the community of the New World believed that man was intrinsically a Jack-of-all-trades and there was no such thing as individual aptitude. This really led to the adoption of the spoils system in politics and the principle of rotation in office. It led to a readiness to change from one occupation to another and to a lack of confidence in the expert in any field. Equalitarianism of this extreme crude variety was asserted by the collective will of the community in order to expunge outright all possibility for the persistence of the petrified principle of privileged classes. The principle of division of labour which is indicated everywhere in nature was thrown overboard along with the privileged classes, in the belief that it was that principle which created them. If such an epoch coincides with that of the introduction of reference service, where success depends so largely on personal qualities, the odds are very much against the furtherance of reference service. When a misfit is recruited the additional strain on those who are of the right variety is not merely that of having to do the work of that misfit, but also that of undoing the mischief that is done to the reputation of the library by the misbehaviour of the misfit.

345 Scaring Away Readers

There is no greater sin than scaring away readers. Some are endowed by nature herself with such unsocial and detestable qualities as to make them permanently unfit for any job that involves contact with the public. Reference service depends so much on the geniality, self-effacement, and untiring energy of the reference staff that nobody should be recruited to the reference section without a thorough test by one who has had experience of reference service and its requirements.

346 Team Spirit

The stuff of which the staff is made, the relation among the staff, and the staff atmosphere, will affect very intimately the service of the library. If these relations are bad, neither good buildings, nor good collections, nor efficient methods will be of use. The members of the staff should be on the most cordial terms among themselves. There should not be the least trace of jealousy or envy. Self should be suppressed to such a degree that every member is prepared to pass off all work as anonymous. Maeterlinck's picture of work in the bee-hive contains the most vivid and accurate description of the spirit that should come over a library staff, if it is to function with maximum efficiency.

CHAPTER 35

SERVICE PROPER

351 Help in the Enunciation of the Problem

The first step in the service to a reader is to help him to enunciate his requirement in exact terms. Many a reader cannot do this by himself. Questions of readers are usually wide of the mark. They are often oblique. But the cumulated experience of a reference librarian with a variety of readers, day in and day out, often enables him to think in consonance with the reader. His discipline in facet analysis in classification enables him to break the vague question of a reader into all its relevant facets. He can then work with the reader in finding out the focus in each of the facets. In this way, the question of the reader can take a clearer shape.

352 Trial and Error

But this may not always clinch the question. A start may have to be made with a provisional formulation of the question. Pursuing the solution along with the reader may lead to successive sharpening of the question. This method of trial and error may have to be adopted in some cases. Here is an example. An old man about to retire from the Indian Civil Service asked for information on iron-works. The *Memoirs* of the Archeological Survey of India describing ancient iron-works and books on modern steel and iron technology had to be gone into with him to know that he was interested neither in ancient iron-works nor in the modern technique of iron work. A further conversation and a display before him of the advertisement pages of architectural periodicals brought light on his face; he picked out a particular picture from an advertisement page showing a good design of iron-railing; and he stated that what he had really wanted was a good picture of iron-railing to help his wife to instruct the contractor to put up an iron-railing in their new house. It is only a sympathetic, patient, and clever questioning, clothed as conversation, which can clinch the specific subject sought by a reader. Even then, it may happen that a prolonged pursuit, by the method of trial and error, is necessary and that specific subject can be reached only when the right book itself is reached. All this may look fearful; but sincerity to help readers, determination to succeed, and perseverance uncontaminated by indolence or impatience, will provide the reference librarian with the necessary acumen to know what exactly a reader wants and what exact book will satisfy his want. Many illustrative actualities are given in the *Reference service and bibliography* [65].

353 Leading to Self-Service

In most cases reference service would really be leading a person to self-service. In school and college libraries, it should be so without exception. Even when the reference librarian has to move with the reader and be by his side more than three fourths of his way to his specific subject and his book, he must know to withdraw himself at the proper time so that the reader has the joy of self-service. The joy of the reference librarian should be derived not only from the consciousness that he himself had practically done everything, but from the sight of the dawn of joy in the face of the reader who has been helped to help himself. Even if the reader's choice of books is not the very best, the reference librarian should resist the temptation to take over totally. The gain in terms of intangibles and personal dignity so obtained outweighs the slight loss in material efficiency.

354 Reach-Me-Down Service

In a few cases the reference librarian will be obliged to find out the information all by himself and pass it on to the readers without much participation of the latter. This should not happen in a school or college library. This may happen occasionally in a public library. This will be the normal form of reference service in a business library.

355 Long-Range-Reference Service

By Long-Range Reference Service is meant reference service which involves tracing information through a long chain of books, periodicals, and other published materials, locating sources of information by prolonged dowsing through varied materials and perhaps even drawing help from other libraries within the locality or within the country, and if needs be even from those in other lands, and even from living persons when books fail us.

356 Ready Reference Service

Reference service may in some cases need only the use of specially prepared reference books or books on current information like directories, almanacs, yearbooks, who's who, atlases, statistical books, encyclopaedias, dictionaries and bibliographies. Finding information from such ready reference books or helping readers to find it is called Ready Reference Service.

357 Service to Absentee Readers

When the enquirer is absent and not available even on the phone, the problem of getting him to enunciate his requirement in direct and exact terms becomes rather difficult. The reference staff do not get the help of the enquirer and have to use their own unaided judgment. In some cases, an intermediate reference by post may become necessary; and in extreme cases, even repeated correspondence. But one compensating factor is that his case need not be attended to at the very moment. It can be taken up as pick-up work and gone into with calmness at leisure, provided it is remembered to dispose it off before the next mail. But even this advantage is lost when the requisition is brought by a messenger. For then the matter must be attended to immediately. In case of enquiry by post, alternative information may have to be given to meet the different interpretations the question admits of. It is desirable to keep a record of the sources of information and of the person who located them as the enquirer is likely to write back for further elucidation.

358 Service to Callers

When the enquirer appears at the library in person and expects the whole tracing to be done by the staff and he is of a class that should be given that form of help, his personal co-operation can be had without difficulty at least at the first stage viz, correct and direct enunciation of the problem. But it is not easy to keep him restful when the information is traced. There are irritating people who demand instant attention and claim to have been waiting for half an hour whereas they had only been in the library for half a minute. A possible remedy is to give some engagement to such flighty enquirers. They may be taken to the shelf of recent additions if they are interested in books. Further, even in the case of this class of people, it is preferable that they should be made to read the information from the book with their own eyes. This will avoid the risk of their turning up later and complaining that they were *given* wrong information. Though there can be no question of legal responsibility if they connect any failure, loss, or discomfiture of theirs with such wrong information, they may be told that the information was perused with their own eyes or copied with their own hands. Though such cases may arise only occasionally, it is better that the reference staff accustom themselves to such a procedure by way of abundant caution.

CHAPTER 36

AFTER THE READER LEAVES

361 Assimilation

Oliver Wendell Holmes has described the man who had an astounding knowledge of every subject under the sun, if its name began with any letter from A to M, but showed an equally remarkable ignorance of every subject which came in the cyclopaedias anywhere between N and Z. Whether such a being ever existed or not, the findings of Jast's probing into his mind are significant. "His mind must resemble an ostrich's stomach, where, if my zoology is correct, everything swallowed, from a bulky beef-tin to a Colt's revolver, is found in its original condition, mingled in an 'admired disorder' but not absorbed" [66]. Similar will be the mental make-up of the reference staff of a busy library unless provision is made for rumination, digestion, and assimilation into the specific skill of reference service.

362 Inner Assimilation

Any skill improves by repetition. But the profoundness which practice secures for skill in reference service is remarkable. To a reference librarian who really enjoys his work every contact with an enquirer and pursuit of every new problem provide an additional opportunity for enrichment. It gives a delightful exercise to his flair. It invariably enhances his mastery over reference books. For the pursuit of a new problem may disclose potentialities which were unnoticed hitherto. How often does not a reference librarian hum to himself "Hallo, does this book contain this ! I had missed it all these days." Sometimes while pursuing a problem, his eye casually falls upon some information which suddenly makes him say to himself "What a pity ! That fat gentleman asked just for this the other day. But none of us could lay our fingers on it. I wonder if I can find out his address and inform him about it. How pleased he will be ! I hope it will not be too late."

363 Nascent Awareness

A reference book cannot be read through. Hence, however

conscientious a reference librarian may be, it is hardly possible to know all its nooks and corners by a formal study at the preparation stage. Absorption of its unusual features or the unexpected pieces of information scattered in it becomes far easier when a nascent awareness is stimulated and maintained at a high pitch by the thrill of grappling with a difficult problem in the presence of an expectant enquirer. A moment's experience or stay at this high level of energy can be far more productive in getting a masterful grasp of a reference book than hours or even days of a dull mechanical poring over its pages. While in such a state, it happens that not only is the particular book on hand rendered transparent and illuminating but it even discloses its integral relation to several other reference books and delightfully lands us at an eminence which gives a clear and lasting view of past reference experiences in almost a prophetic inter-relation with what awaits in future. It is impossible to describe this supreme type of experience in full detail as it is so essentially conditioned by its concreteness with all its infinite shades of context, which goes into our very being but gets distorted by any attempt at generalization or abstraction. Every reference librarian should strive, invoking the full weight of his will, to realize this delightful state of contact with the readers and the books in his daily life.

364 Sharing with Colleagues

Another phase of assimilation is sharing with the brother members of the staff one's new discovery either of reference books or of particular enquirers or even of human nature in general. This does not mean that it becomes the reference staff to discuss the enquirers in a vein of waggishness. All that is meant is that it is helpful to inform all the colleagues about what has been sensed about their temperament, range of interest, capacity of self-help, and what is particularly profitable, the reciprocal help which the staff could get by serving certain well-informed enquirers. Information of this kind will be of much value in making the future contracts with the enquirers easy, pleasurable, and profitable to all concerned. Imagine the pleasant reaction which the enquirer will experience if at his next call at the library, he is met by some other member of the staff with genuine familiarity and without once again being subjected to all the ordeal of first contact. A library is a human institution and every such human touch tones up its functioning. Apart from this very desirable human side of the sharing of every experience with colleagues, there is also an economical side. The time and energy spent by one member of the reference staff in hunting up a difficult question should be made to yield a greater profit than that of merely serving one new enquirer who prompted it. His finding should be made known to the other members if it is worth that. Further, all new discoveries incidentally made out of reference books used should also be passed on to the colleagues so that they may also benefit by them.

365 Recording and Filing

Another mode of assimilation relates to elusive facts which are disentangled from unexpected sources under the stimulus of the enquirer's presence and which may easily be forgotten or be requisitioned only occasionally. Virtually, they belong to long range reference service but get spotted out by sheer chance in ready reference service. All the experience in long-range service needs to be recorded and filed in the reference cabinet. The details of this process may be as follows. The call number, the heading, the title and the exact page reference of every reference located *en route* should be recorded. Whenever warranted, the technical section should be advised about the extra analytical cards desirable to be added to the catalogue cabinet. In other cases, the fullest possible record should be made in the reference cabinet. Wherever necessary even reference to the file relating to the question may be entered. Such a record of questions dealt with gains in importance as it increases in bulk. If carefully built up, it would avoid the labour entailed in unearthing an answer to the same question twice over. It may also be of help in shortening the work involved in pursuing other related questions that may turn up from time to time.

366 Conversion

A systematic recording of findings in long-range reference service eventually converts long-range reference questions into ready-reference questions. This conversion will be of particular value when some topic begins to engage public attention. Its pursuit may be long-range reference service in the case of the first enquirer.

Many sources may have to be looked up to find the information. But its record will be of use for ready reference service when other enquirers bring up the same topic.

367 Enrichment of Stock

A library may repeatedly get a class of enquiries needing help from sources outside the library. If this happens, it is an indication for the library to add the necessary source books to its own stock. The reference staff should be sufficiently aware and alert to use the assimilation stage for this purpose.

CHAPTER 37

JOY OF REFERENCE SERVICE

371 Scar of Misery

It is difficult for a librarian to escape being misunderstood or misinterpreted by some reader or other. Sometimes, it leads to an unseemly situation on the floor of the library. It makes one feel miserable. But it is not all one-sided. Probably for every one such mishap, there are hundreds of pleasant experiences. But the scar of misery lasts longer than the feel of a kind touch. A librarian should learn to heal quickly the wound occasionally caused by unreasonable readers. To minimize its recurrence, a librarian will have to be firm. To be firm without offence, to combat the momentary unreasonableness of a reader without losing him as a customer, and to be good, kind, and helpful to readers without passing for a simpleton totally insensitive to bullying, is an art difficult to practise. However, there are many compensations in the life of a reference librarian.

372 Beaming Faces of Readers

The greatest joy recurring several times every day is the joy of seeing the faces of a reader expand with the joy of having got from the library the exact book service or information service needed by him. To get this joy I used to sit at a particular spot in the Madras University Library. It was at the end of the catalogue room where the door to the stack-room was located. In the stack-room, there were always able reference librarians to receive readers and help them to find their books. It was a joy to see reader after reader come out of the stack-room with a heap of books in the hands and a beaming joy in the face. Occasionally, a reader would come with empty hand and a disappointed face. That was my opportunity. A few minute's talk with him, scanning the catalogue cards with him, looking up a few bibliographies with him, walking into the stack-room along with him, and trying this book or that with his participation, often got him the right book. Then, the sign of joy in his face used to be all the greater for all this delay in getting the service.

373 Gratefulness of Readers

There is a peculiar advantage in the present library situation in India, in this respect. The few large libraries with books on diverse subjects and of diverse standards exist only in big cities. The city-bred People of our country today have had no experience of free public service in any matter. They would also have missed the free community service still lingering in our villages, though considerably attenuated in the course of the last few decades. Even the service in temples, which used to be free a few years ago, has been converted into service for payment, except for a short duration in the day when the crush of the poorer people becomes unbearable, because they are all obliged to come within a short duration of time. Therefore, the free service of books by a library is accepted with an exaggerated expression of gratefulness. Even keeping the library open for 13 hours each day and on all the days of the year without exception, elicits admiration. The late Mahamahopadhyaya Dr U V Swaminatha Ayyar, the well-known octogenarian Tamil scholar, drew a parallel to it from a Tamil verse of the medieval days, which eulogizes a king, the doors of whose palace were never closed at any time on any day, lest a deserving guest or scholar should be denied attention, and made to go disappointed.

374 Thankfulness of Readers

We had a system of home-delivery service in Madras City before World War II. Book-consciousness had not then sprouted among the people in the City of Madras. The reason for this was simple. There was no free lending library service till the Madras University Library liberalized its rules and began to lend books to any graduate or any scholar. On account of the lack of book-consciousness, the library carried books to the houses of readers at intervals. Few readers knew what books to ask for, or what books existed. For the habit of going to the library was not there. A member of the staff was put in charge of the home-delivery service. His duty was not merely the routine of charging and discharging the books. He had also to select books for each reader without any help from him. To enable this to be done with increasing efficiency and exactness, the same person was continued in this work for several years. He cannot be said to have been a widely read man himself. And yet he developed an uncanny sense to spot out the right books for the right readers. He developed this sense by trial and error. We had a column in the home-delivery slip in which the reader was asked to state whether the book sent was to his liking and if he preferred any other subject or any other style or any other author. Sankaran, the home-delivery librarian, used to scan these columns each evening when the book-carrier brought back the bundles of returned books. The column for suggestions was often unmarked by pen or pencil. But by and by, we could make some inference from the way in which the books had been handled if at all, by the readers. With all that, our selection was not far from a random hit. And yet, whenever any member of the library staff was met by a reader on the road, he was thanked for sending the very book he wanted ! Though the staff was paid miserably — mostly 30 to 40 rupees a month — such unsolicited thanks were a valuable source of joy that kept them on to sanity, in spite of their grinding poverty. The staff of the administrative office in the university even began to envy the library staff, when they saw men of position and power usually charged with a forbidding aristocratic aloofness speaking to Sundaram, or Sankaran with familiarity as if they were equals. It is true that shaking hands or exchanging smiles or words with a rich man does not clothe the child or get better food at home. All the same, it did give some consolation and joy. Above all, it did enable them to walk erect.

375 Service to the Unlettered

But even a greater joy was brought by the joy of the poorer people — and of even unlettered people — on getting the information needed by them. One example: An unlettered farmer came to the library one evening. He came from a distant city — Salem. He was growing onions; and Madras City was the chief market. He found a fall in his business. His suffering increased. He came to Madras to study the cause for the trouble. He found out that the public had begun to switch over from bulky white bulbs to tiny bulbs with a deep red colour. He felt that he should introduce that strain in his garden. He did not know how to do it. A distant relative of his, with whom he was staying, was a student in the university. He turned the farmer on to the library. The huge building, the serene silence in the reading room, and above all, the "fear of officials" discouraged him from entering the library.

He was skulking in the entrance lobby, with roaming eyes. I came on my round. The timidness of his eyes and the uncouth borrowed shirt on his body betrayed him. I asked him to come in. He crossed the wicket gate trembling with fear. Fortunately, he spoke my language. In a few minutes, the only three pamphlets we had on the subject were found out for him. They were in English. He did not know English. I translated the essential portion for him. His eyes widened and radiated joy. That night he called at my house with his student-host. He expressed his hope of being saved from ruin. I asked the student to borrow the pamphlets from the library and give his guest a full translation. The combined look of joy and gratefulness on the face of the farmer filled me with an everlasting joy. His face is still clear before my mind's eye; and it still fills me with joy.

376 Deferred Joy

3761 Anonymous Service

The left hand should not know the service done by the right hand. This is an old standard of conduct. Another more explicit statement of this ideal is that one's own mind should not remember the service done by one self. The other day a London paper reported an unknown man who jumped into the Thames, pulled out two drowning persons, and went away without even mentioning his name to anybody. We read a parallel story in the life of the Tamil saint Sundarar who flourished several centuries ago. Such an absolute effacement of self, and practice of anonymity, cannot easily be obtained. Such instances are indeed rare. But certain professions are more favourable for the development of doing service without the consciousness of doing it.

3762 Unconscious Service by Teacher

The teaching profession has occasionally such a chance. One instance has been recorded by the Head Master of an English Public School [67]. He was working as a priest on the western front in World War I. He met an old pupil of his serving as an officer. He invited him for lunch. After lunch he told him, "Bobby, I feel miserable in this trench-war. But you look so cheerful. Who taught you this fortitude?" Prompt was the reply, "You taught me, Sir." The Head Master disowned having taught anything which was of no avail to himself. But the officer said, "You didn't teach that in words, your whole way of life taught that to me — your detachment and your inner joy born of helping others, and the radiation through your face."

3763 Unconscious Service by Librarian

. The library profession has many more chances for such unconscious help being given to people. When we are conscious of any good being done, the ego in us makes us expect a return or at least gratitude. This is demoralizing. Its dangers are estimated to be so serious that in the *Aditya-hridayam* — the gene-like essence of prayer — God is invoked to kill in us any sense of dwelling on, or even becoming conscious of ungratefulness on the part of anybody. Though prepared not to expect gratitude from the individuals concerned, the ego looks at least for some public acknowledgment or recognition or lime-light of some sort. If even that is not forthcoming, the ego makes one go about bragging about one's own good deeds. It is indeed difficult to escape this self-damage of the ego when good is done consciously. If good happens without our knowledge, we escape such a self-damage. The greater the delay in the good done being brought to our knowledge, the smaller is the chance for the self-damage to take shape. The time-factor is thus very important. In the library profession, there is a great chance for the time-factor to be too long for the self-damage of ego to come into play. The mind is well sterilized with the advance of age, before a librarian gets any report of any unconscious good done. When we hear it at that stage, we get at best pure joy, totally free from gratification to one's own self. Life in library service can chasten one in that way. Here are a few instances. I mention them merely as instances of harmless deferred joy, in order to assure new aspirants to library profession that work in a library is not a mere fruitless, soul-killing routine, but that it does carry real service with it, though fortunately we are unconscious of it and thus happily escape the self-damaging effect of being conscious of it.

3764 Salem Gardener

It was 1938. A bright looking young man of about 35 walked into my room with the freedom of familiarity. But I could not recognize him. I took him to be a casual reader and asked if I could help him. He said with a smile, "Probably you do not recognize me. Yes. It will be difficult for you. For I was then poor, ill-clad, famished, and perhaps the very embodiment of worry and misery." Then he showed me the seat where he used to sit in the reading room. Then he narrated his own story. He was then an unemployed graduate . . . it appears I used to cheer him up and suggest some reading course. One day, his eyes fell on an illustrated article on fruit-crops in the *National geographical magazine*. It appears that I then found a gleam of cheer in his face and asked him if he would care to read more books on fruit culture. . . . Ultimately he settled down as a successful fruit-grower.

3765 Florida Gardener

It was 1950. I was working in the study-room allowed for me in the Columbia University Library in New York. A middle aged man called on me. He introduced himself as an Albany man. His story was most interesting. In 1926, he migrated to Florida to do tropical gardening. He applied to his local library for literature on mangoes. His librarian had written to me at Madras. I seem to have suggested three small books. These books started him in his life. I could remember none of these things. But he was dead certain. He knew my name. It was a delight for him to see my picture in the Albany papers. He did not wish to miss the chance to meet me "his benefactor !" in person, who came to his town after quarter of a century quite unexpectedly.

3766 Everywhere Experience

Immeasurable is the deferred joy contributed by hundreds of persons met with, in the several cities of India, in railway carriages and in the aeroplanes, and in the Indian Embassies abroad. Their names are not known. We had got out of touch with one another for a long stretch of years. But the first thing they do is to ask about Sundaram and other reference librarians of the Madras University Library and then give delightful anecdotes about the service they have had in the University Library.

3767 Faith and Good Cheer

The library profession in India is still thin. Many of the libraries are not yet geared to service. This creates pessimism in young entrants to the profession. Here is a typical sentence taken from a letter received from a student who had passed out in the previous year. "I have resumed duties to work as a part of an antidiluvian machine. I hope good time will come." My assurance to them is: Begin intensive reference service to readers. Do not wait for your chief to ask you to do it. He will not prevent your voluntary service. That will hasten the advent of good times. Work with faith, hope, and good cheer. Your deferred joy will become immeasurable.

377 Honorary Reference Service and Vana-Prastha

The joy of reference service should be particularly welcome to the honorary workers drawn from activated community-potential as suggested in section 257. They are persons with leisure heavily hanging on them. They are persons fixed into the habit of active life. After retirement, a sense of boredom and ennui depresses them. This can be warded off by an hour or two of reference service in the local library. This will also build up an atmosphere of respect for them among the people of the locality. The members of the local panel of honorary reference librarians may meet occasionally and exchange their experiences. Such an exchange will give them ideas to do the work better. It will also increase their zeal for drawing joy from reference service. This would amount to a modern version of the *Vana-Prastha* life, practised by our ancestors.

CHAPTER 38

REFERENCE BOOKS

381 Poverty in India

Ready reference books took shape only during the last 200 years. But India had been in a state of cultural exhaustion during this period. Therefore, few reference books are produced in India. India is therefore poor in reference books. Consequently, our reference librarians feel like distributors of drinking water in a land of drought. But they should not fall into a mood of despair. Till now, our people felt little need for information. But the country is now awake. The people have begun to feel their thirst for information. The poverty of reference books will therefore be removed soon.

382 First Step

As a first step, we should make use of the reference books in the English language. The information contained in them should be relayed to the readers in their own languages. Further, much of our reference work will have to be done as if it were of the long-range kind. As and when a particular investigation is successfully completed, the results should be recorded in reference slips, as suggested in section 365. As the reference cabinet formed of them grows, much of the reference work will gradually change over into the ready reference kind. This happens even in developed countries. Its happening will have to be more frequent in newly developing countries, without reference books of their own.

383 Collective Action

The first generation doing reference service should cumulate all its experiences of disappointment caused by the absence of reference books. The State Library Association and the Indian Library Association will have to play an active part in bringing all such experiences of disappointment to the notice of the public, the publishing trade, and the National and Regional Book Councils.

384 Magnitude of the Task

There is need for a large variety of reference books — encyclopaedias, directories, yearbooks, atlases, tables, statistical data, digests, and bibliographies, besides linguistic dictionaries. No doubt, we should begin with reference books of the generalia kind. But, we should eventually produce them in each of many subjects — engineering, technology, agriculture, animal husbandry, medicine, various arts and crafts, literature, religion, philosophy, education, geography, history, economics, sociology and law. The magnitude of the task can be inferred from the fact that in 1940, there were about 2,500 reference books in the English language. Their distribution by subjects was as follows [68].

Subject	*Number of Reference Books*	*Subject*	*Number of Reference Books*
Generalia	201	Δ Spiritual Experience	14
A Science (General)	23	N Fine Arts	63
B Mathematics	93	O Literature	189
C Physics	14	P Linguistics	765
D Engineering	160	Q Religion	115
E Chemistry	26	R Philosophy	7
F Technology	25	S Psychology	5
G Biology	3	T Education	10
H Geology	14	U Geography	129
I Botany	16	V History	28
J Agriculture	30	W Political Science	5
K Zoology	15	X Economics	178
L Medicine	103	Y Sociology	28
M Useful Arts	111	Z Law	80
		Total	2,500

385 Past Achievement

We have now general encyclopaedias in Hindi, Bengali, Marathi.

And Tamil, Telugu and Malayalam encyclopaedias also are in progress. We have a Marathi encyclopaedia on Physical Exercise. A factual account of the struggle of Dr S V Ketker in publishing the first Indian encyclopaedia — the Marathi encyclopaedia — early in the present century forms interesting reading. All honour is due to that pioneer who depended on his own initiative and industry in achieving this huge task [69]. Our linguistic dictionaries are still very few. There is an atlas in Hindi. There is hardly any reference book in particular fields. There is thus much work to be done in the field of reference works.

PART 4

CIRCULATION WORK

CHAPTER 40

MODEL LIBRARY RULES

400 Introduction

Assuming that the reader has been helped by proper reference service to pick out the book he wants, let us next examine the routine involved in allowing him to take it home for reading. The latest, simplest and cheapest method of issue work is the "Tickets Method". This method mechanizes a good deal of the routine involved in loan-work or Circulation Work as it is called. It saves the time of the reader and the staff. It also eliminates possibility for the violation of some of the rules and makes the detection of violation of some others automatic. Before going into the details of this method of issue, it will be an advantage to give a set of model rules governing circulation work as well as other matters connected with the use of a public library.

401 Hours of Opening

11 The hours, when the . . . library will be open to the public, shall be fixed by the Library Committee from time to time.

12 The Library Committee has decided as follows for the time being.

The library shall be open to the public on all days from (7 A M to 9 P M)

Note: The loan counter shall be closed half an hour before the closing of the library.

402 Admission to the Library

21 No person, who is not of sound mind, nor cleanly in person, nor properly dressed, shall be admitted into the library.

Note: The decision of the librarian, or of his deputy during his absence, in regard to these matters shall be final.

The rules may provide for admission by special permit in the case of specified classes of persons, such as non-tax payers, strangers, etc.

22 A person desirous of using the library shall enter his name and address legibly in the gate register kept for the purpose. Such

entry shall be taken as an acknowledgment that the person agrees to conform to the rules of the library.

221 Sticks, umbrellas, boxes and other receptacles and such other articles as are prohibited by the circulation staff shall be left at the entrance.

222 Dogs and other animals shall not be admitted.

241 Silence shall be strictly observed in the library.

242 Spitting and smoking are strictly prohibited.

243 Sleeping is strictly prohibited.

251 No person shall write upon, damage, or make any mark upon any book, manuscript, or map, belonging to the library.

252 No tracing or mechanical reproduction shall be made without express permission from the librarian.

253 A person shall be responsible for any damage or injury done by him to the books or other property belonging to the library. He will be required to replace such books or other property damaged or injured or to pay the value thereof. If one book of a set is injured, the whole set shall be liable to be replaced.

254 Before leaving the library each person shall return to the circulation staff any books, manuscripts or maps, taken by him for consultation.

26 Cases of incivility, or other failure in the service, should be reported immediately to the librarian, or his deputy during his absence.

403 Loan Privilege

4031 Membership

31 Any of the following is entitled to take out books on loan on enrolment as a member of the library:

1 Any tax-payer residing or having his place of business within the area of the library.

2 Any person living within the area of the library and guaranteed by any tax-payer resident within the area of the library.

3 Any person employed in an institution within the area of the library and guaranteed by the head of the institution.

311 To get enrolled as a member, a person shall fill up and sign a Form of Enrolment, which can be had free of cost at the library counter [and make a cash deposit of Rs. . . . . .].

Note: I do not recommend the portion of the above rule which is shown within square brackets.

4032 Reader's Tickets

32 Each member shall be given as many reader's tickets as the number of volumes, he is entitled to have with him on loan at one time.

321 The tickets of a member will be valid for twelve months. They can be renewed by filling up a fresh Form of Enrolment and returning to the librarian all the expired tickets along with it.

322 A book will be lent to a member only in exchange for one of his tickets. This will be handed back to the member when he returns the book, unless it is returned after due date, in which case the ticket will be handed back only after overdue charge is paid.

[33 A week's notice shall be given before a deposit is withdrawn. No deposit shall be repaid until all the books outstanding against the member and all his member's tickets have been duly returned and all the dues from him are paid.]

Note: This rule will be deleted if the portion of Rule 311 shown in square brackets is deleted.

4033 Loss of Tickets

34 A member who has lost a ticket shall make a written report of the same to the librarian.

341 Three months' time shall elapse after the date of such notice, before a duplicate can be issued. During this period, the member shall attempt to trace and recover the ticket if possible and send a second report at the end of the period, stating the result of his endeavours.

342 If the ticket has not been traced, the member shall give an indemnity bond in the prescribed form and pay a fee of ... for each duplicate ticket required.

343 After the receipt of the indemnity bond and the fee, the duplicate ticket will be issued.

[35 If a member, who has lost one or more of his tickets, applies for withdrawal of deposit amount, no action will be taken on such application till the expiry of six months after the report of loss of ticket. If the ticket is not recovered by the member before the end of that period, he shall give an indemnity bond in the prescribed form in respect of the lost tickets. After the receipt of the indemnity bond, the application for withdrawal will be dealt with in the usual way.]

Note: This rule will be deleted if the portion of Rule 311 shown in square brackets is deleted.

404 Conditions of Loan

41 Each member may have out on loan not more than . . . separate volumes at one time. He must make his own arrangement for the conveyance of books to and from the library or any of its delivery stations, except that in the case of invalid or lady members, books may be delivered once a week at their residence on payment of an advance quarterly subscription of . . . .

42 Before leaving the counter, the member shall satisfy himself as to whether the book lent to him is in sound condition; and, if not, he shall immediately bring the matter to the notice of the librarian or his deputy in his absence; otherwise he is liable to be held responsible for the replacement of the book by a sound copy.

421 If one book of a set is injured or lost, the member concerned shall be liable to replace the whole set.

422 The value shall be immediately paid to the library. It will be returned after the book or the set is actually replaced.

43 Periodical publications, directories, works difficult to replace, and such other works, as may be declared reference books by the librarian, shall not be lent out.

44 Members are not allowed to sub-lend the books of the library.

45 All books on loan shall be returned at the expiration of a fortnight from the date of issue.

451 Books temporarily in special demand may be lent for such shorter period as may be necessary or may be temporarily declared reference books under Rule 43.

452 Loans may at any time be terminated by order of the librarian.

46 If a book is not returned to the library when due, an overdue charge of five naye paise per volume per day shall be levied.

47 Loan may be renewed for a further period of one fortnight provided:

1 The renewal application reaches the librarian not less than three and not more than five clear days before the date on which the book is due;
2 No other reader has applied for the book in the meantime; and
3 Not more than three consecutive renewals shall be allowed for the same book without its production to the library for inspection.

In case condition (2) is not satisfied, the librarian shall cause a letter to that effect to be posted to the member concerned and the book shall be returnable on the due date.

48 A member against whom any overdue or other charge is outstanding shall not be allowed to borrow books [or withdraw his deposit] until he has paid the amount due.

405 General

51 The librarian may refuse, under special circumstances, admission into the library to any person or the use of any book without assigning any reason therefor.

52 The library Committee may refuse, under special circumstances, any application for the privilege of loan of books without assigning any reason therefor.

53 The Library Committee may grant special loans on such conditions as it may prescribe.

54 Any infringement of the rules will render the privilege of admission to and of borrowing books from the library liable to forfeiture.

406 Sentinel at the Rubicon

The counter is the Rubicon. The Circulation Staff are the sentinels watching and regulating the entrance and the exit of the users of the library. They should have all the loyalty and the precision of sentinels. And yet they should remember their being employees of the humane library department and not of the military department. They should be courteous without being lax, strict without being offensive, and friendly without becoming chatty. The rules of the library should be enforced in this way.

407 Vigilance of a Sentinel

The Circulation Staff should have all the vigilance and circumspection of a sentinel. Their responsibility is particularly heavy in an open access library. Nobody should be allowed to get in or get out except with their consent and under their surveillance. No book should be allowed to be taken out of the library or brought in without their permission. For an open access library implies *extreme vigilance* at the entrance and exit, and *extreme freedom* in the inside of the library to all readers. To mechanize the going out and the coming in of books, the "Reader's Ticket, Book Ticket" method of issue is being used currently. This method secures the automatic enforcement of many of the rules of the library.

408 Variety of Functions

In addition to playing the role of humane sentinels, the Circulation Section has the following variety of functions connected with the observance and enforcement of the rules of the library:

1 Maintaining all the records relating to all the thousands of users of the library;

2 Admitting users as members of the library and dealing with their withdrawal;

3 Maintaining all the records about the loan of books including inter-library loan, overduing, and collection of overdues;

4 Taking charge of all the books returned after consultation by users; and

5 All the work connected with the bespeaking or reservation of books by users, and for staff purposes.

CHAPTER 41

CIRCULATION APPARATUS

410 Parts of the Circulation Apparatus

The parts of the circulation apparatus fall into the following groups:

1 Materials to be carried by the book ;
2 Materials to be carried by the reader ; and
3 Other materials needed at the counter.

411 Materials Carried by the Book

The parts of the circulation apparatus normally to be found in the book are the following:

1 Date Label; and
2 Book Ticket.

4111 DATE LABEL

The code number for *Date Label is* O61. It is of octavo size. It should be pasted in the book so as to be its first leaf. It should consist of a sheet of 16 pound white printing paper 19×11.5 cm. 4 cm of its bottom should be turned over. This turned portion should be pasted along the edges so as to form a pocket whose mouth is 6.5 cm wide. This is to hold the book-ticket when the book is inside the library. A picture of it is shown in the next page. The turned flap should be printed in 8 point type and the rest of the label should be ruled as shown in the picture in the next page.

4112 -BOOK TICKET

The code number for *Book Ticket is* A62. It is of abnormally small size. It should be made of Manilla paper in the form of a pocket. This is to hold the reader's ticket when the book has gone out of the library. The back-fold should be 7.5×4.5 cm. The front-fold should be 4×4.5 cm. The exposed portion of the inside of the backfold should have the class number of the book in the first line, its book number in the second line, and its accession number

Date Label

7 MAR 1960			
23 MAR 1960			
9 APR 1960			
12 APR 1960			
27 APR 1960			

22
N60
136,241

22 N60
136,241

BANGALORE
PUBLIC LIBRARY

Date of release for loan

22 Feb 1960

This book should be returned on or before the date last stamped above. An overdue charge of 5 naye paise will be levied for each day the book is kept beyond that date.

in the third line. The frontfold should have the name of the author or its substitute used as the heading of the book in the first and second lines, its short title in the third line, and the series of the book, if any, as the last line. The picture of the date label opposite shows the portion of the book-ticket, projecting outside the pocket in the date label.

4113 Book-Pocket

Till now the usual practice has been to have a separate Book-Pocket to hold the book-ticket. It is made of Manilla paper; It has suitable dimensions to contain the book ticket. The practice has been to paste it inside the front cover of the book at a distance of 2.5 cm from the bottom-end and centered between the two side-edges. The alternative suggested in Section 4111 is cheaper and neater.

412 Materials Carried by the Reader

Each member should be given as many reader's tickets as the rules of the library allow. The code number for the *Reader's Ticket is* A61. It is of abnormally small size. It should be made of thick bristol board or its equivalent, say about 0.3 cm thick. The reader's ticket should be capable of being inserted into a book-ticket with ease. It should be 6×4×0.3 cm. One side should have the crest of the library printed in the centre. The words "Not transferable" should be printed above the crest and the name of the library below the crest. The other side should be left blank. The number of the ticket will be written in the first line, the name of the member in the second line, and the forenames or the initials within brackets in the third line. The address of the member should be written after these. The accompanying picture shows the two sides of reader's ticket, a book-ticket, and a book-ticket with the reader's ticket inserted in it.

4121 Ticket Number

The following interpretation of the ticket number in the picture shows how a ticket number is to be constructed:

006 = Expires in June 1960.
D62 = Member's main interest is Machine Tools.

12 = Twelfth member admitted in June 1959.
3 = Third ticket of the member.

4122 Automatic Control

It may be explicitly stated here that assuming for definiteness that a member is given three reader's tickets at any time the number of library books in his possession *plus* the number of free tickets with him, should be equal to three. If he has three books, he will have no free tickets. If he has two books, he will have one free ticket. If he has one book, he will have two free tickets. If he has no book, he will have all the three tickets with him. Thus Rule 32 of the Rules of the Library is automatically enforced.

4123 Colour Scheme

The following is a model colour scheme for tickets :

Children's Tickets	Red
Fiction Tickets	Yellow
Ordinary Tickets	Green

Usually even an ordinary book can be taken on an yellow ticket. But no fiction can be taken on a green ticket. If there are other privileges like loan of periodicals other suitable colours may be used to indicate such privileges. The colour scheme also helps automatic enforcement of rules.

22
N60
136, 241

RANGANATHAN
(S R)
Library Manual

Ranganathan series in
library science, 6

Book Ticket

22
N60
136, 241

006D62.12.3
YOGESHWAR
(T R)

RANGANATHAN
(S R)
Library Manual

Ranganathan series in
library science, 6

Coupled Ticket-Pâir

Not transferable

BANGALORE

PUBLIC LIBRARY

Reader's Ticket (Back)

006D62.12.3
YOGESHWAR
(T R)
775 Seventeenth
Cross Road
Bangalore 3

S R R

6 June 1959

Reader's Ticket (Front)

413 Materials Needed at the Counter

The counter should be provided with the following materials:

1 Trays to file reader's tickets;
2 Rubber dater and inking pad;
3 About 100 Twin-Tokens of the size and shape of Book Tickets and Reader's Tickets made of Manilla paper and numbered 1 to 100; and
4 Tokens for the custody of private property like umbrellas, sticks, boxes;
5 Date guides numbered 1 to 31; and
6 Over-due guides marked 5np, 10 np, etc.

414 Ticket-Trays

About a dozen primary charging trays are necessary. Their inner dimensions should be 25×5×4 cm. Three or more secondary or sorting trays are necessary. These should be triple trays. The inner dimensions of each member of the triple tray should be 45×5×4 cm. There should be three (or as many as may be necessary, depending on the number of members) tertiary or filing or charge trays. Each of them should be a 9-ple tray. The inner dimensions of each member of the 9-ple tray should be 45×5×4 cm. Each 9-ple tray as a whole may be of the inclined sort — the nearer edge resting on a reeper 4 cm high.

415 Conscience Box

Near the entrance wicket-gate, there should be a conscience box — a locked box with a small slit in its lid as we have in temples to collect offerings — into which the members who have delayed the return of books beyond the due date may drop their overdue charges. After practising the Victorian method of formally collecting the overdue charges with formal receipts and maintenance of separate accounts, libraries have learnt that

1 the game is not worth the candle; and
2 a splendid opportunity for the development of civic conscience is thereby being lost.

The conscience-box method is now adopted even for the collection of bus-fares in America. Our libraries should straightway begin with trust in this manner. Trust will beget trust.

CHAPTER 42

CHARGING WORK

421 Mode of Presenting

Members should be trained to present the books to be charged — i e taken home on loan — in a helpful way. They should present them with the front cover thrown open and one of their reader's tickets placed on it, so that the man at the counter can easily read the date label. Of course, they should also be trained to respect the rule of queue. If the book is in a damaged condition, set it aside for binding and tell the reader that it can be taken after repair.

422 Charging and Vigilance

For each book, rapidly tally the call number and the accession number on the book-card with those on the date-label. If they are alright, insert the reader's tickets into the book ticket, taking care to see if the class number of the book has reasonable correlation with the member number of the reader. If it is satisfactory, stamp the due-date in the earliest vacant compartment of the date-label. While doing so, release the wicket-gate. Allow the reader to pass out. Hand over the book to him. Insert the coupled ticket-pair in the charging tray. Any discrepancy in the call numbers and member numbers should be disposed of quickly. If it is too complicated, pass it on to others, as the stream of members crossing the wicket-gate should not be held up and stagnated by tumbling over one case. Without offence but with extreme vigilance, watch every person crossing the wicket-gate, whether taking a loan or not, and make sure that he does not carry away with him, unauthorized, any book or reading material of the library either forgetfully or wilfully.

423 Issue of Bespoken Book

When a reader calls for a bespoken book, take back his bespeaking card, satisfy yourself that he is the right person and issue it in the usual way. If there is a red slip with a name other than his in the book ticket, retain it while charging.

424 Sorting

As pick-up work whenever you are free from readers, arrange in their classified sequence the coupled ticket-pairs collected in the charging tray. Mark the loan-counting-sheet for them by putting against the appropriate subject a vertical stroke, except that the fifth stroke should be a horizontal one across the preceding four. This facilitates counting in blocks of five. As the statistics are being marked for each book, transfer the coupled ticket-pair to the sorting tray and file it by its class number.

425 Unusual Period of Loan

Care must, however, be taken in the case of a book loaned for an unusual period. The coupled ticket-pair must be filed, immediately after charging, behind the proper date-guide in the charged-tray at the entrance counter, after marking the statistics in another colour.

426 Daily Statistics

At the end of the day, total up the statistics. Tally the total number of issues with the number of coupled ticket-pairs standing in the sorting tray. Investigate and set right discrepancies if any. Remember that the coupled ticket-pairs mentioned in sec 425 will cause discrepancy. Transfer the coupled ticket-pairs to behind the correct due-date in the charged tray.

427 Closing Routine

Before closing down, change the dater to the due-date corresponding to the next working day. Put up a new counting-sheet for the next day. See that the charging counter is cleared of all accumulated materials and kept in a clean condition to start work on the next day.

428 Cumulation of Statistics

Add up the statistics and post the figures in the Daily Statistics Register. At the end of each week, month, and year, write the cumulative total.

CHAPTER 43

DISCHARGING WORK

431 Essential Items of Work

Discharging work consists of

1 Renewal of loan;
2 Charge of private property of readers;
3 Discharging of loan;
4 Recovering overdue books; and
5 Other routine.

The man in the discharge counter is the first person whom the reader meets in the library. He should therefore give him a genial welcome, answer his queries and make him feel like walking into the library and accepting its service. At every hour, the hour should be entered at the end of the last filled-up line in the gate register.

432 Opening Routine

As the first thing in the morning, pick out, from the coupled-ticket-pair standing behind the date-guide of the day, those that have white slips in them. Hand them over to the charging assistant so that he may renew the loans.

433 Genial Reception

When a reader approaches the entrance wicket-gate, receive him in a genial way. This does not mean getting into conversation with him. Take charge of all his private property including books, sticks, umbrellas, bags, boxes and receptacles of all sorts. Give him a token in exchange. Place its twin on his property. See that he fills the gate-register correctly and fully.

434 Discharging

If the reader has a library book to return, he should be trained to present the book in a helpful way. He should present it with the front cover thrown open so that the man at the counter can easily read the date-label. He should also be trained to respect the rule of the queue. From the last due-date stamped on the date-label and the call number of the book written on it, locate its coupled ticket-pair. Lift it up. Insert the book ticket into the pocket in the date-label, provided the accession number in the book-ticket is the same as that on the date-label of the book. If it is not, you have picked out a wrong coupled ticket-pair. You must restore it to its place and begin again. If it is alright, pull out the reader's ticket from the coupled-ticket-pair. Hand it over to the member or his agent asking him to verify whether the ticket is the right one. Release the wicket-gate and admit the person inside the library. The book-ticket will stay inserted in the pocket at the bottom of the date-label of the book.

4341 Returned Volumes

If the book-ticket does not contain a red slip, place the book on the returned-book-shelf. If it contains a red slip, it is a bespoken book. Deal with it as provided in chap 44. As and when the returned-book-shelf within the counter gets filled up, the books in it should be transferred to the returned-books-bays in the stack-room.

4342 Auxiliary Work

If the date-space in the date-label of the returned book has been filled up, paste down a new date-label. Enter the call number and accession number of the book at the proper places in it. If the book is in a damaged condition, keep it aside in the damaged-books-shelf. If it had been bespoken, write to the member concerned that it had been set aside for repair.

4343 Overdue Book

If a book returned is overdue, its coupled-ticket-pair will be behind an overdue-guide marked in naya paise. Before handing over the ticket to the reader, suggest to him gently to drop the coins into the conscience box, if he does not do so himself. The old method had been to collect the overdue charges from him and give him along with the ticket a defaced overdue-stamp of the correct value. And even older still was the practice to prepare a receipt in the miscellaneous receipt book, give the original to the reader and retain the duplicate as office copy. If the reader has not brought cash, write the amount due from him on a slip of paper. Initial and date it. Attach it to his ticket with a jem-clip. File the ticket in the kept-tickets-tray alphabetically by the name of the reader. Ask the reader to recover his ticket when he pays his overdue charges.

435 Rush Hour

In rush hours, the process of locating the coupled-ticket-pair may hold up readers at the entrance-gate resulting in a long queue and the break-down of their patience and temper. A similar undesirable situation may also be created if any casual mistake had occurred in the arrangement of the coupled-ticket-pairs in the charged tray and you have to fumble about for the correct ticket. This fumbling in the presence of readers will induce confusion and a sense of inferiority complex which will worsen your capacity for work. All this is undesirable. It is to obviate all these undesirable contingencies that you are provided with a supply of numbered twin-tokens. The moment you feel that stagnation begins, insert the pocket-member of one of the numbered twin-tokens into the book-pocket at the bottom of the date-label of the book returned. Hand over its plain member to the reader in exchange for the book. Request him to take his ticket when he leaves the library, or if he wants to go back immediately, the next time he calls at the library. Don't put such a book on the shelf reserved for books returned. Put all such books on the shelf for Held-up Books. When you get respite from the marching-in of readers, take up in succession each of the books in the held-up-books-shelf. Locate its coupled-ticket-pair with composure. When it is found, insert the proper book-ticket in the book-pocket, having taken out of it the pocket-member of the twin-token. Insert the reader's ticket into that pocket-member. Place the book on the returned-books-shelf or bespoken-books-shelf or damaged-books-shelf as the case may be. File the coupled-ticket-token in the held-up-tickets-tray in the sequence of the numbers on the token. When the reader calls for his ticket, collect from him the plain-member of the twin-token given to him in exchange for his book. Pick out from the held-up-tickets-tray the corresponding coupled-ticket-token. Hand over the ticket to the reader. Couple the numbered tokens. File the coupled-token-pair in the proper place in its tray.

436 Trimming the Charged Tray

From time to time close up the coupled-ticket-pairs in the charged tray so that they all stand erect and fill up each tray tightly. In so doing, do not move more than five coupled-ticket-pairs at a time. Otherwise they may slip out and cause disorder, delay, and confusion.

437 Renewal

If a member or his representative asks for renewal of a loan and if it is due on that very day, locate the coupled-ticket-pair. If it has no red-slip indicating having been bespoken, pass it on to the charging counter for charging. If it has a red-slip, inform the person that the renewal is not possible.

4371 Deferred Renewal

If the book is due on a later date, insert a white slip into the coupled-ticket-pair. This will remind you to renew it on its due date. If the book is already overdue, suggest that it is so and that the overdue charges should be dropped into the conscience box. If the coupled-ticket-pair has a red-slip, inform the member orally or by letter (if he had written for renewal) that the renewal is not possible.

438 Closing Routine

4381 Insertion

As the last item in the day's work, insert, at the very end of the charged-tickets, the date-guide of the day on which the books charged in the course of that day will fall due. Get the sorting tray from the colleague at the charging counter. Transfer all the tickets in them to behind that date-guide.

4382 Change of Overdue Guides

Beginning with the highest denomination, replace each overdue guide by the one showing the next higher denomination of money, if the next day is a working day. If it happens to be a holiday, the overdue guides used for replacement should be the appropriate ones. Put the guide for 5 naye paise just behind the date-guide of the next working day.

4383 Count of Overdue

Enter in the overdue-tickets-register the number of coupled-ticket-pairs standing behind each overdue guide.

4384 Overdue Notification

Write out an overdue notice card for each of the coupled-ticket-pairs standing behind the overdue guides of 10 naye paise and 50 naye paise. Despatch them.

4385 Registered Notification

Send a registered notice for each of the coupled-ticket-pairs standing behind overdue guides of one-rupee.

4386 Other Steps

In the case of those which lie behind overdue guides of 1.50 rupees, make a personal call on the members and take every other necessary step such as taking the help of the guarantors or others to recover the books.

4387 Putting up Gate-Register

Put up the gate-register sheet for the next day.

4388 Damaged Books

Transfer the books in the damaged-books-shelf to the Binding Section.

CHAPTER 44

BESPEAKING WORK

441 First Routine

Whenever a person desires to bespeak a book, give him a bespeaking card. Ask him to enter the call number, author and title of the book, and his own address in the proper places, and to affix the proper postage stamp in the proper place. In token of your having satisfied yourself that the person has filled up the necessary particulars correctly and affixed the stamp, initial the card at the left hand bottom corner and stamp the date of the day just near it. Then place the card in the temporary bespeaking box. If there is already a card with the same call number, put the figure 2 or 3, etc as the case may be, after the date stamp.

442 Locating

As pick-up work, take each of the cards out of the bespeaking box. Locate in the charged tray the coupled-ticket-pair which has the call number mentioned in the bespeaking card. Prepare a red-slip with the name of the bespeaking member and the date of bespeaking adding the serial number thereafter if there is one. Insert this red-slip inside the book-ticket. If the book-ticket is not found in the charged tray but the book is in the bespoken sequence, insert the red-slip into its book-ticket. If the book is not traceable at all, search for it, and do the needful. Enter near the right hand bottom corner of the bespeaking card, the date on which the book is due back in the library. Insert the bespeaking cards in the bespeaking cards box. All the cards in it should stand in the sequence of the class numbers of the books bespoken. If there be two or more bespeaking cards for one and the same book, arrange them among themselves in the sequence of the dates on which the bespoken cards were received. If there be two or more bespeaking cards for one and the same book and with one and the same date stamp, arrange them among themselves in the sequence of the digit entered after the date stamp. Put in the serial numbers after the due date in each of the cards.

443 Bespoken Books Shelf

The bespoken books returned to the library are to be arranged in the Bespoken Books Shelf near the entrance-gate in five groups, viz,

0 Zeroth group consisting of the books whose bespeaking cards have not yet been forwarded;

1 First group consisting of the books whose bespeaking cards were forwarded on the day;

2 Second group consisting of the books whose bespeaking cards were forwarded one day earlier;

3 Third group consisting of the books whose bespeaking cards were forwarded two days earlier; and

4 Fourth group consisting of books whose bespeaking cards were forwarded three days earlier.

The books in each of the groups are to be kept in the sequence of their call numbers. The groups are to be separated by guides. A guide is just a strip of card board 15×5 cm with the group number written prominently at both ends.

444 Notification

Towards the end of the day but in good time to catch the last mail of the day, for each of the volumes in the zeroth group, pick out the related bespeaking card from the bespeaking cards box. If there be two or more bespeaking cards of the same volume, pick out the one which is the senior-most as determined by the serial number after the due date entered at the left hand bottom corner. Tally the volume with the entry in the bespeaking card. Sign and despatch the bespeaking card to the member concerned.

445 Changing Group Guides

As soon as all the bespeaking cards are despatched, release all books behind the group guide numbered 4. Examine if they have been bespoken by others, and if so, transfer them to the zeroth group to be newly formed thereafter. If not, place them in the temporary replacing table. Then, shift the group guides in the appropriate manner — i e shift guide '4' to the place of guide '3'; guide '3' to the place of guide '2'; guide '2' to the place of guide

'1'; guide '1' to the place of guide '0'. Place guide '0' so as to cover the books, whose bespeaking cards are to be forwarded on the next day.

CHAPTER 45

LOST OR DAMAGED BOOKS

451 Action to Be Taken

Occasionally a reader may lose a volume of the library or damage it. In the former case he should be asked to supply the library with a fresh copy. In the latter case, the treatment to be given will depend upon the extent of damage. The volume may either be repaired locally, or if the damage is too serious, the reader may be asked to furnish the library with a fresh copy.

452 Special Deposit

If the decision is to get a fresh copy from the user, find out the published price of the book from the Accession Section or from trade lists, as the case may be. If the book is a rare one, it may be necessary to estimate the current price of the book from second-hand catalogues. If the decision is to have the book repaired locally, get from the Binding Section the estimated cost of the repair. In any case, make a liberal estimate so as to avoid the contingency of recovering excess amount from the user at a later stage. It is always easier to refund the balance rather than recover the excess.

4521 Advice About Special Deposit

As soon as the estimated cost is obtained, inform the user concerned in person, if he is present in the library, or by letter about the amount and ask him to pay the amount as a special deposit immediately.

4522 Receiving Special Deposit

As soon as the user brings the special deposit, receive the amount. Prepare and give him a receipt for the amount. The amount is to be transmitted to the Finance Section at the end of the day along with the miscellaneous collections.

4523 Release of Tickets

As soon as the receipting special deposit is over, pick out the related coupled-ticket-pair. Place the book-ticket in the lost-volumes-sequence. Return the reader's ticket to the member. If it is a case of damaged volume, it may happen that the user is not a member. In that case, simply transfer the book card to the lost-volumes-sequence.

453 Overdue Levy

There is the question, how long overdue charges should be allowed to accrue in the case of a lost or damaged volume:

1 Overdue charge may be made to accrue till the fresh copy arrives; or

2 The levy of the overdue charge may be stopped with effect from the date of payment of the special deposit; or

3 The levy of overdue charge may be stopped with effect from the date of notice of loss.

The adoption of the first alternative is rather too hard in Indian libraries. For a fresh copy of the book has often to be procured from foreign countries. It takes not less than six weeks for the fresh copy to arrive. It is doubtful whether it is desirable to continue to levy overdue charge for such a long time.

A more humane alternative seems to be the adoption of the second one. But there is a curious abuse of this alternative by certain unscrupulous members. In this alternative, it is open to a member wanting to retain a book for a long time after the due date, report loss of the book, pay the special deposit, and produce the old copy after he no longer requires it, with the story that he has recovered it somehow. Some members succumb to the temptation to do this, especially in the case of books of topical importance and particularly text-books which are of great importance in connection with examinations. I wonder whether this abuse may not be guarded against by providing that, in case a user returns the old library copy, he should pay the overdue charges till the date of return. Of course in this case we have no means of distinguishing genuine loss and recovery from pretended loss and recovery.

The third alternative is not desirable. Because special deposits are not easily forthcoming unless the overdue charge is made to accrue until the date of payment of special deposit. The library has to wait indefinitely long to get the special deposit.

454 Replacement

In the case of a lost book, either ask the reader to purchase a fresh copy or take his written consent for the library to purchase it on his behalf. As soon as the fresh copy arrives, pick out its book-ticket from the lost-book-sequence. Attach the date-label. Enter the accession number in the usual places. Insert the book-ticket into the pocket at the bottom of the date-label. Advise the reader that the book had been replaced. Settle his special deposit account. The damaged copy may then be returned to the member concerned with the following endorsement written on its title page:

This copy has been replaced by a fresh copy by Mr .... Hence, this copy is given away to Mr .... This is no longer property of this library.

Librarian

(Date) **(Name of the Library)**

455 Unprocurable Book

If the book is not procurable even second-hand, write off the book from the stock of the library. Appropriate the special deposit to the library fund.

456 Repair

In the case of a damaged book, as soon as the repair has been completed, inform the person concerned about it and settle his special deposit account.

CHAPTER 46

MEMBERS

461 Admission

When a person desires to become a member of the library give him two application cards. When he gives them back duly filled, examine carefully if all the items have been filled up. Verify the accuracy of the statements and also the signatures contained in them whenever necessary. If there is any discrepancy, get it rectified by the applicant. As soon as you are satisfied that everything is in order, send him into the library to acquaint himself with the arrangement and to get initiated into the library set-up and apparatus. Another member of the staff — the reference staff — may be asked to help him in this.

4611 Guarantor's Signature

Remember that in the case of a person who is not a tax-payer of the locality, he should be asked to obtain the guarantor's signature on one of the application cards.

462 Preparation of Tickets

When he is thus taken care of otherwise, prepare the necessary number of tickets of the proper colour in accordance with the rules. Each member should be given a Member-Number. Apart from the serial admission number which will be put in the application cards, the member-number also should be in it. It will be a great convenience if the member-number is so constructed that it is a short representation in ordinal numbers of the year and month in which his tickets will expire and should be returned for renewal and the main subject of interest of the reader, as determined by his vocation and other factors. The example given in section 322 will make this clear.

The life of a reader's ticket may be fixed as 1, 2, or 3 years according to local conditions. The tickets should be initialled and dated by the librarian. When the member comes back to the counter, hand over the tickets to him.

4621 Filing Application Cards

Towards the close of the day, take the application cards of all the members admitted in the course of the day. Arrange one set alphabetically by the names of the members. Arrange the other set by the Member-Numbers. File the former in the alphabetical register of members. File the latter in the classified register of members.

463 Renewal of Membership

The persons at the charging and discharging counters should detect the Reader's Tickets which are in or after the month of their expiry. The members concerned should be advised to present all their tickets at one time and get them renewed for a further period. As the tickets are renewed, their old application cards may be transferred to their respective new sequences with a note of their dates of transfer and with any alternations that may be necessary in them. It may be a good habit to make a list of the expired admission cards lying in the classified register; find out the members concerned, and get the tickets renewed.

464 Lost Tickets

The experience with cases of lost tickets in the Madras University Library is of some interest. For some years, the following practice was adopted. Whenever a member notified loss of tickets, he was asked to report at the end of three months the result of his endeavour to trace them out. If, at the end of that period, he was unable to trace them out, duplicate tickets were given without any charge. It was found that this privilege was abused in several ways. After taking the duplicate tickets, the old tickets were also presented. The tickets reported to be lost were sometimes presented by the relatives of the members, the relatives stating that the member gave them the tickets for their use. Some members reported loss of tickets repeatedly almost every year. While the tickets of some members were locked up in the library against overdue charges, they used to come months later with the story that the tickets were lost. Due to one cause or other, notice of lost tickets came to be received almost every week.

Then, it was felt that something should be done to help the formation of a higher sense of responsibility in the matter of library tickets. The practice introduced was to charge a fee for the issue of duplicate tickets and to ask the members to execute an indemnity bond. No doubt, it is not happy to have this procedure. But this practice had the desired result. Notification of loss of tickets fell down largely in numbers.

4641 Observation Slip

When a member notifies loss of a ticket, send him a copy of the rules regarding loss of ticket and the procedure to be followed. Then prepare an Observation Slip. This should have the number of the ticket in the first line, the name of the member in the next line, and the date of notice of the loss of ticket in the third line. The Observation Slips should be kept in the Observation Slips Box in a classified sequence.

4642 Detection Work

As a pick-up work, the person at the discharge-counter should examine the charged tickets-tray to find out if any of the lost tickets lies charged. The man at the charging counter should also have before him a list of the numbers of the lost tickets to facilitate detection in case any of them is presented. When any ticket is presented, it must be filed in the kept-ticket-tray with the necessary note explaining the circumstances of detection. The owner should be notified about it. If any mal-practice is suspected, it should be pursued in a proper way.

4643 Duplicate Ticket

At the expiry of three months, or whatever period is provided therefor in the rules, the member concerned may be asked to make a report about the results of his endeavour to trace the lost ticket. If it is still not found, he may be furnished with a draft form of indemnity bond and asked to produce the bond on the appropriate stamp paper. If the bond is in correct form, he may be asked to pay the duplicate ticket fee prescribed by the rules and then a duplicate ticket may be given to him with the word "duplicate" written across it.

465 Overdue and Other Collections

The Circulation Section is likely to collect money as overdue charges, special deposits, and fees for duplicate tickets. Open the conscience box before the Accounts Section closes for the day. Hand over to the Accountant the total sum received on all the three heads mentioned above. The date and the amount should be entered in the Transmission Register and the signature of the Accountant taken on it in token of his having received the amount.

466 Overdue Stamps

In case the conscience box system is not introduced, but the overdue-stamp system is adopted, the Circulation Section should take a permanent advance of overdue stamp books worth Rs 5 or any other amount fixed according to local conditions, from the Accountant. Every evening the maximum integral number of rupees contained in the overdue collections of the day should be given to the Accountant and overdue stamp books of equal value should be taken.

467 Receipt Book

If the antiquated receipt book system is still insisted on, the entire collections of the day should be remitted to the Accountant each day and the signature of the Accountant should be received not only in the Transmission Register but also on the back of the counter-foil of the last receipt covered by the amount. The Transmission Register may give also the inclusive receipt numbers covering the amount remitted.

CHAPTER 47

FORMS AND REGISTERS

In what follows if the first letter of the code number is 'A', the form is of abnormally small size. If the first letter of the code number is 'C', the form is of card size 75×125 mm. If the first letter of the code number is 'Q', the form is of the quarto size. If the first letter of the code number is 'S', the form is of the folio size.

A66 *Overdue-stamp*. Overdue-stamp should be designed in a form similar to a postage stamp with the coat of arms of the library as the device. The value of each label should be marked as 5 naye paise. They should be bound in booklets of Re 1.

C612 *Bespeaking card*. Printed. 8 point type. Bristol board. White.

One side is reserved for call number, author, and title. The text of the form is as follows:

(Name of the library) **(Date)**

Dear Sir,

The book mentioned on the other side is now available in the library. Kindly arrange to take it within three days.

The book will not be issued unless this card is produced.

Librarian

***Note*: 1 Write the address on the other side and affix necessary postage stamp;**
2 This card can be used for registering one volume only.

The left half of the other side should have the following words printed:

Call Number

Author

Title

The right half is reserved for address.

C61 *Overdue-notice card*. Printed. 8 point type. Bristol board.

White. The text of the form is as follows:

(Name of the library) (Date)

Dear Sir,

The undermentioned book/books due from you on .... has/have not yet been returned. Kindly return it/them immediately along with the overdue charges.

C62 *Application card*. Printed. 8 point type. Bristol board. White. Tray. The text of the form is as follows on one of the sides:

(Name of the library) (Date)

Adm Numb Memb Numb

Name in block letters (write last word first and the other words or initials after it in circular brackets)

House address

Business address

Vocation or subject of main interest

The second and the later lines may be printed so that the last line ends near the bottom of the card. This will leave ample space between the first and the second lines to write revised admission numbers and member-numbers for a number of years.

The text on the other side of the card should be as follows. The unwanted part will be struck off.

I request to be admitted as a member of the ..... Public Library and I agree to abide by its rules. I am a tax-payer and I reside in Numb .... of Street of Ward Numb ....

Date Signature

I am a tax-payer and I reside at Numb .... street of Ward Numb ...... The person mentioned above is known to me. I recommend that he be admitted as a member of the library.

Date Signature

C64 *Lost ticket observation slip*. Stencil. Ledger paper. Box. The row headings are to be as follows:

Name of the member
Number of the ticket lost
Date of notice
Date of report of the endeavour to trace the lost ticket
Date of issue of duplicate
Remarks

Q64 *Overdue register*. Printed. 8 point type. Ledger paper. White. Loose leaf binder.
The number of rules below the column headings is to be 10 on each side.
Row headings near the top are to be as follows:

(Name of the library) (Date)
Address . . . . Name . . . .
Deposit Numb Numb and nature of tickets

Below that the following column headings are to be printed:
Call number (4 cm); Due date (2.5 cm); Return date (2.5 cm); Days overdue (1.5 cm); Overdue charge R Np (2.5 cm); Date of collection (2.5 cm); Receipt number (2.5 cm); Remarks (2.5 cm).

Q66 *Miscellaneous receipt book*. Printed. 8 point type. 21 lb printing paper. White. To be bound in booklets of 50. Each sheet is to consist of a receipt form and its counter-foil. The boundary line between the receipt form and the counter-foil is to be perforated. The text of the receipt form is as follows:

(Name of the library)

Ser Numb
Received from . . . . the sum of R. . . . . Np . . . . as per details given below:
Special deposit
Fee for . . . duplicate ticket
Overdue charge on a book due on . . . . (Omit this if overdue stamp or conscience box is used)
Date

Chief of Circulation Section

Circulation Assistant

Librarian

S61 *Gate register*. Printed. Display type. 21 lb printing paper. White. To turn on the longer edge. The number of horizontal lines below the column headings in each side is to be 15 and are to be numbered 1 to 15. The columns are to be parallel to the shorter side.

The column headings are to be:

Ser number (2.5 cm); Name in block letters (7.5 cm); Full address (15 cm); Qualifications (4 cm); Token number (1.5 cm); Remarks (4 cm).

The text of the form above the column headings is to be as follows:

PLEASE WRITE LEGIBLY **(Name of the library)**

Enter your name and address in token of your agreeing to abide by the rules of the library.

S62 *Loan counting sheet*. The vertical columns may show either each hour or longer intervals for the period when the library is open each day. A sufficient number of columns may also be provided for the totals at suitable intervals, say one at 9 A M, another at 12 noon, another at 3 PM, another at 6 P M, another at 9 P M, and another for the grand total. In addition it may be advisable that columns may be opened to note the actual number of readers in the library at some important moments to be decided according to local conditions. The row-headings should be the symbols for the main classes of subjects and such of the sub-classes as are of special interest to the locality. In recording the count of books issued, in a particular subject in a particular hour or time interval, the first four strokes may be vertical and the fifth a horizontal one across these four. This will facilitate counting. A portion of the loan counting sheet is shown below as a sample.

			3 PM — 6 PM	
V W			 11	7 2

S63 *Consultation counting sheet.* This may be similar to the Loan Counting Sheet.

S64 *Circulation diary* (Daily). The main headings of the columns are to be the symbols for the main classes of the subjects and such of the sub-classes as are of special interest to the locality. For each subject heading, the sub-headings should be "Consultation", "Loan" and "Total". There should also be the following additional headings: Grand total with the sub-headings "Consultation," "Loan" and "Total"; Total Number of Readers; Receipt of Inter-Library Loan; and Issue of Inter-Library Loan. The row-headings should be the dates of the month with additional rows interpolated at proper places — for the total of the week and cumulative total for the month at the end of dates 7, 14, 21, 28 and the end of the month.

S65 *Circulation diary* (Monthly). The monthly Circulation Diary should have column-headings similar to the daily circulation diary. Its row-headings should be the months with progressive totals, that is to say January: February; Cumulative total; March; Cumulative total; etc.

S66 *Routine diary.* The column headings should be:

1 *General Correspondence*

11 Authorization letters received; 12 Authorization letters disposed; 13 Other letters received; 14 Other letters disposed; 15 Letters originated; 16 Reminders sent.

4 *Renewal and Bespeaking*

41 Renewal requests received; 42 Renewals done; 43 Renewals rejected; 44 Bespeaking requests received; 45 Bespeaking cards sent; 46 Bespeaking cards untraced.

6 *Overdue Cards*

61 First reminder sent; 62 Second reminder sent; 63 Third reminder sent; 64 Registered reminder sent.

4 *Admission*

41 Tax-payers; 42 Others.

5 *Renewal*

51 Tax-payers; 52 Others.

6 *Loss of Tickets*

61 Tickets lost; 62 Lost tickets detected; 63 Duplicates issued.

7 *Loss of Books*

71 Books lost; 72 Books damaged; 73 Special deposit cases; 74 Books replaced.

CHAPTER 48

FILES

481 File Numbers

The following table gives a scheme for numbering the files of the Circulation Section. The meanings of the terms will be found explained in section 508.

Name	*Class Numb*	*Filing Characteristic*
Use	61	Rules
Member	611	Member
Consultant	612	Consultant
Study group	614 (followed by the class number of the subject)	Leader
Ineligible	615	Correspondent
Enquirer	618	Enquirer
Bespeaking cards	6234	Nil
Inter-library borrowing	625 (followed by the class number of the subject)	Heading
Lending and borrowing libraries	652	Library

482 Transfer to Record

All the files of this section are to be transferred to the record sequence one year after it is closed.

483 Destruction of Record

The files relating to used or permanent bespeaking cards returned by members may be destroyed after one year. All other files may be destroyed after three years.

PART 5

WORK BEHIND THE SCREEN

CHAPTER 50

INTRODUCTION

501 General and Distinctive Work

A Library shares many items of administrative routine with other offices, for example, those relating to personnel, finance, accounts, correspondence, printing, stationery, supplies and services, and building and equipment. A library is usually a dependent body. Therefore, the routine about most of these items may have to be in conformity with that of the parent-body. In the case of a public library, the Local Body is likely to be the Local Library Authority. It prescribes the routine. A systematic account of these items can be found in Part 3 of *Library administration*. We shall confine ourselves here largely to the distinctive library routine. These relate to books and periodicals, their selection, purchase, inclusion in stock or accessioning, payment, preparation for dues, arrangement in the stack-room, and binding. In regard to these, there is some difference between books *qua* books and periodicals. In the case of the latter, the finished volume does not come out at once, but in succession in the form of fascicules issued at regular — and more often irregular — intervals. These have to be gathered together, as soon as the title-page and index arrive, and made into a volume. Further, the issues should be made available as and when they come and not allowed to be idle until a volume is completed and bound. The work behind the screen should be done systematically and expeditiously. For, the maximum possible time should be saved to attend to readers, in conformity with the Fourth Law of Library Science. Further, every item of routine should be revised, to avoid errors. Otherwise, the cumulation of errors through time will be injurious to the efficiency and the reputation of the library.

502 Branch Library

A branch library should have only the following items of work behind the screen:

1 The receipt of the current issues of periodical publications;

2 Maintenance of the stack-room;
3 Maintenance of the building and the stores.

All other work behind the screen should be done by the central library. As a result, the staff of a branch library should be able to devote practically all its time to circulation work, reference service, and extension work. This will satisfy the Fourth Law.

503 Central Library

Even a city or district central library should spend only minimum time in classification and cataloguing. This will be made possible by the system of centralized classification and cataloguing coming into vogue in the country. Thus the books will arrive at the city and district central libraries with the call numbers printed in the back of the title-page and tooled on the spine. Printed catalogue cards for all the book entries will also come along from the State Central Library. At any rate, they can be bought from that Library.

CHAPTER 51

BOOK-SELECTION

511 First Step

The first step in the distinctive part of library administration relates to book-selection. This is conditioned by three factors:

1 The demand, in the light of local interest, in different areas of the field of knowledge.

2 The supply or the extent and nature of the availability of books in the market, preference always being given to sumptuous editions on good paper with large type and plenty of illustrations; and

3 The total finance available and the proportion in which it is allocated to different subjects and standards in relation to the strength or weakness of the already existing collection in the various subjects and standards.

512 Ascertaining Demand

The subject-distribution of the circulation of books in the library will give a picture of the demand current in the locality. The library should also anticipate potential demand by studying the happenings in the locality, in the country and in the world, and the special festivals and celebrations expected to occur in the year. The amount for books should be allocated for different subjects in the light of the details arrived at in assessing the demand. Without making undue deviation from the prevailing reading standard and taste, the library should seek to elevate them progressively, in small *quanta* by its book-selection standards.

513 Sources

The chief sources for selection of books in English are the *Bookseller* and the *Publisher's circular* of Great Britain and the *Publisher's weekly* of the United States, which are weeklies; also the *English catalogue* of Great Britain and the *Wilson's catalogue* of the United States, which are available as annuals. The chief sources for selection of books published in India are the *Quarterly* list of publications issued by the Registrars of Books of the Constituent States and the Indian National Bibliography and the State Bibliography of each State publishing it. Other sources of both kinds of books are the catalogues of individual publishers and booksellers; the bibliographies in books; independent bibliographies; and book reviews in periodicals. The Sunday editions of the *Dailies* in India contain literary pages in which reviews are published.

514 Suggestion Tray

Books of probable interest to the readers are likely to be brought to the notice of the library by the readers themselves. When the suggestion reaches the library, a book selection card should be prepared and filed in the suggestion-tray in a classified sequence.

515 Weeding Out

The printed sources should be systematically filed on shelves. As and when a new edition of the source arrives, the old edition should be discarded in the case of ephemeral materials or removed to the bibliographical collection if they are worth the retention.

516 Routine

The sources for book selection should be scanned systematically as and when they become available and a book-selection card should be prepared for each selected item. It should be roughly classified and its standard symbol (like elementary, ordinary, advanced, and so on) should also be tentatively put on the card. These cards should be filed in a classified sequence in different sets according to the standard. The accumulated cards should be discussed at convenient intervals — say once in a month on the appointed day — with the concerned specialists and the sanction of the Library Committee or the Librarian, as the case may be, should be obtained for the finally prepared Indent.

517 Forms and Registers

C12 *Book Selection Card.* Printed. 6 pt type. Bristol Board, white for purchased books, green for gift books. Red for bound volumes of periodicals. The text on one side should be as shown below:

The text on the other side be as follows:

Ac N Don N Wl N
Cl N
Auth

Title

Size Coll Ed Yr
Pub Pub price

Series etc

Review
Reference
Vendor Cost

Indian
Foreign

Order N
Voucher N

	Date	Units
Sel		
Apprd		
Order		
Recd		
Paid		
Accnd		
Cut		
Clasd		
Cat		
Shld		
Bound		
Wl		

Q12 *Book selection consultation letter form.* Stencil. 21 lb. Printing paper. White. The text of the form is as follows:

Subject: BOOK SELECTION

I have the honour to enclose herewith (number) book selection cards in (subject) for your consideration. Please be good enough to sort them into the three groups, "approved", "deferred", and "rejected". The three groups may be separately bundled and sent to me along with a covering letter embodying your recommendation.

The balance available for purchase of books in your subject within the current financial year is Rs....

Expecting your reply within a week.

S13 *Indent noting form.* Stencil. 21 lb. Printing paper. White. The text of the form is as follows:

Outside N — Dated...
File N — Date of receipt...
Subject: Indent for books

Librarian's note	*Office note*
	N of items recommended N of items already available or on order N of items recommended for duplication Estimated cost of the items not in library Rs Estimated cost of the duplications recommended Rs Total estimated cost Rs Allotment for books Rs Amount already appropriated Rs Balance available Rs Remarks

Library Committee's decision

Note: If the librarian is the sanctioning authority, the last line may be omitted. In the first column, the words and "Sanction" may be added after "Note".

S15 *Daily diary.* Its headings should be the following:

11 Letters received
121 Letters replied
122 Letters filed
141 Letters drafted
142 Routine letters issued

15 Reminders sent
21 Indents called for
22 Indents received
31 Book selection cards checked with selected cards tray
32 Book selection cards checked with order tray
34 Book selection cards checked with bills on hand
35 Book selection cards checked with catalogue

S16 *Weekly diary.* This should show the number of book selection cards written. Its headings must be the symbols for the main classes of classification used.

418 Files

Name	*Amplifying device*	*Filing characteristic*
Sources	Subject Device or/ and Language Device	Correspondent
Selection	Subject Device	Do
Indent	Do	Do
Allotment	Do	Do
Outward enquiries	Do	Do
Inward enquiries	Do	Do

All these files may be transferred to the record sequence one year after it is closed. They may be destroyed after three or five years according to convenience.

CHAPTER 52

BOOK-ORDER

521 Introduction

The work of ordering books in Indian libraries is at present more difficult than it is elsewhere. It is English and American books that figure most in them. Thus, the chief book-markets are thousands of miles away in far-off London and New York. As a result Indian Libraries are not able to get books on approval or to choose between different editions by actual inspection of books. The task of deciding whether a new edition is substantially different from the one already in the library becomes extremely difficult. The Book-Order Section in Indian libraries has therefore to take a much greater responsibility and put in much more work in checking the indents with the stock, than in European and American libraries. Of late however, a few enterprising booksellers have begun to stock general books in important state capitals, such as Bombay, Calcutta, Delhi, Lucknow and Madras.

In the matter of Indian publications, the situation is even worse. The publishing trade is not yet properly organized in India except for text-books. In many cases, the author himself has to play the role of publisher and bookseller. He may live in an out-of-the-way place, and as may be expected, he has not developed business methods. Not infrequently it happens that he does not respond at all to orders.

522 Standing Vendors

It is a moot point whether it is advantageous for a library to buy its books directly from the publishers or through a standing vendor. In the case of most books, there may be an advantage to have a standing vendor. The Library Authority should select the standing vendor once in three years. The choice should be settled by the competence of the vendor to make complete and prompt supply. There should be a clause in the contract for the cancellation of the contract for delay of more than three months. After the introduction of net-book agreement, the monetary terms of the contract will be simple and uniform. Even till then, the pestering practice of calling for tenders for every order should not be adopted.

5221 Contract

It is necessary to stipulate certain conditions of a bibliographical nature in appointing standing vendors. They should be asked to undertake the following responsibilities:

0 The contract is liable to be cancelled if the supply is not completed within three months of the order;

1 Every volume should be carefully collated before being sent. If any defect is discovered at this end, they should take back the defective copy and supply a sound copy at their own cost, including the to and fro freight;

2 The latest edition of the book is to be supplied, unless there are specific instructions to the contrary,

3 If the order contains a note that a certain edition of a particular book is already in the library, they should find out if the later edition in the market is substantially different from the one in the library. If not, the book should not be supplied, but an advice should be sent. In cases of doubt, they should state the case and supply the book only after receiving a confirmatory order;

4 If the book is a reissue of another book under a different title, they should advise the library about it and send the supply only after receiving a confirmatory order;

5 If a book is an off-print from a periodical publication or another book, they should advise the library about it and send the supply only after receiving a confirmatory order;

6 If a book is really a foreign publication, though listed in the trade lists of their country by the local representatives of the foreign publisher, they should advise the library about it and send the supply only after receiving a confirmatory order;

7 If there is any difference in the name or in the spelling of the name of the author or in the title, they should advise the library about it and send the supply only after receiving a confirmatory order;

8 If any book occurs in more than one order or is covered by any of the standing orders, only one copy should be sent and

a second copy should not be sent without getting a confirmatory order; and

9 In all these cases, if they send a wrong supply, they should take it back at their own cost.

523 Second-hand Books

In the matter of out-of-print books, it is best to obtain quotations from different second-hand booksellers and decide the vendor in each case on its merits, rather than appoint a single standing vendor. Very often the catalogues of the second-hand booksellers may obviate even the necessity for enquiry. But these catalogues should not be relied upon, if the amount is considerable. It may be possible to get better terms by obtaining competitive quotations.

524 Ordering

It is desirable that order-work is distributed evenly throughout the year and an order is sent out regularly once in a week or a month on an appointed day. The routine for each order may be as follows: Arrange the finally sanctioned book-selection cards alphabetically by the names of authors and check carefully to eliminate unintended duplications of all kinds. For this purpose, check with the

1 Catalogue of the library;
2 Standing-order-cards;
3 Outstanding-order-cards;
4 Bills awaiting payment; and
5 Exchange list of the library if any.

Separate the cards for the books which can be got as gifts and apply for them. Type four copies of the order-list for the surviving cards, send one with the order to the vendor. Leave one for use in advising readers. Use the third as office copy. File the fourth copy behind a guide showing the week in which the supply is due. This will be used for the Vigilance Work described in section 526.

The corresponding book-selection cards now gain the status of order cards. Insert these in their proper alphabetical places, in the order tray which contains the outstanding cards.

5241 Standing Order

It is desirable to give standing orders for the following classes of books:

1 *Series-books*, i e belonging to a series all the volumes of which the library has decided to buy;
2 *Multi-volumed books*, i e books in two or more volumes all the volumes of which are not published simultaneously;
3 *Instalment-books*, i e books published in successive parts or fascicules which should be accumulated in the library and bound after the title-page arrives;
4 *Subscription-books*, i e books for which advance payment is to be made either in full or in part before actual publication.

525 Receiving the Supply

When the supply arrives, arrange the books in the sequence in which they are entered in the bill. Lift the order card of each book from the order tray and insert it on its title-page. If there is no order card for a book, it has been either already paid for or it was never ordered. When all the books have got their respective cards, carefully collate the books, scrutinize and approve them only if they answer to every detail furnished in the respective order cards. Then pass the books on for classification, cataloguing, and shelf-registering. Defects may also be detected at this stage. Hence, defer cutting, stamping, accessioning and payment till those processes are over. Retain the order cards with you. They form the control to ensure that all the books come back for accessioning. Various difficulties may crop up in this work. These are enumerated and the means of dealing with them are given in Chapter 24 of the *Library administration*.

5251 Supply of Standing Order

The procedure for receiving supplies of standing order, and watching their regular supply, should be similar to the one described in section "53 Periodical Publications".

526 Vigilance Work

As soon as a book order is sent out, file the fourth copy of the order in the Book-Order Vigilance Pad behind the week-guide of the due date of supply. The files behind a week-guide are to be arranged on the basis of the following successive characteristics: (1) Vendor; (2) Order Number; and (3) Order Date. The due date also should be filled up at that time. The items received should be ticked as and when the supply or report arrives. It may not arrive all at one time. In every week in which some items lie unticked, shift the vigilance order copy to the proper place behind the next week-guide. After the supply is completed it may be destroyed.

527 Forms and Registers

C24 *Standing order card.* Manuscript. Bristol board. White. Tray. Front side 7 lines. Back side 18 lines.

Row headings at the top of the front side:

First line: Series Heading

Second line: S O N . . . dated . . . Period

Third line: Vendor . . Note

Column headings for the remaining part of the first side and for the back side:

Serial Vol N (12 cm). Accession N (18 cm). Voucher N and Date (25 cm). Call N (30 cm). Heading (30 cm). Price (6 cm).

Q235 *Order form to standing vendors.* Stencil. 21 lb. Printing paper. White. The text of the form is as follows:

Subject: Book Order

Please supply the . . . Library under the usual conditions with the books in the enclosed lists, viz

Order Number Dated Remarks

S25 *Weekly diary* (*Routine*). Its headings should be the following:

11 Letters received
121 Letters replied
122 Letters filed
141 Letters drafted
142 Routine letters issued
15 Reminders sent

21 Indents received
22 Indents returned
323 Book order cards checked with outstanding order tray
327 Book order cards checked with standing order cards
34 Book order cards checked with bills on hand
3495 Book order cards checked with exchange list
35 Book order cards checked with catalogue
38 Book order cards checked with shelf
41 Standing orders issued for series books
42 Standing orders issued for multivolumed books
43 Standing orders issued for instalment books
44 Standing orders issued for subscription books
5 Order cards filed
7 Ordinary books received from vendor
71 Series books received from vendor
72 Multivolumed books received from vendor 6664
73 Fascicules of instalment of books received from vendor
74 Subscription books received from vendor
754 Volumes and cards transmitted to the accession section

S26 *Weekly diary* (*Subject*). Its headings must consist of the symbols for the main divisions of the book classification used or some suitable modification of them.

528 Files

Name	*Class Number*	*Filing Characteristic*
Standing vendors	21 (Subject Device)	Vendor
Standing vendors (Second hand books)	218 do	do
Enquiries and quotations	22 do	Heading
Ordinary books ordering	23 do	Vendor and date of order
Ordinary books order doubt clearing	234 do	Heading
Series ordering	241 do	Series heading
Multivolumed books ordering	242 do	Heading
Instalment books ordering	243 do	do

Prepublication ordering	244	(Subject Device)	Heading
Gift books	28		Donor
Outward enquiries	291		Correspondent
Inward enquiries	292		do

The files may be transferred to the record sequence one year after disposal and destroyed five years thereafter.

CHAPTER 53

PERIODICAL PUBLICATIONS

530 Introduction

Periodicals are prone to develop idiosyncrasies of several kinds. Of these, irregularity in publication and supply affects the administrative routine most. If the non-receipt of a particular issue is not brought to the notice of the publisher promptly, there is a great probability of the library never getting it. Hence the greatest amount of vigilance and promptness is necessary in dealing with periodical publications, and it must be achieved without undue dependence on mere memory. It is best done by means of a simple Three Card System. A card 125×75 mm will last for 6 years for weeklies and for twenty-five years for monthlies, if they are ruled on both sides. It may not be worth-while to bind and preserve all the periodicals. What must be preserved should be decided by the authorities.

531 Renewal Order

It is desirable not to change the list of current periodicals violently from year to year. A periodical which it has been decided to have bound and preserved should not be light-heartedly discontinued in one year and renewed in another year. Thus most of the periodicals should be given a standing order. It is conducive to good business to send a renewal order once in a year on an appointed day and call for bills for subscription. For subscriptions of most periodicals are payable in advance. This is enforced by the publishers since they cannot otherwise decide how many copies they should print. Foreign periodicals will, therefore, have to be renewed even in October so that payment may reach the other side before the year begins. For convenience of routine it is better to renew Indian periodicals also in October.

532 Three Card System

The prompt receipt of the current issues of each periodical publication is to be watched with vigilance. Vigilance is best practised by the Three-Card System in a big library and by a Two-

Card System in a small library. One of these cards is called the Registered Card. Its use is described in section 533. Its structure is given in section 537. The second card is called the Check Card. Its use is described in section 534. Its structure is given in section 537. The third card to be used in a large library is called the Classified Index Card. Its use and description can be found from **Chap** 23 of *Library administration.*

533 Registering

As soon as the mail arrives each day, after satisfying yourself that each packet is addressed to the library, open the wrapper of each and insert it in the periodical. Arrange the periodicals alphabetically by the title. The rest of the work is to be done for each periodical successively. Collate it, and see if any abnormalities need attention. Note them at the top of the back of the front cover. Put all such cases aside in the deferred tray. If it is normal, pull out its register-card. If it is not a duplicate copy, make the necessary entry in the register-card. Taking the class number from the register-card, write it near the right hand top corner of the front cover of the periodical. If the issue is not the one immediately after the one last registered, the entry should not be made in the next vacant horizontal line but in the line that would be appropriate to it. Write a reminder card for the earlier issue not received and put it in the week's current box for despatch. If it is a gift periodical and if an acknowledgement is due, write out the acknowledgement and put it in the week's current box. If the title-page, contents, and index are due but have not come, write a reminder card for them also and put it into the week's current box. Stamp on the covers, on all the plates and on the first and the last pages of the periodicals registered and enter the date of receipt on the cover.

534 Vigilance

As soon as a periodical is registered, pick out its check-card. It should be found among the cards lying behind the current week's guide. Transfer it to behind the guide-card of the week in which the next issue is due. For example, if we are now in the first week of March, the current week's guide-card will be 3.1. If the periodical is a weekly, the check-card should be transferred to behind the guide-card 3.2. If the periodical is a monthly, the check-card should be transferred to behind the guide-card 4.1. If the periodical is a quarterly, the guide-card should be transferred to behind the guide-card 6.1, and so on. If the check-card is not found behind the guide-card 3.1, look up the register-card for the date on which the preceding issue was registered. Add the period of the periodical to the number of that week. The result will show the guide-card behind which the check-card could be found.

5341 Notifying

On the last day of the week for each of the check-cards still lying behind the guide-card of the week, write out a reminder card. Fill up in each check-card the details about the reminder. Then transfer all the check-cards to behind the next week's guide-card.

535 Display

If any sheet in any of the periodicals registered is loose, fix it up. The Laws of Library Science require that all the periodicals should be promptly registered and displayed for the use of the public. A compact display table for periodicals was designed by me in 1937. It is now being widely used all over the world. A picture and the specification for it is given in Annexure 2 of my *Five laws of library science*, ed 2, 1957. It adds to cleanliness and strength without taking away the distinctive look of each periodical if it is encased in a plastic cover now available in all suitable sizes with Libraco Company of England. Otherwise, leave the periodical as it is without any cover. Arrange the periodicals in the classified sequence. Take them to the display-table. In the case of each, take out the preceding number lying on it and insert the current one. All the older numbers collected in this way should be distributed in the loose-numbers-shelf, so that they may be readily available for consultation.

536 Rounding-off

5361 Completion of Volume

As soon as the title-page and index are received for a volume of a periodical, register it, collect together all the issues covered by the title-page and index, collate them, and bundle them up.

At the end of the week get accessioned and catalogue each completed volume of a periodical that the library has decided to keep permanently.

5362 Faulty Cases

All faulty cases due to wrong delivery, defects found in cumulation, duplication, and all other cases should be attended to each week.

5363 Payment of Subscription

Every week collect the bills received for payment of periodicals. For each bill examine the register-card. See if the subscription has not been paid already. See also if the claim is for the correct amount. Certify in the bill that the amount may be paid. It will be good to have a rubber stamp for it with the headings:

1 Volume last paid;
2 Date of last payment;
3 Amount of last payment;
4 Volume for which claimed;
5 Amount claimed; and
6 Explanation of discrepancy if any.

As soon as payment is sanctioned, note on the register-card, the voucher-number and its date.

5364 Accessioning

As soon as a cumulated volume is accessioned, note the accession number in the registration card against the number of the volume.

5365 Cumulative Index

Scan through the pages of the periodicals received, for announcement of cumulative index. If any such index is announced, take steps to order for it.

5366 Loose Numbers

Lending of loose numbers of periodicals or newspapers is not generally allowed in public libraries. However, we have found a tendency in the libraries of many of the developed countries to lend out current issues of periodicals after they had been on the display-table for at least one week in the case of weeklies and for one month in the case of monthlies and periodicals of longer periodicity.

537 Forms and Registers

C32 *Renewal order card.* Printed. 8 point type. Bristol board. White. The text of the form is as follows:

Reference: This office standing order No . . . dated . . .
Kindly renew, on behalf of the . . . library the subscription to . . . for volume/ year . . . and send your bill in duplicate for payment as usual.

C331 *Register-card.* Printed. 6 point type. Bristol board. White. 7 lines in the front page and 14 lines in the back. Gift cases, black border. Back side, column headings only. The text is as follows:

Title			Payment	
			Vol or Year	Voucher N & Date
Vendor				
Cl N	Period	Order N & Date		
			Ann Subs	

Vol & N	Date of pub	Date of rect	Vol & N	Date of pub	Date of rect

C332 *Check card.* Printed. 6 point type. Bristol board. White. 14 lines on each side. Gift cases, black border. The column headings are as shown below:

Heading **Period**

Vol and N	Date of Rem	L's Initials	Vol and N	Date of Rem	L's Initials	Vol and N	Date of Rem	L's Initials	Vol and N	Date of Rem	L's Initials

C34 *Binding peculiarities slip.* Manuscript. Ledger paper. White. The row headings in the form are as follows:

1 Title
2 Volume number
3 Year
4 Class number
5 Covering material
6 Clubbing or splitting peculiarities, if any
7 Assembling peculiarities, if any

C361 *T C I Reminder card.* Printed. 8 point type. Bristol board. White. The text of the form is as follows:

I have to inform you that the Title Page, Contents, and Index to Vol. . . of the . . . have not yet been received here. Kindly despatch them at an early date.

C362 *Non-supply card.* Printed. 8 point type. Bristol board. White. The text of the form is as follows:

I have to inform you that No . . . of Vol . . . of the . . . was the last part received. Kindly bring the supply up to date and send future parts as issued.

C363 *Gap-in-supply card.* Printed. 8 point type. Bristol board. White. The text of the form is as follows:

I have to inform you that N . . . of Vol . . . of the . . . has not yet been received though a subsequent part is to hand. Kindly fill up the gap in supply at an early date.

Q32 *Standing order form.* Stencil. 21 lb printing paper. White. The text of the form is as follows:

Subject: PERIODICAL PUBLICATION ORDER

Please supply to this library the undermentioned periodical publication. The supply is to begin from the first issue of Vol . . . Year . . . Each issue is to be supplied promptly as and when published. The title-page, contents, and index relating to each completed volume should be supplied as soon as they are published.

The non-receipt of an issue, if any, will be notified either immediately on receipt of the latter issue or within three months after its due date, when it is known to us.

The cost of a volume is to be recovered by sending a bill in duplicate in advance, after the completion of the volume and supply of the title-page, contents, and index.

This may be treated as a standing order until counter-manded.

S32 *Weekly diary*: It should have the following headings:
11 to 22 same as for S 25 of Book Order Section
31 Order cards checked
32 Orders issued
4 Volumes made up
45 Binding slips written
46 Accession cards written
47 Made up volumes transmitted
48 Accession numbers noted
52 Cumulative indexes ordered
53 Cumulative indexes received
7 Bills passed

S33 *Daily receipt diary*. It is to show the number of periodical publications received from day to day. Its headings must consist of the symbols for the main divisions of classification system used or some suitable modification of them.

538 Files

Name	*Class Number*	*Filing Characteristic*
Standing vendors	31 (Subject device)	Vendor
Sources, enquiries and quotations	32 do	Title
Indent	33 do	do
Current periodicals	34 do	do
Finance	36 do	Correspondent
Back volumes	37 do	Title
Outward enquiries	391 do	Correspondent
Inward enquiries	392 do	do

The files are to be transferred to the record sequence one year after it is closed. The records may be destroyed after five years.

CHAPTER 54

ACCESSIONING

541 Accession and Donation Number

Every volume to be included in the stock of the library must receive a serial number called Accession Number. Donated books must receive a Donation Number, in addition to the accession number. Cumulated volumes of periodicals should also receive accession numbers and if necessary also donation numbers, if the volume is to be bound and preserved in the library.

542 Accession Numbering

As soon as the classification and cataloguing of books and completed volumes of periodicals to be preserved are finished, arrange the purchased books in the sequence of their entry in their related bills, and the periodicals and the donated books in the sequence of their call numbers. Use the order cards of the purchased books as their accession cards. Write green and red accession cards for donated books and for periodical publications respectively. Arrange also the related shelf-register cards, the accession cards. and the catalogue cards in an exactly parallel sequence. Look up the accession cabinet for the last accession and donation numbers which had been already given. Starting with the next numbers, assign the accession number, and donation number if warranted, in correct numerical sequence in each of the shelf-register cards, the accession cards, and the main catalogue cards.

543 Numbering the Books

Then copy the accession number, and also donation number in the case of gifted books, class number, book number, one below the other on the back of the title-page of each book. The collection symbol also should be written. The class number should begin just half an inch below the central line of the back of the title-page. If that place happens to be printed over, start it as near that place as possible. If the book has no title-page write these numbers on the top of the first page leaving space for at least two lines between the top-edge of the book and the call number.

Write these numbers also at a certain other conventional place in the book, say the bottom of page 50.

544 Passing of Bill

As soon as the writing of the numbers of the purchased books is over, write the accession number against the respective items in the bills for the purchased books. Strike off the items not supplied or rejected and make the consequential changes in the total amount of the bills. Then pass the bills for payment with the remarks "Brought into stock register. Bill may be paid."

545 Accession Register

On receiving accession numbers, the order cards attain the status of accession cards. File all the accession cards in the sequence of their accession numbers in the accession cabinet. This must be kept under lock and key, as these cards constitute the basic record of the books in the library, giving, as it were, a complete history of the respective books.

Further details of this routine and the complications which may arise are discussed in Chap 24 of *Library administration*.

547 Diary

S41 *Accession diary* (*Weekly*) to show the numbers of volumes accessioned. Column headings should be:

Accessioned, Donated, Purchased, Periodicals, Books.

CHAPTER 55

PREPARATION OF THE BOOKS

551 Easing

The books themselves should be prepared. Ease the back by opening the book somewhere in the middle, placing it on a flat table and gently running the thumb from the top to the bottom along the inner margin, working your way through the book to the two covers, turning a few leaves at a time, and simultaneously pressing. As the glue at the back of the volume is likely to have hardened, this easing work has to be done in a very careful and gentle way, so that the back of the book does not break.

5511 Cutting Open

Cut open the pages with a cutting bone and not with a finger or a pencil as the latter will spoil the edges and even damage the text in books with narrow margins.

552 Stamping

Then put the library stamp, without disfiguring printed matter, in certain conventional pages such as the lower half of the half-title-page, the lower half of the back of title-page, the top of the first chapter, the bottom of the earliest chapter that ends after the fiftieth page, the bottom of the last page, each map, plate, etc. and so on.

553 Tagging

After the stamping is over, stick a tag on the back (spine) of the volume. If there is a jacket, remove it temporarily for this purpose and replace it after the tagging is over. Apply tag exactly 2·5 cm above the bottom of the book. It will be convenient to have a piece of metal, 1·5 cm wide and bent at right angles with each of the arms exactly 2·5 cm long to mark the position for applying the tag.

If the volume is too thin to have the tag on its spine, fix it on the front cover close to the spine, adjacent to the position it should have occupied on the back. Write the call number on the tag.

554 Date-Labelling

As soon as tagging is over, fix the date-label to the volume. The date-label is to be gummed only at the top and bottom corner of the left edge and it is to be fixed on the very first page after the cover, whether that page is an end-paper, half-title page, or even the first page of the text. Then write the book-ticket and insert it into the pocket at the bottom of the date-label. Enter the call number, accession number, and the date of release on the date-label. Now the book is ready to reach its destiny — which is reader's hand — and to rest on the shelves of the library when not solicited by readers.

555 Classification and Cataloguing

As it has been already indicated in section 542, classification and cataloguing is done even before the book is accessioned. But, the preparation work mentioned in sections 551 and 554 should be done only after accessioning is done. All this work should be done on a weekly basis like most other work in a library. Every attempt should be made to round off the week's work without any arrears.

This work will require constant use of the library catalogue. It is therefore necessary that, in addition to the catalogue in cards for public use, there should be a copy of it in slips for office use.

5550 Process Slip

Insert in each volume a process slip, i e, a slip 125×75 mm. Even a waste slip with one side blank will do. On this slip various notes regarding the volume should be entered. Ultimately this process slip will have to be used for preparing the monthly statement of amendments to the Classification Code and the Catalogue Code and destroyed thereafter. Draw a vertical line dividing the length of the slip exactly into two parts. Reserve the left hand side for noting cross references. Divide the right hand half into three compartments by three horizontal lines. Use the first compartment to indicate class index entries, not requiring consolidation, the second to indicate cross reference index entries, the third to indicate the book index entries or main entries or class index entries. Any further notes which arise in the course of classification and cataloguing should be entered in this slip.

5551 Classification — Routine

Sort rapidly by their main classes the volumes to be accessioned in the week. Then decide the class number of the books one by one. If any volume is elusive and requires detailed study, or appears to call for the creation of a new class, put it aside temporarily in the group of deferred volumes. For normal books, determine the call number and write it at the leading line of the process slip. Add the appropriate sequence number wherever necessary. By examining the main slip in the office-copy of the catalogue, see that the class number you give is consistent with the old placings. If there is any catalogue slip in the same ultimate class and with the same book number as the volume on hand, add the appropriate digit as the accession part of the book number. In cases of doubt compare the old books with the new ones. Note down on the process slip notes for cataloguing work. As soon as each volume is thus treated, pass it on with the process slip for cataloguing.

After all the normal volumes are dealt with take up the more difficult volumes and proceed with them when the catalogue cards of the other volumes are being written.

55511 Amendments Noting

If any addition or amendment is made either to the rules or the schedules in the Classification Code, note them down in the official interleaved copy of the Classification Code.

55512 Source-Slips

If any source outside the volumes classified and outside the common reference books is used in determining the class number, note it down with details on a source-slip 125 × 75 mm. The source-slip should contain in successive sections the call number of the volume classified, the call number of the source, the heading of the source, its short title, and the exact page reference. All such source-slips should be filed away in a classified sequence in the source-slips tray.

5552 Cataloguing — Routine

Sort out the classified volumes according to their cataloguing difficulties. The following groups may arise:

1 *Fresh cards group* consisting of volumes which are in familiar languages and whose process slips do not indicate consolidation of cards;
2 *Consolidation group* consisting of volumes which are in familiar languages and whose process slips indicate consolidation of cards and periodical publications;
3 *Linguistic fresh card group* consisting of volumes in unfamiliar languages which do not require consolidation of catalogue cards;
4 *Linguistic consolidation group* consisting of volumes in unfamiliar languages which require consolidation of catalogue cards; and
5 *Refractory group* consisting of volumes of unusual cataloguing peculiarities.

Deal with the first four groups first so that the maximum number of volumes can be pushed forward without any delay.

55521 Amendments Noting

If any amendment in the Cataloguing Code is arrived at in the course of the week, note them down in the official interleaved copy of the Catalogue Code.

55522 Sources Noting

If the data for cataloguing has been taken from any source outside the book, prepare a source-slip and file it in the source-slip tray mentioned in 55712.

5553 Checking Work

All the class numbers and cataloguing entries must be carefully checked preferably by a second person, and if no second person is available, by the same person at a later time.

5554 Typing

If the catalogue cards are handwritten, get the slips for the catalogue for office use copied out from them by typing. If the catalogue cards themselves are typewritten, the slips for the office copy may be carbon copies.

5555 Insertion Work

After all the volumes are completed and accession numbers are written in the main cards and the shelf cards, sort out all the catalogue cards according to the nature of their entries and insert them in the cabinets containing the public catalogue. Do similarly for the slips forming the catalogue for office use. The filing of the shelf-cards is described in section 56.

55551 Guide-Cards

It will be a good practice to review the guide-cards in the cabinets of the public catalogue once in a year. New guide-cards might be necessary or experience might have suggested changes in the existing guide-cards.

556 Correction Work

All the old volumes set aside for correction of class number or catalogue entries should be dealt with similarly.

557 Forms and Registers

The description of catalogue cards is usually given in books on cataloguing. The code numbers for the different types of cards are given here. They are all 125×75 mm.

C51 *White cards* for main entries and book index entries.

C52 *Mild-pink cards* for cross reference entries and cross reference index entries.

C53 *Guide cards.*

C54 *Black-edged white cards* for class index entries.

C55 *Catalogue slips.*

S52 *Volumes diary* (*weekly*). Its column headings are to be the symbols for the main classes or any modification of them. and in addition "Total number of volumes".

S53 *Cards diary* (*weekly*). Its headings are to be:

1 Main cards;
2 Cross reference cards;
3 Class index cards;
4 Book index cards;
5 Cross reference index cards;

6 Shelf register cards;
7 Total number of cards;
81 Number of periodical publication cards consolidated;
82 Number of other cards consolidated;
83 Total number of cards consolidated.

S54 *Correction diary* (*weekly*). Similar to the volumes diary.

458 Specification for Card Cabinet
To Hold Cards, 125×75 mm

1 The card cabinet is to consist of two parts: 1 cabinet proper; and 2 a table on which the cabinet proper rests.

2 The cabinet proper is to contain 24 drawers — four columns of six drawers each.

21 The external dimensions of the cabinet proper are to be:
Breadth 2 ft 4½ inches.
Height 2 ft 7½ inches.
Depth 1 ft 11 inches.

22 The planks used for the two sides, top and bottom, are to be 7/8 inch thick and that used for the back 5/8 inch thick.

23 The front side of the cabinet is to be partitioned by three vertical planks 7/8 inch thick and 4 inches in breadth to secure four columns of sockets and by five horizontal planks 7/8 inch thick and 3 inches in breadth to secure six rows of sockets, to contain the drawers.

24 The front of each socket is to be connected with the back plank of the cabinet by two cross-bearers (one on the left and one on the right) 7/8 inch thick and 1 inch wide.

25 The cross-bearers are to be provided with two brass cylinders, each 9½ inches apart over which the drawer is to slide.

3 The internal dimensions of each socket holding the drawer are to be:
Breadth 6 inches.
Height 4½ inches.
Depth 1 ft 10½ inches.

4 Each drawer is to have the following internal dimensions — breadth 5 inches and depth 1 ft 8 inches. The side and back planks used for the drawer are to be ½ inch thick and only 2¼ inches high. The front plank of the drawer is to be 6¼ inches in breadth and

4¼ inches in height so as to cover the socket exactly. The bottom of the drawer is to be fitted with two reepers of ½ inch thickness and 1 inch breadth properly centered. A brass rod ⅛ inch in diameter is to run right through the centre of the drawer to lock up the card contents. To the rod projecting at the front plank of the drawer is to be screwed a screw knob. A fly nut is to be screwed to the rod projecting at the back plank of the drawer. To prevent the drawer when drawn from falling out of the socket, a self-locking catch is to be fixed into the socket to the right side at a depth of 1½ inches. A notch is to be cut in the further end of the right hand side of the drawer. The catch is to fall in that notch and lock up the drawer automatically. On the front plank of the drawer, just above the centre, a brass label holder to hold a label 1¾ inches by 1¼ inches is to be fixed. Just below the label holder a ring is to be screwed to serve the purpose of a handle to pull out the drawer. Each drawer is to be provided with an adjustable card rest (5×3 inches and 1 inch thick at the bottom and tapering towards the top) the cross section of which is to be a right angled triangle, the hypotenuse forming the front side over which the cards should rest. The card rest is to be provided with a hole in its centre through which the central rod of the drawer is to pass. The card rest is also to be provided with a bolt so that it may be bolted to the left side plank of the drawer where holes are to be provided at intervals of 1 inch.

5 Locking arrangement of the cabinet: The vertical plank between the first and second columns of drawers and that between the third and fourth columns are to be provided with two U shaped rings each 1 ft 7½ inches apart. Two brass plates 2 inches wide and 2 ft 2½ inches long with two rectangular holes each, at required intervals to take in the U rings are to be applied to the U rings to lock up the cabinet. Four locks (one to each U ring) are to be used for locking.

6 The table on which the cabinet rests is to have the following dimensions:

Height of the table 1 ft 10¼ inches (including the top plank).

The dimensions of the top plank are to be in breadth 2 ft 5¼ inches and in depth (the side corresponding to the depth of the cabinet) 2 ft.

Thickness of the plank 7/8 inch.

The dimensions of the frame work of the table (excluding the plank) are to be 2 ft 4½ inches × 1 ft 11 inches.

Legs, at the top, 3 × 3 inches.

Legs, at the bottom, 2½ × 2½ inches.

7 The wood used for the cabinet is to be well-seasoned teakwood.

8 The contractor is to be responsible for any crack that the cabinet may develop within a year of supply.

9 The cabinet is to be coated with wood oil.

10 The cabinet is to be delivered at the library, free of delivery charges.

11 The metal portion of the cabinet is to be of well-tempered brass.

12 The dimensions of the drawers and the sockets, and of the cabinets, as a whole, are to be quite exact so that the drawers of the cabinets may be interchanged among themselves and with the drawers of the cabinets of the specifications already in the library without any difficulty whatever.

CHAPTER 56

MAINTENANCE WORK

560 Introduction

The books should be arranged on the shelves so as to fulfil the Fourth Law of Library Science, viz, "Save the time of the reader". Reference books like encyclopaedias, dictionaries, current year-books and directories, and recent additions should be located in a prominent place as near the entrance as possible so that those who come for ready-reference alone may do so quickly and without disturbing the serious readers. The arrangement of the other books in the stack-room itself requires special skill. The arrangement cannot be permanent in the changing library world. It will have to be judiciously varied and readjusted from time to time. Several factors will have to be examined from time to time for this purpose. One would very much like to have the books and periodicals arranged in the sequence of the subjects in the schedule of classification for the mere satisfaction of having them arranged in strict accordance with the schedule sequence. But the standard helpful sequence of the main classes found in the schedules of classification is seldom strictly parallel to the popular sequence. Nor is the popular sequence a permanent one. It does and must change with time.

561 Formation of Collections

Hence, the rigid arrangement of main classes by their numbers results in wasting the time and energy, not only of the reading public, but also of the reference staff. In an arrangement like this, a majority of readers may have to waste their time and energy in walking unnecessarily great distances to get at their books. The reference staff also are affected in the same way, as their movement is dependent on the movement of the readers. It is quite necessary to break the schedule-sequence and judiciously repermute the main-classes on the shelves. For example, literature, as the most popular subject attracting the greatest number of readers, may be located as near the entrance as possible, irrespective of its proper place in accordance with the schedule of classification. Other subjects may be arranged at distances from the entrance varying inversely with their popularity. Any one arrangement should not be considered as final (merely on the ground of unwillingness to undertake additional labour). Its utility must be constantly tested by experience in the light of the statistics of issue. Any reshuffling of subjects found to be necessary should be immediately carried out even at the cost of additional labour and time, as the convenience of the readers is the convenience of the library.

562 Multiplication of Collections

The collection of books of current interest may be called the Main Collection. There may be a second collection consisting of periodicals and serials and a third one made of books of archaic interest and hence of comparatively infrequent demand. These may be called Secondary and Tertiary Collections respectively. A suitable symbol may be put above the class number of a book in all but the main collection to indicate the collection to which it belongs. Such a collection symbol may not be necessary in a bound volume of periodical, as its very look will show that it is a periodical.

5621 Closed Collection

Again, certain types of books, if they are put in open access shelves, are likely to be adversely affected by their being mal-handled by a few black sheep to such an extent that they are of no use to others who really want them. In this category we may include Fine Arts books, books full of art plates, and books of pornographic interest. Such books may be kept in a non-open-access or closed collection (not necessarily in closed shelves). By a closed collection is meant that readers will not normally be allowed to have direct or open access to the shelves containing it, but will obtain their books in most cases by the old application slip system. This restriction may be waived in the case of certain classes of responsible readers. This closed collection arrangement gives us control over the use of these books. Fine Arts books will be exposed to loss of plates if they are placed in the open access shelves. Similarly all pages savouring of obscenity are systematically purloined (to satisfy the morbid curiosity of the black sheep) from otherwise scientific treatises. A monumental example of this in the Madras University Library was Havelock Ellis' *Psychology of sex*. Previous to its withdrawal from circulation, it was in so much demand that it was treated as a reference book and kept on the issue counter. Every other reader would ask for "Ellis". Such books also should be taken over to the closed collection. Such a closed sequence may be called a Special Collection. Their book numbers may be put between two horizontal parallel lines to indicate their location.

5622 Abnormal Size Collection

To come to the actual arrangement of books on the shelves, it is quite necessary to see that the shelves present an aesthetic appearance. This presentable appearance is of extreme importance in an open access library; for, the first thing that creates a good impression in a reader is the trim condition of the shelves with sufficient direction guides, bay guides, and shelf guides. It is a most unsightly thing in a library to see on the shelves giants, pygmies, and weaklings, all in a conglomeration minus the respect due to their ordinal arrangement. Hence, all volumes which, on account of their size and weight, preclude easy handling should be kept in a separate collection — this may be called Oversize Collection. The bottom-most plank throughout the book-racks may be used for this collection. To indicate their location, their book numbers may be overlined. Pamphlets and miniature volumes may be kept in a closed collection. This may be called Pamphlet Collection or Undersize Collection. Their location may be indicated by the underlining of their book numbers. If this is not done, such volumes invariably get themselves squeezed and even lost, either amidst other volumes or in the pockets of book-vandals.

563 Temporary Collections

The above mentioned sequences by no means exhaust the collections to be maintained in a growing library. While these sequences are of a permanent nature, need is felt for the formation of certain temporary sequences.

5631 Correction Collection

If the library makes any attempt whatever to keep itself abreast of the times, there will be constant need to revise the class numbers assigned to the books in stock, in the light of the experience gained in serving the books to the readers and in consequence of the realignment and reorientation of the divisions of knowledge brought about now and then in the learned world. Change in cataloguing policy, which should be occasionally necessary, may require the revision of the catalogue entries of certain books. When groups of books are segregated for correction of class number or catalogue, they have always a tendency to stay for long, away from the stack-room. Special steps have to be taken to call for them at systematic intervals. It is better to make a separate collection of them. This may be called Correction Collection. They should be constantly watched and pushed forward.

5632 Binding Collection

Another factor which calls for a temporary collection is one of necessary occurrence in a popular library, which gets its books well-used and well-thumbed. As the books get worn out by such legitimate use, it falls to the lot of the Maintenance Section to play the role of the family doctor to such books. At the right time, the Maintenance Section is to send such books to the hospital on medical leave. The process of relieving them, keeping them in mind when they are patients in the bindery, and reclaiming them promptly when their treatment is over, is best regulated by looking upon them as forming a Temporary Collection, called the Binding Collection. Here again, it is likely that more than one monthly batch will be in the hospital simultaneously. The binding collection should therefore have a number of sub-collections. It may also be wise to have their call numbers re-examined and reshaped before they are sent away to the bindery, as they are likely to have their call numbers marked permanently on their back in glittering letters of gold when they come back hale and healthy from their sojourn in the bindery.

5633 Topical Collection

Apart from finding for every reader his book and for every book its reader, the Reference Section has also to satisfy the Fourth Law, viz, "Save the time of the reader". In certain situations, the Reference Section can achieve maximum result in this matter, if and only if the co-operation of the Maintenance Section is forthcoming. This co-operation, the Maintenance Section can and should easily offer. One of the vital reasons for maintaining the shelf register in cards on the basis of "one volume, one card", is the extreme mobility that it gives to the arrangement of books. The Maintenance Section should exploit this mobility for the benefit of the readers by freely forming Special Temporary Collections to meet the special demands that may arise from time to time. A few concrete examples will make this clear. When a special course of lectures on educational experiments was being delivered to a large class of teachers, the syllabus of the lectures was perused in advance. In consultation with the lecturer, all the books in the library, with a bearing on the course of lectures were assembled together, and put in a special cup-board as a special temporary collection dubbed Educational Experiments Lecture Collection. The Principle of Parallel Movement enabled the Maintenance Section to form such a sequence and have easy control over it, thus enabling the Reference Section to serve the teachers attending the lectures with the least loss of time. Apart from the saving of time, the psychological effect was felt to be much more vital. The data on which a topical collection may be broken up may be written on the date-label and encircled.

5634 Occasion for Topical Sequence

Every class of library, which wants to function up, will find occasion to form such Topical Collections from time to time. Local festivals, local celebrations, and, any other important local event will give the occasion to the library to form such temporary topical collections. The discussion of a Bill or any momentous resolution that may come up before the legislature may prove to be an occasion to form such a temporary topical collection. The rush of enquirers and the pressure of time in a Legislative Council Library would make the work of the librarian inefficient, if not impossible, if such temporary topical collections are not intelligently sensed and formed in advance and their formation would be impossible even if they are sensed, but for the extraordinary power which is given to him by this wonderful invention, by the library profession, of this extremely mobile shelf-register-in-cards, and the equally facile Principle of Parallel Movement. Perhaps, the value of the freedom to form such temporary topical collections at pleasure will be most appreciated in business localities, whose patrons know best the value of time and indeed look upon time as money and money as time.

564 Principle of Parallel Movement

Having been obliged to disturb the schedule sequence and to arrange the books in so many collections, it is a great responsibility for the Maintenance Section to maintain correct sequence in the shelves and to see that every book is in its correct place. The mechanical apparatus invented by the library profession to cure this is what is known as the Shelf Register. It is made up of cards of standard size, viz, 125 × 75 mm, written on the principle — one title, one card — with the call number in the leading line. These shelf register cards are kept absolutely parallel to the books on the shelves, which means that they are to be arranged in an equal number of collections. What is more, except when the books leave their proper place on the shelves to get into the hands of a reader, every movement of the books should be controlled and imitated by an exactly parallel movement among the shelf register cards. The discovery of this Principle of Parallel Movement has turned out to be panacea of most of the ills in the management of the books in the library and brought in its train the inevitable genesis of the Maintenance Section. The shelf register cabinet is the hub of the stock in the library and correspondingly the Maintenance Section is the hub of the staff of the library.

565 Guides

The Maintenance Section should put up guide-boards to places like reading room, periodicals room, catalogue room, stack-room, etc, so that readers can by themselves find their way about in the library. Within the stack-room itself, there should be tier-guides and gangway-guides showing the subjects in the respective tiers and gangways. There should also be bay-guides in each bay showing the subjects contained in it. It has been found from experience that each bay-guide may have to be in at least six lines. All the above mentioned guides may consist of thick card boards 35 × 12 cm covered with white paper. Each bay, whose standard width is about 1 m will require two guides. The legends, which should consist of the class numbers and their equivalents in the natural language, may be stencilled on these guide-boards. Each shelf-plank also should have shelf-guides. As the standard length of a shelf-plank is about 1m, it is found helpful to have an average of three shelf-guides in a plank. These shelf-guides may be strips 125×12mm cut from white Bristol boards. Discarded catalogue-cards with one side blank may be used for cutting these strips. The shelf-guide also should give the class number and its equivalent in the natural language. Since we have said that on an average there will be one shelf-guide for every 25 cms of shelf-plank, it is obvious that in a stack-room accommodating 25,000 volumes, about 3,000 shelf-guides will be needed. It is not an easy matter to maintain these shelf-guides. As the books will be frequently moving forward as a result of new accessions, these shelf-guides also will have to be frequently moved forward and adjusted. This will add to the task of maintaining the shelf-guides. The best way of facilitating this work is to provide wedge-shaped grooves along the front edge of shelf-plank in which the shelf-guides can be slided.

5651 Adjustment of Guides

It must be a matter of prestige for the Maintenance Section that no guide tells a wrong tale. The shelf-guides will have to be carefully watched and adjusted, from time to time, into their proper position. The bay-guides may not require such frequent attention. But whenever books have to be transferred from one bay to another the bay-guides should be immediately corrected. The gangway-guides and the tier-guides will not require even as much renewal as the bay-guides.

5652 Reshuffling

To take away from the monotony of the appearance of shelf-arrangement, to exploit the Principle of Novelty, to help every book to get its reader, and to keep step with the slowly changing scale of popularity of subjects with the reading public, it will be desirable to reshuffle the disposition of the subjects in the stack-room at suitable intervals. Once in five years the whole library may have to be reshuffled. Every year some particular region may have to be reshuffled. Whenever such wholesale re-arrangement takes place, the bay-guides and the gangway-guides will have to be mostly re-written.

5653 Renewal of Tags

The tags on the backs of books should be rapidly reviewed each day. The entire stack-room should be covered in this way at least once in a month. During this review, all worn-out tags should be replaced by fresh ones and the call numbers copied on them. All the newly written call numbers should be verified by somebody else or by the same person on the next day before the volumes are back on the shelves.

5654 Open Access without Guides

It is sheer callousness to adopt open access system without plenty of guides, or even if there are guides, to leave the guides unchanged in an ever-changing library. It will be frustration to readers. It will even irritate them. It will bring odium on the library staff. There is no doubt that maintenance of plenty of guides in their right places will consume considerable staff-time. Library authorities should take this into account in providing staff. But on the side of the staff also, they should have a sense of value which is sufficiently compelling to make them feel miserable even if one guide is in the wrong place or one plank is without guides.

566 New Books

The work of absorbing the accession of the week into the stock should be done on a weekly basis. As soon as the preparation of the new volumes of the week is over, sort them out according to their collections. In each collection arrange the volumes by their call numbers. Do similarly for their shelf-cards. Tally them. Books of a normal nature fit for display in the recent additions shelf should now be separated with a parallel separation of shelf-cards. These separated shelf-cards should be put in the recent additions box behind the guide "Collection 0". Take this box and the new volumes to the recent additions shelf which should be in the first row of shelves in the stack-room. Pull out all the volumes corresponding to the shelf-cards behind the guide "Collection 2". As each volume is pulled out, turn its shelf-card in its own plane through a right angle so that it stands on its shorter edge. If any volume is not to be found, trace it out. After all the books have been traced out, transfer the guide-card "Collection 1" to the place where the guide-card "Collection 0" is, transferring the latter to the end of the current week's cards. Put the current week's books, meant for display, on the recent additions shelf in the classified sequence.

5661 Released Books

Hand over to the counter all the released books which have been bespoken. Take the remaining books along with the other books of the current week and shelve them in their proper places. Take out from the recent additions box the shelf-cards which are standing on their shorter edges and put them along with the shelf-cards of the week's additions which are not to be put on the recent additions shelf. File these cards in the proper places in the shelf-register cabinet.

5662 Used Books

56621 Consulted Books

Every hour, walk round the reading room and collect the books left by readers on their respective tables after consultation. Enter the statistics in the consultation counting sheet and shelve the books in the returned-books-shelf in a roughly classified sequence. This shelf may be in the first row of shelves in the stack-room.

56622 Borrowed Books

The books returned by members at the discharging counter should also be brought to the returned-books-shelf at convenient intervals and shelved in a roughly classified sequence.

56623 Replacing

Readers should be allowed to take away for consultation on loan any books lying in the returned-books-shelves. There is no gain in segregating them and keeping them away from the use of readers until they go back to their permanent places in the stack-room. On the other hand since the books in the replaced-books-shelves will be popular ones, there is every chance that many of them will go into reader's hand in the course of the day and that the books to be actually replaced will be considerably reduced in number — resulting in the saving of the time of the staff. But the volumes which stay back in the returned-books-shelf should be replaced in their permanent places once in a day at an appointed hour. This hour should be the slackest hour in the library.

5663 Correction

For all the volumes taken out for correction work, transfer the shelf-cards to behind the correctly dated guide-cards in the correction collection. When these volumes come back after correction, shelve them in their proper places and file their shelf-cards also in a parallel manner. Periodically the shelf-cards in the correction collection should be checked and steps should be taken to round off the work without undue delay.

567 Rectification and Verification

In an open access library, readers are never allowed to replace books on the shelves. They have freedom only to pick out books from the shelves. In spite of this convention, books do get mixed up as a result of the reader's browsing round the stack-room. Even apart from criminally-minded people deliberately putting a book in quite a distant place, the unintended misplacements within the same shelf-planks would in the long run mount to very near chaos. Unless the books are put back in proper sequence periodically, readers will be put to much difficulty; nor can the library staff find books easily. The process of restoring order among the books is called Shelf-Rectification. There is also need for periodical Stock-Verification. This is normally done once in a year. This practice usually involves much disturbance in the rhythm of the work of the library. Some libraries go to the criminal extent of closing down to the public for the period of stock-verification. This practice violates all the Laws of Library Science. The necessary shelf-rectification and stock-verification can be combined into a single process. In other words stock-verification will be automatically done not merely once in a year but even more than once if shelf-rectification is properly designed and correctly carried out.

5671 Cycle for Shelf-Rectification

All the regions of a library may not be equally prone to disturbance by readers. The main collection will be the most disturbed. The closed collection will not be disturbed at all. The secondary and the tertiary collections will be disturbed much less than the main one. It is desirable that shelf-rectification should be done in the main collection at least once in a month. That for the secondary collection may perhaps be done once in six months. It may be enough to attend to the other collections once in a year. But, the frequency of periodical dusting and cleaning of these collections should be in just the reverse sequence. This is because in the main collection the books are constantly disturbed by the readers themselves and dust and insects cannot therefore accumulate very much. But in the other collections they will accumulate.

5672 Daily Quota

The daily quota of the region for shelf-rectification can be arrived at by taking the total length of shelving to be rectified and the period in which it should be done. Each day, take out the shelf-register trays for the day's quota. As far as possible make the end-points of the quota the end-points of convenient subjects. The rectification-work should be done by two people.

56721 Checking with the Charged Tray

One of the persons should read out, from the charged tray at the counter, the call numbers of all the book-cards lying within the range of the day's quota. As each call number is read out, the second person should turn its shelf-card through a right angle in its own plane so as to stand on its shorter edge.

56722 Other Preliminary Checking

Do similarly for all the books of the concerned region, lying in the bespoken collection or among the books returned or being consulted by readers.

56723 Final Checking

Then take the trays to the region of the stack-room to be checked. One person should go on reading the call numbers of the books on the shelves. The other person should go on looking up and pushing towards himself, the corresponding shelf-register cards. If any shelf-register card standing on its shorter edge intervenes, it must be turned down to its normal position. If the book corresponding to any shelf-card lying in the normal position is not read out by the man at the shelf, that shelf-card should be turned so as to stand on the shorter edge. The result will be that at any moment the cards that stand on the shorter edge in the checked region will be those of untraced books. On the other hand the cards which stand on the shorter edge in the unchecked region will be those of traced books. As the checking proceeds, misplaced books will happen to be read out by the man at the shelf. It may happen that the card of a misplaced book is found standing on its shorter edge in the checked region. It may then be restored to its normal state of standing on the longer edge. It may also happen that the shelf-card of a misplaced book is in the unchecked region of the tray. If so, ask the man at the shelf to shelve the book at the proper place. If any reader takes away a book of the unchecked region of the day's quota, before he leaves the region, the shelf-card of the book may be turned so as to stand on its shorter edge. Thus there will be no obstruction whatever for readers to use any book they like when the shelf-rectification *cum* stock-verification is proceeding. As soon as the checking of the day's quota is over, enter in the investigation note-book the details of the cards standing vertically on their shorter edges; and then restore the cards to their normal position. Insert the shelf-register tray in its proper place.

56724 Untraced Books

Investigate the items untraced with the aid of the investigation note-book. As each item is traced, restore it to its proper place and strike out the entry in the investigation note-book. The items that do not get traced out within the year should be taken as lost books.

56725 Speed of Rectification

Experience has shown that, if the classification scheme used is an individualizing one like the Colon Classification with the book number designed in an organic relation to the class number, it is sufficient if the book number alone is read out. All that is needed is to have an occasional check-up by reading the whole class number. Even the occasions for it are automatically indicated when some difficulty arises. The number, for the book numbers on the backs of books alone to be strictly parallel to the book numbers in the shelf-cards without the class numbers also being strictly parallel, is negligibly small. This makes shelf-rectification expeditious. Nearly a thousand volumes can be done in an hour. This means that by doing shelf-rectification work for one hour a day a cycle of 25,000 volumes can be checked in a month. The main collection in most of the public libraries is not likely to exceed 25,000 volumes.

568 Binding

An important part of maintenance work is to keep the books in a physically fit condition. The standard of artistic binding of books for private use — which means very sparing use — is quite high. But re-inforced library binding to stand constant wear and tear has not yet come into vogue in India. Even concepts like split boards and French joints are unknown. The necessary materials of good quality are not easily available. It is therefore necessary that the most detailed specification should be given for library binding. It would be a good policy to ask the binder to take personal instruction from the librarian. A specification of library binding is given at the end of this chapter for ready reference. Each library should also train some member of the staff to make petty repairs. A stitch in time saves nine, as the saying goes.

5681 Damaged Books

As already stated in sections 331, 33231 and 33286, the damaged books should be picked up by the circulation staff and segregated for attention. It is also desirable to walk round the stack-room and pull out books needing re-binding. All the cumulated volumes of periodicals intended to be preserved will require to be bound. It is again a matter of policy whether a book should be sent to the bindery after the publishers' case is worn out or even at the beginning before it is released for circulation. We are of the opinion that the life of the book will be considerably lengthened if the latter course is adopted. If we can get books from publishers unbound in sheets, it is well and good. In Norway where few publishers agree to do so, we found that the Director of Libraries ruthlessly pealed off the publishers' cases as soon as the books arrived from the publishers. He even employed a fairly large staff to do this pealing work ! In any case books in paper covers should not be released for the use before being bound. At the same time every book may not need costly library binding. In the case of books of passing interest, particularly ordinary fiction, usually printed on bad paper, it may be cheaper to buy additional copies than to have them bound in the library style.

5682 Volumes for Binding

Perhaps binding work is best done on a monthly basis. As soon as the quota for the month has been collected, arrange them in a classified sequence. Take out their shelf-register cards and form a binding collection of them. Scrutinize the volume from the point of view of their binding peculiarities and form them into homogenous groups. Arrange the volumes in each such group in classified sequence. Prepare binding slips for each of them. Make an order copy for binding from out of these slips. Ask the binder to come to the library and collate all the volumes. If any volume is defective, decide whether it is worth binding. If it is, note the defects in its binding slip. Hand over the volumes to the binder. Keep the slips in the *binding box*.

5683 Bound Volumes

Before forwarding begins — that is, before the covering material is applied — inspect the books in the bindery to see if the specification has been fully followed. When the bound volumes come back to the library, check them with the binding slips, scrutinise if the tooling has been properly done, insert the books in their proper places, merge the corresponding shelf cards in their proper places, and check the binder's bill with regard to style of binding and the rates claimed.

5684 Specification for Re-inforced Library Binding

56841 Assembling

1 *Collation.* All books received by the contractor are to be examined and collated and any found to be imperfect or seriously

damaged are to be returned unbound to the librarian. Torn leaves and plates are to be neatly repaired.

A periodical shall not be held to have been collated properly nor to be perfect, unless all the parts of a volume are bound in correct order of pagination and the usual title and contents pages and indexes are inserted in the proper places. Unless each imperfect and damaged book is reported upon to the librarian and unless the librarian has instructed the contractor to proceed with the work on such books, the bill will not be paid for any such books bound or repaired.

2 *Wrappers and advertisements* in periodicals and books are to be bound in, if the contractor is instructed to do so; otherwise, they are not to be bound in.

56842 Stitching

3 *Sewing*. Books printed on paper of good quality are to be sewn one sheet on (except where thinness of paper makes it necessary to sew two sheets on) with unbleached thread of suitable thickness over unbleached linen tapes. Books printed on soft, spongy or brittle paper are to have the sections lined at inner and outer folds with strips of thin but tough paper before they are sewn. All sections broken at the back are to be lined with tough paper or linen strips, and where necessary neatly overcast on modern methods of cross stitching before being sewn to the tapes. The first and last sections of all books are to be enclosed at back in linen strips. All separate leaves, plates, maps, plans, etc, are to be mounted on guards of linen or tough thin paper and to be sewn in. Pasting on is not to be permitted. Double plates are to be guarded at the fold. No charge is to be made for the first dozen plates so guarded in each book. For books up to post octavo ($6\frac{1}{4}'' \times 3\frac{7}{8}''$) three tapes, one-quarter inch in width, are to be used. For books of crown octavo ($7\frac{1}{2}'' \times 5''$) four tapes, one-quarter inch in width, are to be used. For books of larger sizes the number of tapes and their width are to be increased in proportion. Two of the tapes are to be placed within one inch of the head and tail of each book.

Straight-line machine stitching will not be accepted.

Books printed on calendared or heavily loaded art paper are to be reported to the librarian and a quotation sent to him for lining each leaf of such books with a linen hinge on a throw-up guard.

4 All folded *maps and illustrations* are to be mounted on jaconet or thin linen of good quality and to be charged for separately.

5 *End-papers.* End-papers are to be of good tough opaque paper of approved mild colour, with at least one plain white leaf between each of them and the printed matter. The end-papers are to be made with strong linen or cloth joints and to be sewn on as a section.

6 *Cutting edges.* Unless otherwise instructed the contractor is to cut edges of books accurately and to take care to leave margins as wide as possible. Unless other instructions are given, the edges are to be sprinkled or tinted with a colour harmonizing with the colour of the materials used for covering.

56843 Forwarding

7 *Forwarding.* Unless otherwise directed, all books should have French joints and tight or close flexible backs with the covering material attached directly to the back. Tapes are to be firmly inserted between split boards. Books bound in quarter leather or in cloth or in buckram are to have the boards slightly rounded at corners and the covering material is to be neatly folded and not mitred.

Leathers are not to be unduly pared down or unduly stretched in covering. The covering material of back is to extend over boards to at least one sixth of the width of the book. All books should open up freely and lie flat.

56844 Lettering

8 *Lettering.* Lettering is to be impressed in best gold directly on to the material which covers the book. The lettering is to be of good size and easily readable; small lettering will not be accepted except on very thin books. No extra charge will be allowed up to and including fifty letters or/and figures.

56845 Size

9 *Sizes.* The size of a book is to be determined by the measurement of the board, the square of which must not exceed one-eighth of an inch in books up to crown octavo, and proportionately for

larger sizes. Extra charges for thickness is to be allowed only when the thickness of the volume exceeds one half the width of its boards. No extra charge is to be made for two or more volumes bound in one, unless the thickness of such a volume exceeds one half the width of the boards. In submitting the bills for work done, the measurement of the board should be given in inches in addition to the conventional mode of specifying the size.

56846 General

10 *Alternative suggestions.* When the preceding instructions are obviously inapplicable to any book or for any reason undesirable, the contractor is to submit suggestions for binding such a book with estimate of cost.

11 *General.* The whole of the work in binding is to be carried out with due regard to the fact that the books will be subjected to hard wear and tear and that the binding is to be permanent. Special instructions, if any, given with reference to particular volumes sent for binding should be faithfully carried out.

56847 Materials

12 *Thread.* To be of best unbleached linen of suitable thickness.

13 *Tapes.* To be of best unbleached linen, of close strong texture and of the specified width.

14 *Glue.* To be best quality flexible glue mixed with copper sulphate to keep off insects.

15 *Boards.* To be good quality mill boards.

16 *Leathers.* The contractor must guarantee or undertake to produce, when required, the guarantee of the firm supplying the leather, that all skins used

1 have been tanned in sumach or oak bark or similar vegetable stuff, or a mixture of them;

2 are free from sulphuric or other deleterious acids;

3 have been dyed with colours that are fast with respect to light as well as moisture; and

4 are genuine as described.

17 *Buckram.* To be linen buckram of best quality.

18 *Cloth.* To be good quality art canvas or imperial morocco cloth fast colour and finish.

19 *Gold.* To be best English gold.

56848 Item for Quotation

10 *Styles and sizes.* All combinations of the following:

1 Style
- 1 Half morocco and calico.
- 2 Half morocco and marble.
- 3 Half calico and marble.
- 4 Full buckram.
- 5 Half buckram and calico.
- 6 Half buckram and marble.

2 Height
- 1 6″ or less.
- 2 Between 6″ and 8″.
- 3 Above 8″.

3 Thickness
- 1 Less than 48 pages.
- 2 Between 48 and 100 pages.
- 3 Between 100 and 500 pages.
- 4 Above 500 pages.

CHAPTER 57

FINANCE AND ACCOUNTS

570 Introduction

The task of raising money, investing funds, managing property, preparing and getting the sanctions for the budget, and all other financial matters relating to a public library usually fall to the share of the Local Body which is the Local Library Authority. Nevertheless there may be some amount of financial work that falls to the share of the library. It will have to do initial work in the framing of the budget. This will have to be done according to the standing instruction of the Local Body. So also it is in regard to accounts. We shall deal here only with the work of primary book-keeping which must be done by the library staff and even here to confine ourselves only to what is distinctively of library nature. Matters relating to pay-bill, permanent advance, miscellaneous receipts, etc, will be regulated by the standing orders prevailing in the Local Body.

571 Double Payment

One of the dangers to be specially watched is double payment. As books and periodicals dribble in, all through the year, special effort is necessary to avoid double payment. Some kind of automatic check, not depending on memory is necessary. With regard to books, control by book-order-cards as described in section 423 will prove effective. If a book arrives and there is no book-order-card for it, you should not improvise a card in order to accept the book. You must have complete trust in the cards-file. Card system of this kind can work only if every routine is carried out thoroughly and faithfully at every stage. If the card is not in the order tray, the presumption should be that the book had already arrived and that the order card had been taken out or that the book is not due on any order. It might be lying in the sequence corresponding to the current week's arrival or it might have been already converted into an accession card and filed in the proper place. In the latter case the card will show the date of payment and the number of the voucher of payment.

In the case of a periodical, the routine suggested in section 5363 will, if faithfully carried out, prevent double payment.

572 Bills Register

Another danger in dealing with supplies dribbling in day after day is that certain supplies are neglected and never paid, at any rate not promptly paid. The best way to control this is to have a properly designed register of bills. As soon as bills are received, couple each bill with its duplicate if any. Group the bills by the parties to whom payment should be made. Arrange the bills in each party's group by the numbers of the order to which they relate. To make this easy the parties should be instructed never to include in any one bill supplies made relating to more than one order. Register the bills in the sequence in which they have been thus brought. Post the register number at the right hand top corner of the bill as well as its duplicate. Then comes the passing of the bills with reference to order-cards for books and register-cards for periodicals as described in section 423 and 4363.

573 Arrangement of the Bills

Tie together all the bills payable to one party. Verify the total of each bill. On the back of the last sheet of the bunch of bills, write the total of each of its successive sheets and total up the figures. Get the posting of the figures and the grand total verified by another person or by yourself at some later time. This must be done both for the original and for the duplicate copy of the bills. If a bill has no duplicate, the duplicate copy must be prepared. Put the pay-order-stamp in a convenient place on the last sheet of the bunch of bills. Also at the bottom of each sheet of the bunch, put the stamp "Included in voucher number . . . ." Write the amount in words in the imprint of the pay-order-stamp. Write the pay order inclusive of remittance charges, if any, at the end of the office copy of the bill. Arrange the bunches in a convenient sequence according to the nature and amount of payment.

574 Voucher

Enter each bunch in a separate line of the register of payments in serial sequence. The serial number, got by it in the register of payments, is called Voucher-Number. Write the voucher-number in the fair copy as well as the office copy of each bunch of the bills and also at the bottom of each sheet in a bunch. Then the voucher is ready for payment. The voucher-number should begin with '1' at the beginning of each financial year.

575 Posting of Voucher-Number

It is at this stage that the voucher-numbers should be posted in all the accession cards of the books and the register cards of the periodicals concerned.

576 Allocation Register

It will be necessary to watch the progress of payment for books and periodicals so that the amount allocated for each subject is not exceeded. This is controlled by allocating the amount of each voucher to the different subjects under the heads "books" and "periodicals" in a special allocation register.

577 Forms and Registers

S9771 *Bills Register*. Printed. 10 point type. 21 lb printing paper. White. Bound book. Folio pagination. 30 lines per page. The text above the column headings and the column headings are to be:

(*Name of library*) Register of Bills Received in....

Register N of Bill (1.5 cm); Date of receipt of Bill (1.5 cm); Outside date (1.5 cm); Outside N (1.5 cm); From whom (5 cm); Purport — Books or Periodicals and main class symbols (4 cm); Amount (2.5 cm); Initials (1.5 cm); Amount (2.5 cm); Draft requisition date; initials (1.5 cm); Script N and Date (1.5 cm); Script received date; initials (1.5 cm); P. O., M. O. N (1.5 cm); Despatch date; initials (1.5 cm); Acknowledgement reminder date; initials (1.5 cm); Acknowledgement receipt date; initials (1.5 cm); Acknowledgement filing; initials (1.5 cm); Remarks.

S9774 *Payments Register*. (Books and Periodicals) Printed. 10 point type. Ledger paper. White. Bound book. Folio pagination. 20 lines per page. The text above the column headings and the column headings are to be as follows:

(*Name of the library*) Payment Register — Books and Periodicals [Year; Date (1.5 cm); Voucher N (1.5 cm); Bill N (1.5 cm); Bill] date (1.5 cm); Party and place (9 cm); Books (5 cm); Periodicals (5 cm); Subjects symbols (6.5 cm); Remarks.

S9776 *Allocation Register*. Printed. 10 point type. 21 lb printing paper. White. Bound book. Folio pagination. 30 lines per page. The text above the column headings and the column headings are to be:

(*Name of library*) Allocation Register (Year)

Month and week (1.5 cm); Voucher N (1.5 cm); Different currencies in which payment is claimed (2.5 cm for each currency) for books; Different currencies in which payment is claimed for periodicals (2.5 cm for each periodical); Total (2.5 cm for each currency); Remarks.

There should be one folio page for each subject and the page allotment should be written next to the name of the subject.

578 Files

The call numbers for files of various kinds have been given in section 48 and at the end of sections whose numbers end with 8 in chapter 5. These numbers are the same as those given in the *Library administration*. Wherever "subject device" is added after a file number, the file number should be amplified by the class number for the subject concerned. For example, 23 is the number for order files, 23R will be the number for order files relating to books in Philosophy. Similarly 34 is the class number for files relating to current periodicals. 34R will be the number for files relating to current periodicals in Philosophy. 21 is the number for files on standing vendors. 23P15 will be the number for files on standing vendors for Sanskrit Books. A full account of the theory of filing will be found in Chapter 18 of *Library administration*.

CHAPTER 58

BUILDING AND STORES

580 Introduction

The main work relating to library building, equipment, stationery, and other articles needed for library use, will be looked after normally by the parent body of the library. However, the library will have some routine connected with them. Before taking up the routine, it may be worth-while to say a few words about some features which are expected in a small library building.

581 Building

There should be a gangway down the wall which is at least 1 m wide in the stack-rooms. This gangway will protect the book-racks from rain and sun. Further as an additional precaution it is always insisted in our country that the lengthwise wall in which these stack-room windows occur should run from east to west. The floor should be sound-proof. Either the pavement material itself should be sound-proof or if it is too costly to get such material in Indian conditions today, the floor should be covered with some matting. Coir matting may be cheap enough and within the means of many of our small libraries. The other details of the building are easily seen from the diagram.

582 Book-Rack

The following is the specification for a unit book-rack:
That standard unit-rack that I have designed for the Madras University Library has two faces. Each face has two bays, so that the unit-rack is a four-bayed rack — two bays on each side. While the height may be 7 ft in adult libraries, it should not exceed 5 ft in children's libraries.

The detailed dimensions of and specification for an adult library unit are as follows:

11 External dimensions 6′ 6″ × 1′ 6″ × 7′.

12 Three uprights, each 2″ × 1′ 6″ × 7′.

13 Seven shelf-planks, each 3′ × 8½″ × 1″.

Two of the shelf-planks are to be fixed ones — one near the top and the other near the bottom. The other five are to be movable ones supported by Tonk's fittings, so that they can be adjusted to an inch. It may be an advantage to provide two spare shelves for each unit.

2 The book-rack is to have sanitary bottom — i e, the lowest shelf is to be fixed at a height of 6 ins from the floor to facilitate cleaning the floor beneath the rack and easy vigilance. The topmost shelf is to be fixed 6 ins below the top of the uprights.

3 To prevent the books on the shelves in one face getting mixed up with the books on the corresponding shelves in the other face, an expanded metal or weld-mesh partition is to separate the two faces. It is to accommodate this frame that the planks are made only 8½ inches broad, thus leaving a gap of 1 inch in the centre of the rack. The partition is to begin only from a height of 6 inches from the lowest fixed shelf and go right up to the lower side of the uppermost fixed shelf. The advantage in beginning it only from a height of 6 inches from the lowermost shelf is that giant folios, which are more than a foot broad, can be made to lie flat, on the bottom-most fixed shelves, extending from one face to the other. If the partition is of steel, it should be coated with an anti-corrosive paint.

4 The front-edge of each shelf is to have a wedge-shaped groove cut in it, to hold shelf-cards. If the groove is carefully cut, the shelf-cards can be easily slided from end to end, as the books are necessarily moved in course of time.

5 The three uprights are bound together by the four pairs of fixed shelves. It would be an advantage to re-inforce this by means of two steel tie-rods binding them together, one at a height of 2½ ft from the bottom and the other at a depth of 2½ ft from the top. To accommodate these rods it may be necessary to make the partition in three parts, the rods running between the frames of the parts.

6 It may be convenient to fix spring blind-holders to each bay to hold maps. At least two maps can be accommodated in front of each bay. The maps are to be normally in the rolled-up position. Whenever necessary, they are to be pulled out for reference and then released.

71 The teakwood used should be well-seasoned and the contractor should make good any crack that it may develop within a year of supply.

72 The length of all the shelf-planks should be quite accurate,

so that they can be interchanged without any restriction.

8 This unit-rack requires about 10 c ft of teakwood. It has 84 running ft of shelf-space. It can accommodate, on an average, 750 volumes. When full of books, it will weigh about 1 ton.

583 Opening Routine

Before opening the main gate, go round the building and see if there is anything abnormal. Ask the night watchman about his observations in the night. Check his work. See if the lock of the main gate is intact and untampered with. Then, examine if the doors and the windows are in the proper bolted position. Then, ask the peon to open them and report to you anything abnormal that he might notice. Ask him to report also all cases of broken panels, broken bolts, hooks, etc. Then, walk through the different parts of the buildings in accordance with a systematic plan, examining if there is any defect anywhere in the electric installation. Examine also if there is evidence of damage done by rats, bats, squirrels, and other similar creatures. Examine also if there is any sign of white ants anywhere. If there had been rain on the preceding day, examine if there are signs of leakage anywhere. Examine if the counter wicket gates are in a sound condition and if they work properly. Examine if all the electric switches are in good working condition. As you go round, if any defects are observed, make an accurate note of the same in your diary. Soon after this proccess is over, take the necessary action about each of the defects noticed. If anything serious is noticed, send word to the librarian immediately. Fill up the columns relating to opening in the diary of the section. Wind the clocks and the time pieces on the due days and set them right whenever necessary. See if the sweepers and cleaners do their routine.

584 Closing Routine

Examine if there is any person in any room or part of the building before it is closed. Ask a peon to go round and close and fix the bolts of all the doors and windows in a systematic manner. Inspect each of the doors and windows and examine if they have been securely bolted. Examine if any inflammable material is lying about loosely anywhere and if it does, have it removed. Put the bait in the rat traps and distribute the traps in the parts of the library, which are known to be frequented by rats. Rats are cunning creatures. It is our experience that we have to change the bait from time to time and also change the places where the traps are placed from time to time. In spite of all the ingenuity that man is capable of, the rodents are uncanny enough to thwart all his efforts, evade his traps and take its toll from some other part of the library. If the building could be designed rat-proof, a good deal of this bother will be avoided.

Take the diary of the section with you and turn the fans and lights off individually after satisfying yourself that nobody is left behind in any part of the library. Then, turn off the sub-main switches. Then turn off the main switch. Then, ask the peon to lock the main door securely. Pull it and see if it is properly locked. Ask the night watchman also to satisfy himself that it is properly locked. Then, seal it up. Then, enter the columns relating to closing, in the section's diary. Send the key and the diary to the person who is to have custody of the same during the night.

585 Stores

The issue of the articles is to be regulated and controlled by a combined stock and issue register. In the case of each article, the following "constants" are to be fixed from experience and suitably changed at intervals in the light of further experience:

1 Maximum to which the stock should be brought up periodically — say, once in a year, the period being determined for each article;

2 The minimum below which the stock should not go, i e, when the stock reaches that figure, steps should be taken for replenishment;

3 The annual consumption;

4 The quantum of issue. It will add to convenience and economy of time, if articles are issued only in a definite number of quanta. The quantum for each article is to be determined according to its nature; for example, catalogue cards are to be issued only in quanta of 100. The indenting section should ask only for 100 cards or multiples of 100 cards. It should not ask for fractions of a quantum. The quantum for writing paper may be 100 sheets; and so on.

In the light of these figures and in the light of the frequency of issue, each article is to be given a certain number of pages in the stock and issue register so that the pages allotted to all the articles are finished off, more or less at the same time.

Apart from this standardization of the quantum of issue, it is desirable that the issue is controlled and standardized from the point of view of time also. It is slovenly and annoying to run out of stock of stationery in the middle of work and to run out to the stores at odd hours. The following sample time-table will illustrate what should be aimed at:

1 11 A M Saturdays filling up indent forms
2 2 P M Saturdays supply of stores in accordance with indents.

This implies that the week's requirements should be anticipated. Over-indenting should be avoided as much as under-indenting.

5851 Stationery Articles

Another important factor in the organization of work regarding stores relates to the storing of the articles. In the case of forms and registers, receptacles of suitable size and shape are necessary. The forms and registers should be arranged strictly in the sequence of their numbers as shown in chapter 47 and in sections 517, 527, 537, 547, 557 and 577. The stationery and other articles should be arranged in some convenient sequence in receptacles of their own which should also be of proper size. The store-room should be kept scrupulously neat and tidy. If the quantum principle of distribution is adopted and if the articles themselves are packed in quanta, the tidiness in storing arrangement will be easily secured. Further, the verification of stock will also be greatly facilitated. Here is a schedule of stationery which may be required in a library.

Straw board
Packing paper (60 lb)
Brown cartridge paper (46 lb)
Bristol boards, 4 sheets thick
Ledger paper 27″×17″ (for printing)
Paper (white) 21 lb 27″×17″ (for printing)
Paper (white) 16 lb 27″×17″
Section paper
Manifolding paper
Carbon paper
Impression paper
Stencil paper
Black ink
Red ink

Rubber stamp ink
Stamping pad
Stencil (Alphabet and Arabic numerals)
Ruler
Twine
Thread
Paper weights
Drawing pin
Tap tag
Pin
Jem clip
Paper clip (steel)
Drying book
Blotting paper
Flat file boards
Hinged file boards
Bound file books
Pencil (black lead)
Pencil (blue lead)
Pencil (red lead)
Pencil (phono) required for writing call numbers also
Penholder
Nibs
Ink bottle
Ink stand
Eraser
Eraser, ink (black)
Eraser, ink (red)
Stencil ink
Punch plier
Needle
Inch tape
Foot-rule
Knife
Scissors
Paper cutter
Dhungry cloth
Umbrella
Wheat flour
Copper sulphate
Phenyle
Soap
Gum bottle
Sealing wax
Sponge
Dater
Calling bell
Typewriter
Typewriter ribbon
Typewriter eraser
Typewriter oil
Benzine oil
Typewriter metal polish
Typewriter brush
Long cloth
Duplicating machine
Duplicator ink
Duplicator obliterine
Roneo pen
Stencil plate
Lamp black
Candle stand
Electric bulb
Cycle, with its tools
Rubber solution
Cycle oil
Valve tube
Pump connection
Metal polish
Grease
Match box
Lantern

Kerosene oil
Polishing wax
Sand paper
Tonk's shelf plates and other similar fittings
Nail puller
Hammer and other tools

It is desirable that the entire stores of the library should be checked at least once in a year. The best time to check it is just before the year's supply is received.

586 Preventive Injuries

5861 Fungus

A group of omnivorous fungus known as mildew or moulds is destructive of paper and leather. They are recognized by the white scars they produce. It grows much when humidity is above 70 per cent and most when it reaches 90 per cent and the temperature is between 25°C and 38°C. Ventilation controls moulds to some extent. To provide for aeration, books must be loosely arranged on shelves. In winter, steel shelves cause local lowering of temperature producing near the books pockets of more humid air.

5862 Book-Worm

Book-worm is the popular name for the larva of beetles. It eats paper and leaves its eggs on the surface of binding or on the edges of books. The eggs hatch within ten days during summer. The larva eats its way into the interior of the book and reaches the surface again when ready for crysalis stage. It has about five life-cycles in a year. Its damage is recognized by the pinholes and tunnels across the leaves of books.

5863 Silver-Fish

Silver-fish has glistening silver-grey scales on the body, long antennae on the head and filaments at the hind-end. It is less than half an inch in length. It hides away all day and feeds on binding, starch, and paper at night and in darkness.

5864 White Ant

White ants are perhaps the most dreadful destroyer, in libraries in tropics. They live mostly on cellulose and paper and board made of it. It is the subterranean species that are most destructive in libraries. As they have a reserve of queen-ants, it is difficult to eradicate them. Like silver-fish, white ant also shuns light.

5865 Foundation

When the building is erected, the earth in the site should be dug up and cleared of nests of queen-ants The soil of the foundation trenches may be soaked with a 20 per cent solution of zinc chloride or copper sulphate. The superstructure should be isolated from foundation by a damp-proof course of concrete slate or asphalt. Stone or burnt brick and lime-mortar or cement alone should be used in construction. Floors should not have cracks or joints. Monolithic concrete should be preferred. The settlement joints and the junction of the floor with walls should be grouted with cement or plastic coal tar. This should be repeated whenever cracks develop. Another preventive against white ants is to treat joints and cracks and crevices with solution of one part corrosive sublimate and 16 parts methylated spirit. All wood-work should be of teak properly treated, for which advice may be taken from the Forest Research Institute at Dehra Dun. The stack-room may be air-conditioned. But this will not be within the reach of our small libraries. The next best is to provide for adequate ventilation, sunlight, and dryness. Napthaline bars, lime, mergosa leaf, and tobacco-leaf have preventive effect. Buckets of coal may keep humidity under control.

5866 Handling of Books

Open access is the best prevention against all the above mentioned ills. In regions into which readers go often, the books are constantly handled and injurious organisms do not find harbour. In regions which contain books not much in use, books must be frequently taken out, cleaned, aired, and exposed to sunlight. Black colour should be avoided in the covering materials of the binding. Red colour has proved to attract insects least.

587 Forms and Registers

C9971 *Indent slip.* Stencil. Ledger paper. White. The column headings are to be as follows:

Article (3 inches); Quantity on hand (½ inch); Quantity required (½ inch); Remarks.

The text above the column headings is to be:

Number and name of the section; initial of the head of the section; date; L's sanction and initials.

C9972 *Monthly supplies indent slip*. Stencil. Ledger paper. White.

The row headings are to be:

Month.

Article.

Successive names of persons or sections.

Total.

L's sanction and initials.

C9975 *Indent consolidating form*. Stencil. Ledger paper. White. The column headings are to be as follows:

Number of form or article (2.5 cm); The numbers of each of the different indenting sections, and lastly, total (1.5 cm for each of of these columns).

S997 *Stock and issue register*. Printed. 10 point type. 21 lb printing paper. Bound book. 30 lines.

The column headings are to be as follows:

Date (2.5 cm); From whom received or to whom issued (5 cm); Receipts (2.5 cm); Issue (2.5 cm); Balance (2.5 cm); Initials of receiver (1.5 cm); Remarks.

588 Files

Name	*Class Number*	*Filing Characteristic*
Indent	9972 (Last digit of the year to which the indent relates)	Correspondent
Forms	9974 (N of the form)	do
Distribution	9976 (N of the article)	do
Sanctioned indents	9977	
Stock verification	9978 (Last digit of the year to which the verification refers)	Correspondent

The files may be transferred to the record sequence at the end of five years and destroyed after three years.

Part 6

LIBRACHINE

CHAPTER 61

LIBRARY SERVICE TO RURAL FOLK

611 Time-Lag

Historically, library service first developed in most countries in cities and towns. It took more than half a century to give library service in equal measure to villages and hamlets. Generally speaking, India cannot be a total exception to this form of evolution of library service. However, there are two factors in India making it possible and necessary to reduce the time-lag between urban service and rural service.

612 Learn by Foreign Experience

It is possible for us to learn from the experience of foreign countries. They had to learn slowly by trial and error. We can skip through some of their stages. In many of the states of USA, the library van is used only to deliver bags of books in a village centre. It is located in a grocer's shop, a barber's shop, or the Church. In Denmark too, the delivery is often to a village library. It is located in the local school. In Great Britain, service is often made directly to individuals in villages by the travelling librarian. The routine involved in each such mode of service is now well known. A knowledge of this routine can give us a better start.

613 Learn from Population Distribution

The distribution of the population of India makes it necessary for us to reduce the time-lag in extending library service to the rural folk. About 90 per cent of our people live in rural areas, as against 20 per cent in England. Let us fix the maximum population test as follows:

Hamlet		1,000
Village		5,000
Town		100,000
City	above	100,000

About 10 per cent of our people live in about 200 cities. About

15 per cent live in about 4,000 towns scattered in a rural setting. About 75 per cent live in about 80,000 villages and 600,000 hamlets. Thus, India cannot be said to touch the fringe of the public library service, till it extends library service to the scattered towns, villages, and hamlets.

614 Arrest of Population Drift

There is a strong drift of population towards cities. Till 30 years ago, the main cause for this drift was the absence of schools in villages. Ambitious families migrated to cities to have their children educated. The better civic amenities of cities began to retain these rural immigrants. Then, the wide-spread link-up of the villages with the cities by bus service gave a greater chance for the rural folk to know the amenities in cities. This intensified the population drift. In the Gandhian period, industrialization is further intensifying this drift. We have learnt from the experience of other countries the almost insoluble problems likely to be introduced by such a drift. Therefore, some thought is now being turned to the arresting of this drift. Power is supplied in villages. Cottage industries are being encouraged. Community Development Plans are being experimented upon. One of the constituents of the anti-drift measure should be the provision of free book service.

CHAPTER 62

CONCRETE CASES

621 Sweden

It has been my theoretical conjecture that nothing will be gained by amalgamating a Rural Central Library with the City Central Library of the place where it is located. My Library Development Plan for our country has proceeded on this assumption. During my visit to Uppsala on 28 June 1948, I found a practical demonstration of it at its Rural Central Library. Here an attempt had been made to make the City Central Library function also as the Central Library for the surrounding rural area. But they had found it necessary to keep the stock distinct. The staff also had to be kept distinct. The only saving was in the salary of the watchman. He was shared by both the urban and the rural wings.

622 Denmark

The Swedish librarians say that they are still in the pioneer period, while they describe Denmark as having books integrated into its cultural life. On 26 June 1948, I visited a typical village library in the parish of Karlebo. Its population was only 2,000. One of the rooms in the parish school housed the library. The headmaster and his wife looked after it. It had about 2,000 volumes. About 60 books were added each year to the permanent collection. The travelling library of the district called six times in a year for exchange of books. The annual issue was 5,000 for a population of 2,000. The library was kept open on Tuesdays from 3 to 5 P M and on Fridays from 5.30 to 7.30 P M. The classification and cataloguing had all been done centrally. The librarian had only to advise readers and look after the issue work. The catalogue was in cards. The Director and the Inspectors of Libraries co-ordinated the work of the rural library system as a whole.

623 England

The rural library system of England has made considerable progress and become quite mature during the thirty-five years which had elapsed since my first visit in 1924. Practically every county has now established its rural library system. They range in type from the Middlesex system at one extreme, which consists of a chain of urban libraries and is a rural system only in the legal sense, to the Hereford system at the other extreme, which is typically rural and has to serve a community scattered over a difficult terrain. Most of the county library systems have already emerged from the initial stage of sending out boxes of books — and have begun to take an assorted collection of about 2,000 volumes in a librachine or library-van down to the villages. Some have also established several branch libraries in the bigger villages and smaller towns in their areas.

624 Typical County Library System

Derbyshire is typical of this advanced type. It finds service from one county-centre expensive and has therefore established regional centres in the branch libraries of centrally situated towns. I was very much impressed by the high level of reading which had been induced by its service. When I was in the librachine which had pulled up at a roadside to serve the neighbouring villages, it was a sight to see crowds of people walking into the librachine for exchange of books. Heavy books in subjects like poetry, anthropology, and animal husbandry were exchanged in large number — and not merely fiction, music and travel. The orderliness and quick despatch of business were impressive.

625 Branch Libraries

The branch libraries were like beehives with a throng of people at all hours. The proportion of children in most of the libraries was remarkable. By engaging myself in conversation with the children, I found how well-informed and widely interested they were. They were all quite familiar with classified arrangement and card catalogue. When I asked some children to pick out for me some books on butterflies and on India, not finding any in the children's collections, they quietly walked into the adult section and brought out the appropriate books without any help from others. This is very significant. Attractive folders and bulletins are freely distributed as appetizers. Artists show much originality in designing and varying the design of such folders.

626 Typical Branch Library

Here is a typical picture of the result of entrusting the task of promoting the perpetual self-education of one and all to the library system and giving the library profession full freedom to do their work as well as they can, without interference from others under the pretext of administrative expediency. Bakewell is one of the villages I visited. Population: 3,000; population of the neighbouring villages, also being served: 7,000. Membership in Bakewell: 100 per cent. Library: in a single room. Shelf-capacity: 8,000 volumes. Average daily issue: 600. Maximum daily issue: 1,200. Annual issue: 180,000 volumes.

CHAPTER 63

VALUE OF FULL LIBRARY SERVICE

631 Informed Mass-Power

The development in the extension of library service to the whole population has happened within a span of twenty years. The benefits of this will become visible in the course of the next generation. If this agency of culture and self-education continues to function at this rate, the enlightenment and efficiency in England will permeate throughout the entire community and step up to a marvellous level. There is no doubt that this is a true and effective means of the cultivation of the mental resources of a nation as a necessary prior step in the cultivation of its material and spiritual resources.

632 Despair Ten Years Ago

In 1950, I wrote in a mood of despair, "When will the statesmen in India realize the importance of this ? When will our Economy Committee develop a proper sense of value ? When will they distinguish between what gives quick but ephemeral political returns to the few money-grubs or power-grubs and what is beneficial in the long run to the people at large ? When will they, for example, give up tying down libraries to archaeological museums and dropping them together into the depths of the future, leaving the next generation to pick them up and develop them if it so wishes. Little do they realize that the world has now reached a stage when a nation, which pushes library provision aside, in order to save its cost for other purposes, is like one whom the common man describes as penny-wise and pound-foolish [70]".

633 Awareness at Top Level

But today we are in a happy position. The elder statesmen in the Planning Commission have become aware of the necessity for country-wide public library service. They have provided liberal sums of money. Nearly two crores of rupees for the development of public library service during the first five year period should be said to be almost generous. They are also keen to place public library service on a statutory basis in each of the constituent states.

634 Leakage

But there is many a slip between the cup and the lip, as the saying goes. This sum is not, in the first instance, being properly transformed into actual book-service. The reasons for this are many. The ministers, who have to carry out the intention of the Planning Commission, had had no chance to have enjoyed, seen, or even heard of a good library service in their earlier years, which fell in the British period. They are, therefore, unable to judge the proposals put up before them by the bureaucracy. In most cases, a tradition has developed that the implementation of library service belongs to the Department of Education. The officers in this Department are equally without any library experience. On the other hand, this century-old Department has developed a great rigidity in outlook. It begins and ends with the enforcement of the account rules, financial rules, and other Victorian rules of procedure. There is also a third casual cause of trouble. Many of the handful of persons, occupying vantage positions in the library profession, are unprogressive. Some are too idle to act up to standards. Some are clever enough to cover up their idleness by specious social contacts and wise talks; and there is no mixture more ruinous to society than the mixture of cleverness, idleness, and garrulousness. Some are swept away by passing considerations of "getting on" with personal coverage at the cost of what can be of lasting benefit to the library personality of the country and "getting honour and getting honest", in that provential way. Therefore, there is now much leakage in the utilization of the money voted for library service.

635 Optimism

The original ground for pessimism expressed in 1950 has now vanished, thanks to the vision of the Planning Commission. Let us be optimistic enough to believe that the pessimism now expressed in section 634 will also vanish soon. The ground for this optimism is the fine professional sense of social values visible in the newer generation entering the library profession. Prompted by this sense of optimism, I am giving in chapter 65 a description of a village library scene which will become a reality within the next few years.

CHAPTER 64

NEED FOR CENTRALIZATION

641 Casual Development

In some States, rural library service has developed in a casual way. This has been largely due to library enthusiasts. All honour to them. But lack of understanding of the economics of public library service has brought this casual development to a dead end. This is seen at its worst in the southern districts of Kerala. In 1956, the southern-most district of Kerala — Kanyakumari — was transferred to Madras. In 1958, the Madras Library Association collected detailed data about the library service in that district [71]. This single district had small independent libraries in one hundred and eleven localities. Only one of these was a big town.

642 Absence of Viability

The following are the averages (in round figures) obtained from the statistical data for each of the one hundred and eleven libraries of the Kanyakumari District:

Stock of books	1,700
Registered borrowers	100
Daily attendance	20
Daily issue on loan	4
Annual income and expenditure (Rs)	200
Cost of annual purchase of books and periodicals (Rs)	100
Annual cost of staff (Rs)	25

These figures speak for themselves. How many new books can a local library get, if it has only a hundred rupees to spend on newspapers, weeklies, monthlies, as well as books ? This highlights the total absence of viability of each small locality as an independent library unit.

643 Dissipation of Reading Urge

The average population of a locality may be taken to be 1,000. If so, a daily attendance of 20 is as high as it can be. It signifies a high reading potential. It is more than potential. It is a measure of the actual manifestation of the urge to read. But the daily issue on loan is only 4. The ratio of loan to attendance is as 1 to 5. This gives a measure of the dissipation of the reading urge. Obviously, the reading urge is dissipated in reading of an ephemeral kind — newspapers and light magazines.

644 Causes for Dissipation

Three causes contribute to this unprofitable dissipation:

1 Inability of a locality to add each year worth-while new books to its stock in sufficient number;

2 Inability of a locality to engage trained staff capable of harnessing the reading urge of the people and diverting it into serious, useful channels; and

3 What is deplorable, failure of the State Department of Libraries to become sensitive of the wastage due to the second cause. If it had thought about it, it would have easily tapped the community-potential of the locality by arranging at least for honorary helpers to readers, as indicated in section 257.

645 Remedy : Viable Unit

We should find a remedy to this pathological state of affairs. World experience gives some indication. There cannot be a satisfactory library service, capable of preventing the dissipation of the reading urge in the people, unless the annual income of a library is above a certain figure. This means that the area served by a library should have a population above a certain figure. About twenty years ago, I had estimated 50,000 as the minimum population that can maintain an independent library service. I had been repeating this all along. But, in the meantime, the cost of books and the cost of staff have more than doubled. Therefore, I should now suggest 100,000 as the minimum population which a locality should have to possess an independent library system. In fact, I should like to re-define a city as a locality with 100,000 as minimum population.

646 Remedy : Staff Budget

There cannot be a satisfactory library service capable of preventing the dissipation of the reading urge in people, unless a half of the annual budget of a library is set apart for staff-salary. This is world experience. We have yet to learn that purchase of books does not by itself amount to library service. The transformation of the money invested in books into book-service to readers costs money. If this latter money is not provided, the former money is only a waste; and it even causes an illusion in the minds of library authorities. This illusion leads to a fatal complacence. As stated at the beginning of this section, half the budget has to be set apart to meet the cost of transformation — this has to be done by the staff — including the processing of books through classification, cataloguing, etc, reference service, circulation, and maintenance. Let us lay bare the full implication of this distribution of the budget. The second half of the budget will have again to be distributed on cost of books and periodicals, and on cost of rent, lighting, postage, stationery, and other contingencies.

647 Book Budget

The following statement about the distribution of the library fund in the USA, should be known to our library authorities.

The 1943 *Post-War standards for public libraries* set the figure for the collection at 25 per cent.

The 1948 *National plan for public library service* suggested 20 per cent for books, periodicals, and binding as a general norm, although noting that it might be "desirable" in large cities to spend only 17.5 per cent for these items.

"*Public library service*, in 1956, suggested 'about one-fifth of the total' for the collection, 'for libraries with support at a minimum level'" [72].

648 The Moral

The moral is that all towns, villages, and hamlets in a district in India, other than cities with a minimum of 100,000 population, should combine themselves into a single library unit. The proceeds of their library taxes should be pooled into a single library fund. The State grant should be put only into this pooled fund. All impersonal activities — such as book-purchase, processing, and maintenance — should be done only by the District Central Library. Service alone should be decentralized. Books should be taken out from the

District Central Library in a librachine — a motor-van fitted as an open access library on wheels — and distributed periodically to the branch libraries in towns and directly to the people in the villages and hamlets.

CHAPTER 65

VILLAGE LIBRARY SCENE

651 Announcement

Here is a typical village library scene. I am looking forward to its becoming common in the next few years. It is 9 A M on Monday. The village sergeant moves from street to street. The beating of his drum draws the children, the women-folk, and the old from out of their homes. He announces the fortnight's call of the Travelling Library at the village centre at 2 P M. There is a stir in the streets. People dart out from one home to another. They exchange notes on their book-needs. The sergeant's drum is heard from amidst the fields. It is nearing 2 P M. The Village Library Committee has assembled. The village headmaster, its secretary, draws up the list for the books to be brought by the Travelling Library in its next visit.

652 Librachine Arrives

The motor-horn is heard from a distance; villager after villager drops in with his library books; there is a throng of people in front of the village temple. The motor-van pulls up. The Travelling Library puts up the maps and charts from the rafters of the front hall of the temple. The gramophone is turned on. The children chirp with joy as they see the cinema projector moved into the audience-hall of the temple. The book-shelves of the motor-van are thrown open. An issue counter is improvised and the headmaster takes charge of it. The people fall in queue and begin browsing amidst the books displayed inside the van. The travelling librarian has a busy time interpreting the book to some, selecting books for others, and noting down the wants of still others. An open-access library on wheels !

653 Librachine Leaves

It is nearing sunset. The travelling librarian returns after finishing his round of visits to the homes. He addresses the public. A discussion follows. This discloses to him the current trend of the villagers' interests. He promises to bring suitable reading materials in his next trip to help them in preparing for their annual drama. The sound-film is on. There is intense attention for one hour. The film shows "good night". There is another rush to the book-shelves in the van. With forethought the travelling librarian had already reshuffled the books in anticipation of the demand induced by the cinema show. The engine of the motor-van begins to throttle. There is a cordial exchange of greetings. The van moves away. The hands wave. The villagers go home books in hand. There is a look of satisfaction in their faces. Small groups halt in the way and stand absorbed in discussion. They glance through each other's books. The life in the village has received its rewinding for the forthnight.

CHAPTER 66

TRANSPORT OF BOOKS

661 Service Point

As seen in Chapter 66, a small stationary, independent library in a locality with less than 100,000 people is not viable. This means that the books of all such localities in a district should be owned in common. The common stock should be housed in the District Central Library. This library is best located at a central point in the district with easy access to all the towns, villages, and hamlets in the district. Each village should have a service point. So also, a few consecutive hamlets should share a service point. A service point may not be able to have a library building of its own. Therefore, it may not be able to have a permanent collection of books. Its people should be served periodically with books from the District Central Library. This calls for periodical transport of books to and from the service stations.

662 Branch Library

In due course, a library building can be put up in each town. There, it can have a permanent collection of reference books and oft-used books. It can then become a branch library. The people of the town can be invited to visit the library and read in its premises besides taking books home. They can be given reference service. A branch library can also make library extension service a regular feature. In short, it can function as the social centre for the town. But, a branch library will have to get its periodical supply of new books from the District Central Library. It will also have to return its books to the District Central Library for distribution to other branches. This calls for periodical transport of books to and from the branches.

663 First Phase of Transport

In the first phase of public library development, finance will restrict the mode of transport of books. We may have to follow the example of Sweden [73]. Books should be exchanged with service stations in boxes or bags through the public bus service.

Each box or bag may contain about 50 books. More books will make the weight too much for convenient handling of the box or the bag. The box must be made extra strong to stand wear and tear. It should have straps to make lifting easy. It should also have a holder for address card. The bag must be made of thick canvas. Perhaps it will be good to have it lined with corrugated packing-card-board, in order to minimize the impact on books. Its flap should have a holder for address card. Exchange with branch libraries need not be equally frequent. Moreover, more books will have to go into each consignment of a branch library. It may therefore be an advantage to hire a vehicle for transport on each occasion. It is totally uneconomical to invest capital on a jeep and spend money on petrol, man-power, and other recurring items. This will be far more costly than hiring transport in the earlier years. In the first phase, the staff of the District Central Library too will have to visit each service station by bus. In his first visit, he must fix some willing local person to take charge of the boxes of books as and when they come, distribute the books among the villagers, collect them after use, and return them in due course. The staff should also visit each service station for public relation and promotion of the acceptance of the book-service.

664 Ultimate Phase

The ultimate phase of library development may be reached perhaps after about 25 years — that is during the time of the next generation of readers. In this phase, public finance would have reached a higher level. Each District Central Library may be able to maintain a few librachines. Each librachine can carry about 2,000 books on its shelves. It will be a library-in-little on wheels. It will admit of open access. It will have an issue counter. A librarian can ride on it to render reference service. He can also use the occasion for public relation work and for promoting local extension service. In the ultimate phase, the librachine can be used also for the exchange of books with the branches.

665 Route of Librachine

The fixing of the route of the librachine will depend on local conditions. If the District Central Library is centrally placed, the route may be radial. Each day, the librachine may visit a few service stations lying more or less in a radial line and return to the headquarters in the evening. Another alternative will be to make the route a continuing one. The librachine may continuously be out in field-service for five days in the week. It may visit a few service stations each day. It may come back on the sixth day. The forenoon of the first day of the week may be spent in the headquarters collecting the books for distribution during the week. The afternoon of the sixth day may also be spent in the headquarters discharging the books brought back. The librachine may be serviced on the seventh day of the week. Its travelling staff will have it as their weekly holiday. There may be combination of these two methods of coverage of the district.

CHAPTER 67

CONTROL OF CIRCULATION

671 Ultimate Responsibility

The records and statistics of circulation should be maintained by the District Central Library. It should devise a suitable method for the collection of the primary statistics getting formed at the service stations and the branches. It should watch the returns obtained from the different service stations and branches, collate them with the data developing in the headquarters, and apply the methods of librametry — the statistical study of library data — to correct any faults discovered and to step up the quality and the quantity of service.

672 First Phase

In the first phase of transport described in section 663, the following routine may be found useful. I found it working satisfactorily in Sweden in 1948. With each box, go three copies of the list of the books sent out. One comes back immediately as receipt. The second has columns for statistics of issue against each item and is returned with the books. The third copy is retained for the case of the service station or branch library. A fourth copy is retained at the Central Library as an office copy and filed in a find-me-out folder under the name of the service station or branch as the use may be. This may be used to prevent sending the same book over again to the same service station or branch. These sheets may be destroyed, say once in five years. Apart from this, the book-card of each book sent out is filed, as in ordinary loan, in a charged tray by due dates and call numbers. This mechanizes the location of the books sent out and forms the basis for classified statistics.

Each book is provided with two book-tickets. When it goes out, it carries with it a second book-card, which the service station or branch uses for its own charging work.

There is a map with tags pinned to the service stations and branches. The colour scheme of the tags shows which branch has a permanent collection and several other features.

673 Ultimate Phase

In the ultimate phase with the librachine, the making of the lists will be unnecessary. But two book-tickets for each book will prove sufficient to control circulation. One will be charged at the headquarters against the particular librachine. The other will go out with the book. It will be used by the counter of the librachine for its charging and discharging work. Thus, clerical routine will be reduced to a minimum.

674 Local Advisory Committees

It is desirable that the District Central Library gets the maximum cooperation from the local public of each branch and service station. It should not develop a bureaucratic attitude and decide everything *ex cathedra* from the headquarters. It should establish a Branch Library Committee in each town. It should also establish a Village Library Committee in each service station. These committees should be encouraged to mobilize their local needs in respect of reading materials and other points in library service. The visiting librarian should meet these committees periodically. This will lead to progressive improvement in the acceptance of library service, in local cooperation, and in the mechanics of circulation work.

CHAPTER 68

SEPARATION OF CITY AND RURAL SERVICE

681 Separation

City library service and rural library service should not be mixed up. Each is viable by itself. There should no doubt be cooperation among them, in inter-library loan and in permanent exchange of books, as between any two library service units in an integrated national library system. But, to put a city library service and a rural library service in the hands of one authority is not helpful. A city has greater capacity of library rate than the rural district. For, there is more business activity in a city, leading to a higher level of income. There is more coherence in a city population. The hunger for books is greater in cities than in villages. There is also a perceptible difference in the reading interests of city folk and rural folk. Books of common interest will have to be duplicated in any case. It is a matter of experience that the organization, mode of service, publicity methods, book selection, and library buildings and fittings have to be different for cities and rural areas. City and Rural Library Systems are too heterogeneous to be looked after with efficiency by a single Local Library Authority. A city library system will develop more easily by itself than when it is tied to a rural library system. Their combination under the Madras Act infests both with the faults of each.

682 No Value in Merging

It may be thought that combining the two services under one Authority may lead to some saving in overhead charges — such as capital cost of the central library buildings and furniture, supervisory staff and janitorial staff. But this is an illusion. The floor area and the shelf-length of a combined building will have to be the arithmetical sum of those for the City and the Rural Central Libraries. Therefore the saving in capital cost will not be appreciable. The nature of the work of the supervisory staff for City Library Service will be essentially different from that for Rural Library Service. The density of population and the variety of interests in a city area calls for day to day contact with the public on the part of the supervisory staff. To have the same supervisory staff to look after several cities in a district will prove futile. Any attempt to save overhead charges by having the same supervisory staff for city service and rural service will be bad economy in the long run. Perhaps there will be a real saving in the janitorial staff by merging the two kinds of central library buildings. But the saving will be too small to compensate for the disadvantages. Secondly, this saving can be ensured even if there are two different Local Library Authorities. This can be done by having the city and the rural central library buildings in the same compound and providing a common janitorial staff. At Uppsala in Sweden, I had an opportunity to study the advantages and disadvantages of combining city and rural library services. I saw something similar in some of the cities of Switzerland also. The staff corroborated the above findings. Indeed, I found that for all practical purposes the two wings of the central library were functioning merely as co-tenants living in the same building. All the disadvantages of co-tenancy also were evident.

683 Madras Experiment

Under the Madras Public Libraries Act of 1948, a single Local Library Authority is provided for the cities as well as the rural areas of a district. This was a deviation from the draft bill furnished by me in 1946. The Select Committee introduced this change in the draft bill. This was in September 1948. I was then away in Europe. The following reason for this change was received by me on 18 October 1948. "Our difficulty has been that we have not been able to levy any cess in rural areas and if they are left out, the effect will be that we have library committees only for the cities and leave out rural areas which, you will agree, is not the proper thing to do. What the Government is now proposing is to levy a cess in the urban areas and contribute a similar amount on behalf of the rural areas so that a good library administration may be built for the district as a whole which will contain representatives of both urban and rural areas." The proposed method of finding money for library service to rural areas does not necessarily require that cities and rural areas should be brought under a single Local Library Authority.

684 Illusion

The merger prescribed by the Madras Act was not, in reality, due to any considerations of advantage in practical working or in overall economy. It was due only to a catch in the administration of public finance. It was based on the assumption that:

1 Library rate in a city or a town can be made a surcharge on property tax;
2 No convenient basic tax could be found in villages and hamlets on which library rate could be made a surcharge; and therefore,
3 The library service of villages and hamlets should be maintained virtually at the cost of the cities and the towns.

No doubt the Act provides for a State grant equal to the proceeds of the library rate. Our tax-pattern makes this supplement a necessity. In fact, it should be three times the proceeds of the library rate in the tax-pattern now prevailing. This was first brought out in 1953 [75]. To claim that, by a grant equal to the proceeds of the library rates in urban areas alone, the government financing the library service of villages and hamlets is wrong.

685 Result of the Experiment

One result of the Madras experiment is that a city should have an independent library system. A city has a good rating capacity. It is closely knit. It is capable of independent provision of many local services, such as water supply, sanitation, maintenance of streets, lighting, and elementary education. Library service too is such a local service. It will not develop properly in a city, unless it is given independent charge of it. Of course, a city will maintain not only a City Central Library, but also branch libraries, on an average at the rate of one for every 25,000 persons in excess of the first 25,000. Thus, in a city too there should be periodical transport of books between the branches and the City Central Library. This should be kept independent of the book transport to rural areas.

686 An Appeal

An appeal, therefore, is made to the other States in India not to copy this feature in the Madras Public Libraries Act of 1948.

They should think out these problems independently. They should not blindly copy the Madras Act either in this matter or in other matters of organization.

PART 7

CLASSIFICATION

Partly based on the Workedout Examples in
SUBJECT CLASSIFICATION PRACTICE
S.R. Ranganathan's Postulational Approach
By
M.A. Gopinath **and** ***M.A. Alar Mel Mangai***

POSTULATIONAL APPROACH TO CLASSIFYING SUBJECTS EMBODIED IN DOCUMENTS IN ANY MEDIUM

71 INTRODUCTION

Classifying a book, essentially the subject embodied in it, is both an art and a science. It involves placing the book and/or its surrogate such that the subject embodied in it gets arranged in a filiatory sequence among the subjects embodied in the document collection, for instance, in a library or in the classified part of the library catalogue or bibliography of the books. It should also facilitate easy identification, access and retrieval of the required document(s) in the collection To assist in this process, a systematic step by step procedure based on a sound theory has been formulated by Dr. S.R. Ranganathan. This is called the Postulational Approach to subject components analysis, re-synthesis and representation. This procedure is independent of any scheme for classification used for assigning class number / call number to a document.

The procedure requires familiarity with the analysis of a subject into its components (facets, isolates, speciators), categorizing the facets, and organizing the components derived by the analysis according to an appropriate Principle for Facet Sequence. In this book, three major classification schemes, namely Colon Classification (CC), Dewey Decimal Classification (DDC), and Universal Decimal Classification (UDC), are used for assigning class number.

According to the Postulational Approach there are nine steps in practical classification. These steps are presented in this section. The notation from any of the schemes for classification can be applied to the Title in Standard Terms. The latter can also be used for deriving subject indexes, say according to the Chain Procedure or its variations (POPSI, PRECIS, KWIC, KWAC etc.) and for preparing subject analytical entries.

72 PRELIMINARY PREPARATION

721 Familiarity with Concepts and Schedules

The beginner should become familiar with such concepts as 'Isolate', 'Facet', 'Basic Subject/Facet', 'Fundamental Categories', 'Speciator', 'Characteristic', 'Simple Subject', 'Compound Subject', and 'Complex Subject'. The definitions and explanations are given in S.R.Ranganathan's *Prolegomena to Library Classification*, edition 3, 1967. The work of and steps in, classifying a subject are divided into three planes: Idea Plane, Verbal Plane and Notational Plane. See Sec 91 Note below.

Before beginning to classify a book, the beginner should have completed the tasks prescribed in Sec BA5 of CC edition 7, vol. 1 and be able to identify the Main or Basic Subject, with which a Compound Subject may go. He/she should also have perused the Schedules in each of the chapters of CC7 Parts D and E. This will help in identifying and locating schedules of isolates derived from the analysis of a Compound Subject to be classified. Familiarity with the Rules for Classification will help in locating any particular rule.

722 Patience and Repetitive Work during the First Few Months

CC7 Sec BB5 gives the Steps 0 to 8 to be followed in classifying the subject of a book. During the course of learning, the beginner should write out each step while classifying the subject of the book. With sufficient practice one can acquire the ability to go through some of these steps mentally. The more the number of books classified systematically according to the nine steps, the firmer will be the foundation of the capacity to classify, and fewer the chances of errors in classifying.

723 Preparation for Classifying the Subject of a Book

The steps of the procedure for classifying, given in CC7 Sec BB5, are only for a simple subject. These steps will not give much difficulty if the beginner has completed the task prescribed in CC7 Sec BA5 satisfactorily.

724 Classifying Complicated Subjects

In a few months, or perhaps even weeks, the beginner will discover what more should be done in the various steps of the procedure for classifying complicated subjects. This will be demonstrated in the later sections of this book.

73 CLASSIFYING A SIMPLE BOOK

The steps are described as a series of directions to the classifier.

Step 0-Raw Title

In most cases the title of the book (other than in the field of Humanities and Literature (Belle lettre)), usually found on its title-page, indicates in a general way the subject dealt within the book. Therefore, the title of the book is the starting point.

Example: "Eradication of virus in rice plants in Japan (1971)"

01 Preparation for Expressive Title

011 Incomplete Raw Title

Often, the Raw Title will not be fully expressive of the specific subject of the book.

012 Basic Subject not Mentioned

Fill up the name of the Basic Subject (BS), if it is not found in the Raw Title. For example, in the above mentioned Raw Title, the name of the (BS) "Agriculture" is absent. This should be supplied. For, every Compound Subject, by definition, should necessarily have a (BS) and one or more isolates.

013 Fill up the Period or Time Element

Obviously, this book will have information about its subject only up to a particular period of time. It is useful to indicate this in the class number. But the Raw Title does not mention the period. Here, it is necessary to peruse the book and find out the period. Before doing so, read the definition of the term 'Last Effective Decade' given in Sec DH41 of CC Ed. 7. For this book, perhaps, the period may be fixed as the decade 1970s.

014 Filling up the Implied but Missing Ideas

Compound and composite ideas should be broken into unit

ideas. If, for instance, you do not know the exact meaning of the term 'Virus', look it up in a dictionary. Virus is a micro-organism causing disease. Therefore, the term 'Virus' in the Raw Title should be changed to "Virus disease". For, surely the book deals with the "Eradication of the virus disease in rice plant".

Step 1 - Expressive Title :

The Title resulting from carrying out the directions given in the sub-sections under Step 0.

For the example given in Step 0, the Expressive Title is:

"*In Agriculture, eradication of virus disease of rice plant in Japan brought up to 1970s*".

11 Preparation for the Title in Kernel Terms

111 Removal of Apparatus Words

Remove the apparatus words from the Expressive Title. In our example, remove the following apparatus words:

"in", "of", and " brought up to" from the Expressive Title.

112 Kernel Term

Each surviving term is denoted as a 'Kernel Term'.

113 Reduction into Nominative Case Singular Form

If any Kernel Term in the Expressive Title is not in the nominative case singular form, change it to that form. In our example, there is no need for this.

114 Capitalizing the First Letter

Make the first letter of each Kernel Term a capital letter. In the example, we then get:

'Agriculture', 'Eradication', 'Virus disease', 'Rice plant', 'Japan', '1970s'

115 Inserting a Full stop

Insert a full stop after each Kernel Term.

Step 2: Title in Kernel Terms :

The title resulting from carrying out the directions given in the sub-sections under Step 1.

For the example given in Step 0, the Title in Kernel Terms is:

Agriculture. Eradication. Virus disease. Rice plant. Japan. 1970s.

21 Preparation for Analysed Title

At this stage, read again in CC7 Sec CN5 and its sub-divisions, Sec CPI, and CPII to understand the idea of the Five Fundamental Categories, "Personality"(P), "Matter"(M), - which may denote either "Matter-Material" (MM) or "Matter-Property" (MP), Energy"(E), "Space"(S), and "Time"(T).

211 Manifestation of the Fundamental Categories

Find out of what (FC) the idea denoted by each Kernel Term may be deemed to be a manifestation. In the example given in Step 2:

1. The idea denoted by the term '1970s' is obviously a manifestation of the (FC) Time;
2. The idea denoted by the term 'Japan' is obviously a manifestation of the (FC) Space;
3. The idea denoted by the term 'Rice plant' is obviously not a manifestation of the (FC) Time, nor of Space, nor of Energy, nor of Matter-Property. Every subject deals with an entity or a group of them - concrete or abstract. The study reported (discourse) is usually about the attributes or properties of the entity and how one or more of them may be used, manipulated, or changed for some purpose. In our example "Rice plant" is such an entity and by Sec CP11 it is deemed to be a manifestation of the (FC) Personality.
4. The idea denoted by the term 'Virus disease', is a disease caused by the micro-organism virus). 'Disease' denotes a particular state of the Personality 'Rice plant'. It is therefore a manifestation of the (FC) Matter-Property. It is a particular type of disease - one that is caused by virus. Therefore, 'Virus disease' is a manifestation of the (FC) Matter-Property.
5. The idea denoted by the term 'Eradication' denotes external action. It is, therefore, a manifestation of the (FC) 'Energy'. Note: Internal action or action taking place within an entity, (e.g cell division, fission, physiology, biochemistry, thought

process, behaviour, etc.) is an attribute of the entity and therefore deemed a manifestation of the (FĊ) Matter-Property and not of the (FC) Energy.

6. The idea denoted by the term 'Agriculture' was introduced in the Expressive Title from the schedule of (BS) (See CC7, Chap CN for the meanings)
7. For convenience, Agriculture is called Basic Facet (BF); Eradication is called (E) Facet; Virus disease is called (MP) Facet; Rice plant is called (P) Facet; Japan is called (S) Facet; and 1970s is called (T) Facet.

213 Putting in Abbreviations

Insert after each Kernel Term, the name of its Facet in abbreviated form as given in CC7, Chap CN.

Step 3 - Analysed Title :

The Title resulting from carrying out the directions given in the sub-sections under Step 2.

For the example given in Step 0, the Analysed Title is:

Agriculture (BF). Eradication [E]. Virus disease [MP]. Rice plant [P]. Japan [S]. 1970s [T]. (See CC7, Chap GP for the meanings of the abbreviations.; peruse Chap. CF also)

31 Preparation for Transformed Title

Read CC7, Sec CP7 and its subdivisions, and learn the sequence in which facets of a compound subject should be arranged.

Arrange, in the correct sequence, the Kernel Terms in the Analysed Title.

Step 4 - Transformed Title :

The Title resulting from carrying out the directions given in the sub-section under Step 3.

For the example given in Step 0, the Transformed Title is:

Agriculture (BF). Rice Plant [1P1]. Virus disease [1MP1]. Eradication [IE]. Japan [S]. 1970s [T].

41 Preparation for Title in Standard Terms

Next, replace each of the Kernel Terms by its equivalent Standard Term as given in the schedules of CC7, as. follows:

411 Basic Subject Term

Look up in CC7, Chap DD, the Schedule of "Basic Subjects, and Partial Comprehensions". The term 'Agriculture' itself is found there. Therefore, this term need not be changed.

412 Rice Plant

Look up in CC7, Chap "EJ Agriculture", the schedule of (1P1) isolates for Compound Subjects going with "J Agriculture". Locate the term 'Rice plant'. You do not find this term. But you will find its equivalent term 'Rice'. Therefore, change the term 'Rice Plant' into 'Rice'.

413 Virus Disease

Look up in CC7, Chap "EJ Agriculture", the schedule of (1M1) isolates for Compound Subjects going with "J Agriculture". Locate the term 'Virus disease'. But you do not find this term. You will find only the term 'Disease'. Under this term you will find the direction:

"Divisions as for Medicine in Chap EL"

Therefore, turn to CC7, Chap "EL Medicine". In that chapter look up the divisions under "4 Disease" in the schedule of (1MP) isolates for Compound Subjects going with "L Medicine". In that schedule locate the term 'Virus' or its equivalent. You will find the term 'Virus' itself. Therefore, this term need not be changed.

414 Eradication

Look up in CC7, Chap "EJ Agriculture" the schedule of (IE) isolates going with "J Agriculture". Locate the term 'Eradication'. You do not find it there. Therefore, look for its equivalent. Look up a dictionary of the meaning of the term 'Eradication', if you do not already know it. The dictionary gives the meanings 'get rid' and 'extirpate'. With these terms in mind again look through the said schedule of (1E) isolates. You will find that the term 'Prevention' comes nearest to it. Change the term 'Eradication' to 'Prevention'.

415 Japan

Look up in CC7, Chap "DJ Space Isolates". Locate the term

'Japan'. You will find it there. Therefore, this term need not be changed.

416 1970s

Look up in CC7, Chap "DH Time Isolates". Locate the decade '1970s' in it. You will find only "N 1900 to 1999". You will also find instructions in CC7, Sec DF34 and DF4 and its subdivisions of the Rules given after the schedules in that chapter.

According to these Rules, the Time Isolate is the decade "197".

Step 5 - Title in Standard Terms :

The Title resulting from carrying out the directions given in the sub-sections under Step 4.

For the example given in Step 0, the Title in Standard Terms is:

Agriculture (BF). Rice [1P1]. Virus disease [1MP1]. Prevention [IE]. Japan [S]. 1970s [T].

51 Preparation for Title in Facet Numbers

For each Standard Term, look up the relevant schedules used

Step 6: Title in Facet Numbers :

The Title resulting from carrying out the directions given in the sub-sections under Step 5.

For the example given in Step 0, the Title in Facet Numbers is:

J (BF). 381 [1P1]. 421 [1MP1]. 5 [1E]. 42 [S]. N7[T].

61 Preparation for Class Number

Look up in CC7, Chap DA, the schedule for Indicator Digits and select the Indicator Digit prescribed for each kind of Isolate Facet.

611 Insertion of Indicator Digit

From each Isolate Facet Number, remove the abbreviation and the full stop. Prefix to each Isolate Facet Number the Indicator Digit appropriate to its (FC).

Step 7: Class Number of a Subject :

The ordinal number resulting from carrying out the directions given in the sub-sections under Step 6.

For the example given in Step 0, the Class Number of the Subject according to CC7 is:

J, 381; 421: 5.42'N7.

For comparison, the UDC and the DC Numbers for the same subject are given below:

UDC 633.18-238-298 (520) "197"

DC 633.189 809 520 904 6

The Isolate 'Prevention' is not represented in the DC Number.

Step 8 - Verification :

81 Facet Analysis of Class Number

Write each Facet Number in the Class Number in a separate line. Write against each Facet Number the abbreviated name of the Facet.

For the example given in Step 0 the Facet Analysis will give:

J	(BF)	5	[1E]
381	[1P1]	42	[S]
421	[1MP1]	N7	[T]

82 Translation into Kernel Terms

Write down the Facet Number in succession given against the Basic Subject Number or the Isolate Number, as the case may be, its translation into English.

For the example given in Step 0, the Translation into Kernel Terms is:

J	Agriculture	5	Prevention
381	Rice	42	Japan
421	Virus disease	N7	1970s

83 Assembly in Skeleton Form

Assemble the Facet Terms assigned in the preceding section, in the sequence indicated by the abbreviated names of the facets. Read CC7, Sec CP7 and its subdivisions for arranging them in a sequence.

For the example given in Step 0, the Assembly in Skeleton Form is:

Agriculture (BF). Rice [1P1]. Virus disease [1MP1]. Prevention [1E]. Japan 1970s. [T].

Here the facet terms are arranged according to the Syntax of CC Language.

84 Transformation according to the Syntax of the English Language

Rearrange the Facet Terms obtained in the preceding section, according to the syntax of the English language, inserting the necessary apparatus words, instead of the abbreviated facet terms and full stop, and change the standard terms into the terms in the original.

For the example given in Step 0, the Translation according to the Syntax of the English Language is:

In agriculture, eradication of virus disease of rice plant in Japan in 1970s.

85 Last Step in Verification

See if the name of the subject arrived at in the preceding section is equivalent to the Expressive Title of the subject of the book classified.

For the example given in Step 0, the title arrived at in Step 84 and the title in Step 1 are equivalent.

86 Rectification

If the name of the subject arrived at is not equivalent to the Expressive Title and thereafter to the Raw Title, an error may have occurred in one step or another, while classifying. Trace it out, rectify it, and verify again.

91 Note

1. The work in Steps 0 to 4 lies in the Idea Plane;
2. The work in Step 5 lies in the Verbal Plane;
3. The work in Steps 6 and 7 lies in the Notational Plane. In this connection, peruse CC7, Chap CE to CM.

4. What we have done in these eight steps is what we generally do when translating from one natural language into another.
5. Here we have translated the name of a subject given in English into its name in the artificial ordinal language of Colon Classification.
6. The first exercise has necessarily to be slow, and it has therefore taken much time. But you should enjoy it as if it were a game in cross word puzzle or as a child would enjoy building a toy with a Meccano Set.
7. As you continue classifying, the time taken will go on decreasing.
8. By the time one becomes a "veteran", the classification would take, in most cases, much less time.

74 CLASSIFYING COMPLICATED SUBJECTS

740 Kinds of Complicated Subjects

For a beginner only two kinds of complicated subjects are discussed here

1. A Compound Subject with an Anteriorising Common Isolate (*See* CC7, DG 3), and certain Personality Isolates; and
2. A Complex Subject with two Phases.

01 Classification of Subject in Each Phase and Assemblage

011 Host Subject and Anteriorising Commons Isolates.

Many of the Anteriorising Common Isolates admit of being fitted with isolates of their own. Therefore, it is convenient to classify the Host Subject and the Anteriorising Common Isolate as two separate processes. Then combine the resulting Class Number and the Anteriorising Common Isolate Number, using the prescribed Indicator Digit for Anteriorising Common Isolates.

012 Each Phase

In the case of a Complex Subject it is convenient to classify the subject forming each phase independently then combine the resulting two Class Numbers, by using the prescribed Indicator digit and the digit representing the kind of Phase Relation involved.

1 Classification of a Subject with Anteriorising Common Isolate

Example: Indian sugar cane journal 1955.

Classification of Host Subject. The Host Subject is "Sugar cane".

By following the steps given in Sec 3 above, we get the results mentioned below:

Step 2 -Title in Kernel terms: Agriculture. Sugar cane

Step 3 - Analysed title: Agriculture (BF) Sugar cane [1P1]

Step 6 - Title in Facet Numbers: J (BF). 311 [1P1]

Step 7- CC Class Number: J, 311.

13 Classification of Anteriorising Common Isolate (ACI)

The Anteriorising Common Isolate part is "Indian Journal 1955-"

On the analogy of the steps given in Sec. 3 above, we get the following:

Step 2 -Title in Kernel Terms: India. Journal. 1955.

From CC7, Chap DM we get the following results in Step 3:

India [1P1]. Journal (AC1). 1955 [1P2].

Step 4-Transformed Title.

From CC7, Chap DM we get the following Transformed Title:

Journal (AC1). India [1P1]. 1955 [1P2].

Step 5-Title in Standard Terms

Periodical (AC1). India [1P1]. 1955 [1P2].

Step 6- Title in Facet Numbers

Read CC7, Sec CU3. The Indian sugar cane journal is taken to be the first Indian periodical on sugar cane. This information may be obtained from the following publications:

1. *Union catalogue of learned periodical publications in South East Asia*; 1952.
2. *World list of periodicals*; (latest edition). and
3. *World list of periodicals*; Ed 10, 2 vol. "*Ulrich's International*" 1972. R.R. Bowker Co., New York Periodicals Directory.

As a result we get for the Chronological Number the digit N. Thus the Title in Facet Numbers is (ACI). 44[1P1]. N [1P2].

Step 7-CC Number: m44,N14 Assembling of Class Number

141 Indicator Digit

From CC7, Chap DA we find that the Indicator Digit for an Anteriorising Common Isolate is "(double inverted comma).

142 Assembled Class Number

Thus, we get the assembled Class Numbers J,311"m 44,N.

2 Classification of a Complex Subject

Research Methodology for Economists

21 Classification of Subject in Phase 1

The subject forming Phase 1 is "Research Methodology".

By following the steps given in Sec. 3 above, we get the following:

Step 1 - Expressive title: In Research Methodology

Step 2 - Title in Kernel terms: Research Methodology

Step 3 - Analysed title: Research Methodology (BF)

Step 6- Title in Facet Numbers: 9f (BF)

Step 7 - CC Number: 9f

22 Classification of Subject in Phase 2

Step 1 - Expressive Title: In Economics

Step 2 - Title in Kernel Terms: Economics

Step 3 - Analyzed Title: Economics (BF)

Step 6 - Title in Facet Number: X (BF)

Step 7: - CC Number: X

The Phase Relation is Inter-Subject Bias Phase Relation

231 Phase Relation Digit

The Phase Relation Digit for Inter-Subject Bias Relation is b. See the table in CC7, Chap DP Phase Relation."

24 Assembling of Class Number

241 Indicator Digit: &

242 Assembled Class Number

The assembled CC Number: 9f&bX.

SUBJECT CLASSIFICATION PRACTICE WORKEDOUT EXAMPLES

WORKED OUT EXAMPLES

Hannaford, Peter. Talking back to the media

Raw Title	: Talking back to the media
Analyzed Title	: Mass communication (BF) Mass media [1P1] USA [S]
Synthesized Title	: 4(BF),1[1P1].73[S]
CC7	: 4,1.73
CC6	: (P).73
DDC 21	: 302.230973 D4=659.444

Hodgson, F.W. Modern newspaper editing and production

Raw Title	: Modern newspaper editing and production
Analyzed Title	: Mass communication (BF) Newspapers [1P1] Editing [E]
Synthesized Title	: 4(BF),211[1P1]:pR6[E]
CC7	: 4,211:pR6
CC6	: 4
DDC 21	: 070.41

Page, Gillian. Journal publishing: principles and practice

Raw Title	: Journal publishing: principles and practice
Analyzed Title	: Mass communication (BF) Periodicals [1P1] Academic institutions (Sp. to 1P1) Publishing [E]
Synthesized Title	: 4(BF),23[1P1]=zB3(Sp. to 1P1):pR7[E]
CC7	: 4,23=zB3:pR7
CC6	: 4
DDC 21	: 070.572

McKean, Charles. The making of the museum of Scotland

Raw Title	: The making of the museum of Scotland
Analyzed Title	: Museology (BF),Museum [1P1],Scotland [S]
Synthesized Title	: 6(BF),1[1P1],565[S]
CC7	: 6,1.565

CC6	: M96.563
DDC 21	: 069.09411

Johnson, Glenn L. Research methodology for economists

Raw Title	: Research methodology for economists: philosophy and practice.
Analyzed Title	: Research methodology (BF) Economics (Inter-Subject Bias Phase Relation)
Synthesized Title	: 9f(BF)&bX(Inter-subject Bias Phase Relation)
CC7	: 9f&bX
CC6	: T480bX
DDC 21	: 330.01

Kumar, H.D. Environmental technology and biosphere management

Raw Title	: Environmental technology and biosphere management
Analyzed Title	: Environmental Science (BF), Biosphere [1P1], Management [E]
Synthesized Title	: AXB(BF),1[1P1],x[E]
CC7	: AXB,1:x
CC6	: G;5:8
DDC 21	: 333.71495065 or 333.9517

Tompkins, Peter and Bird, Christopher. Secrets of the soil: new solutions for restoring our planet

Raw Title	: Secrets of the soil: New Solutions for restoring our planet
Analyzed Title	: Soil Science (BF), Soil [1P1], Conservation [E]
Synthesized Title	: AXD(BF),1[1P1],k7[E]
CC7	: AXD,1:k7
CC6	: J:1:7
DDC 21	: 333.7316 or 363.73968

Ray, R.K. and Others, Ed. Materials for the third millennium

Raw Title : Materials for the third millennium
Analyzed Title : Materials Science (BF),Materials [1P1]
Synthesized Title : AXE(BF),1[1P1]
CC7 : AXE,1
CC6 : F,0Z
DDC 21 : 620.110905

Roitman. Introduction to modern set theory

Raw Title : Introduction to modern set theory.
Analyzed Title : Arithmetic (BF) Integer [1P1] Algebraic [Sp to 1P1]
Synthesized Title : B1(BF),3[1P1]-2[1P1]
CC7 : B1,3-2
CC6 : B13:2
DDC 21 : 513.12

Gardner, B.J. Radical theory, 1989

Raw Title : Radical theory
Analyzed Title : Algebra (BF) Radical theory(System Speciator to BF)
Synthesized Title : B2(BF) -N8(Sys.Sp.to BF)
CC7 : B2-N8
CC6 : B2N8
DDC 21 : 512.4

Magnus. Matrix differential calculus with applications in statistics and econometrics

Raw Title : Matrix differential calculus with applications in statistics and econometrics.
Analyzed Title : Analysis (BF) Differential calculus [1P1] Statistics(Inter-Subject Bias Phase Relation) Econometrics(Later part)
Synthesized Title : B3(BF),21[1P1]&BT(Inter-Subject Bias Phase Relation)+XYT (Later part)

CC7	: B3,21&bBT+XYT
CC6	: B321 0b B28
DDC 21	: 515.33

Weaver, H.W. Theory of discrete and continuous Fourier analysis

Raw Title	: Theory of discrete and continuous Fourier Analysis.
Analyzed Title	: Analysis (BF) Fourier [1P1] Distribution of value [1MP1]
Synthesized Title	: B3(BF),6M[1P1];5[1MP1]
CC7	: B3,6M;5
CC6	: B36M
DDC 21	: 515.2433

Beale, E.M.L. Introduction to optimization

Raw Title	: Introduction to optimization.
Analyzed Title	: Operations research (BF) Linear programming [1P1]
Synthesized Title	: BTT(BF),1[1P1]
CC7	: BTT,1
CC6	: B28
DDC 21	: 003

Clemson, Barry. Cybernetics: a new management tool

Raw Title	: Cybernetics: A new management tool
Analyzed Title	: Cybernetics (BF)
Synthesized Title	: BV(BF)
CC7	: BV
CC6	: D6291,78
DDC 21	: 003.5

Kapur, J.N. Mathematical modelling

Raw Title	: Mathematical modelling.
Analyzed Title	: Cybernetics (BF) Model [1P1]
Synthesized Title	: BV(BF),8[1P1]

CC7 : BV,8

CC6 : B

DDC 21 : 003.5 [OR]511.8

Dormand, J.R; Woolfson, M.M. The origin of the solar system: the capture theory

Raw Title : The origin of the solar system: the capture theory.

Analyzed Title : Astrophysics (BF)Solar system [1P1]

Synthesized Title : BYC(BF),H[1P1]

CC7 : BYC,H

CC6 : B9:6

DDC 21 : 523.2

Cohen-Tannoudji, C; Dupont-Roc, J; Grynberg, G. Photons and atoms: introduction to quantum electrodynamics

Raw Title : Photons and atoms: introduction to quantum electrodynamics.

Analyzed Title : Physics(BS) Quantum theory(System Speciator to BS) Electricity physics(Canonical Sp.to BS) Electrodynamics [1P1]

Synthesized Title : C(BS)-N(Sys.Sp.to BS)-6(Canonical Sp.to BS),11[1P1]

CC7 : C-N-6,11

CC6 : CN1,6

DDC 21 : 537.67

Grasso, Vincenzo, Ed. Electronic structure and electronic transitions in layered materials

Raw Title : Electronic structure and electronic transitions in layered materials.

Analyzed Title : Physics of properties of matter (BF) Solid state [1P1] Physical property(CMPI) Structure (Sp.to CMPI)

Synthesized Title : C2(BF),11[1P1];c1(CMPI)-b68(Sp.to CMPI)
CC7 : C2,11;c1-b68
CC6 : C21:8
DDC 21 : 530.41

Kastner, Marc A, etc, Ed. Disordered semiconductors

Raw Title : Disordered semiconductors.
Analyzed Title : Semiconductor physics (BF) Semiconductor materials [1P1] Amorphous (Sp. to 1P1)
Synthesized Title : C6T2(BF),0Z[1P1]=156(Sp. to 1P1)
CC7 : C6T2,0Z=156
CC6 : C6
DDC 21 : 537.622

Urry, Grant. Elementary equilibrium chemistry of carbon

Raw Title : Elementary equilibrium chemistry of carbon.
Analyzed Title : General chemistry (BF) Carbon [1P1] Chemical equilibrium [1MP1] Oxidation [E]
Synthesized Title : E1(BF),140[1P1];2143[1MP1]:811[E]
CC7 : E1,140;2143:811
CC6 : E140:214-81
DDC 21 : 546.6815

Burgess, J. Ions in solution: basic principles of chemical interactions

Raw Title : Ions in solution: basic principles of chemical interactions.
Analyzed Title : Physical chemistry (BF) Solution [1P1] Ionisation [1MP1]
Synthesized Title : E2(BF),2[1P1];2136[1MP1]
CC7 : E2,2;2136

CC6 : E:2136-22
DDC 21 : 541.34

Jenkins, R. X-Ray fluorescence spectrometry

Raw Title : X-ray fluorescence spectrometry.
Analyzed Title : Analytical chemistry (BF) X-ray spectrometry [1P1]
Synthesized Title : E3(BF),553[1P1]
CC7 : E3,553
CC6 : E3,E53
DDC 21 : 543.08586

Ioffe, I.I. Application of pattern recognition to catalytic research

Raw Title : Application of pattern recognition to catalytic research.
Analyzed Title : Synthetic chemistry (BF) Catalysis [1P1] Research [CEI] Pattern recognitions [CEI] (Tool phase relation)
Synthesized Title : E4(BF),8H[1P1]:aR[CEI]&ebTB1[CEI]
CC7 : E4,8H:aR&ebTB1
CC6 : E:88
DDC 21 : 541.395

Schugerl, Karl: Bioreaction engineering: reactions involving microorganisms and cells

Raw Title : Bioreaction engineering: reactions involving microorganisms and cells.
Analyzed Title : Chemical engineering(BS) Biochemical engineering(Specials Sp. to BS) Reactions (CEI)
Synthesized Title : EX(BS)-9G(Specials Sp. to BS):ea(CEI)
CC7 : EX-9G:ea
CC6 : E9G:(D)
DDC 21 : 660.63

Kennedy, J.F, etc, Ed. Wood and cellulosics: industrial utilisation, biotechnology, structure and properties

Raw Title	: Wood and cellulosics: industrial utilisation, Biotechnology, Structure and properties.
Analyzed Title	: Technology (BF) Cellulose [1P1] Molecular structure [1MP1] Utilisation (CEI)
Synthesized Title	: F(BF),96Z[1P1];17[1MP1]:xc(CEI)
CC7	: F,96Z;17:xc
CC6	: F6894
DDC 21	: 661.802

West, Roger. Philosophy and evolution: the evolution of philosophy and the philosophy of evolution

Raw Title	: Philosophy and evolution: the evolution of philosophy and the philosophy of evolution.
Analyzed Title	: Biology (BF) Body, Organism [1P1] Evolution [1MP1] Philosophy, Metaphysics(Inter-Subject General Phase Relation)
Synthesized Title	: G(BF),1[1P1];66[1MP1]&aR3(I-S General P.R)
CC7	: G,1;66&aR3
CC6	: G1:660aR3
DDC 21	: 128

Glover, D.M. DNA cloning: a practical approach

Raw Title	: DNA cloning: a practical approach.
Analyzed Title	: Cytology (BF) DNA [1P1] Cloning(Copying) [CE1]
Synthesized Title	: GT(BF),332[1P1]:ag2[CEI)]
CC7	: GT,332:ag2
CC6	: G1133:7

DDC 21	: 571.6

Taylor, A.E.R,; Baker, J.R, Eds. In-vitro methods for parasite cultivation

Raw Title	: In-vitro methods for parasite cultivation.
Analyzed Title	: Microbiology (BF) Micro-organism parasite [1MP1] Cultivation (CEI) Experiment (CEI)
Synthesized Title	: GV(BF),0Z[1P1]-03 Parasite(Sp to 1P1):g3(CEI):aR3(CEI)
CC7	: GV,0Z-03:g3:aR3
CC6	: G1:564:f3
DDC 21	: 577.857

Jiemba, Patrick K.. Environmental microbiology principles and applications

Raw Title	: Environmental Microbiology Principles and Applications
Analyzed Title	: Microbiology (BF), Environment, Biosphere (inter subject bias phase relation)
Synthesized Title	: GV(BF)&bAXB(BF),1[1P1]
CC7	: GV&bAXB,1
CC6	: G21;5
DDC 21	: 579.17015

Marre, Jacques. The structural analysis of granitic rocks

Raw Title	: The structural analysis of granitic rocks
Analyzed Title	: Petrology (BF) Granite [1P1] Structure [1MP1] Analysis (CEI)
Synthesized Title	: H2(BF),1731[1P1];2[1MP1]:aR8(CEI)
CC7	: H2,1731;2:aR8
CC6	: H21731
DDC 21	: 552.3

Royal Society. Tectonic settings of regional metamorphism: proceedings of a royal society discussion meeting in association with IGCP project no.235

Raw Title	: Tectonic settings of regional metamorphism: proceedings of a royal society discussion meeting in association with IGCP project no.235.
Analyzed Title	: Structural geology (BF)Metamorphism [1P1] Geomorphology (Inter-Subject General Phase Relation)
Synthesized Title	: H3(BF),5[1P1]&aH4(I-S General P.R)
CC7	: H3,5&aH4
CC6	: H340aH4
DDC 21	: 551

Cullen, Michael. Our electrical environment: a new insight into nature

Raw Title	: Our electrical environment: a new insight into nature.
Analyzed Title	: Meteorology (BF) Electrical phenomena [1P1]
Synthesized Title	: HV7(BF),626[1P1]
CC7	: HV7,626
CC6	: U2862
DDC 21	: 551.56

Willis, J.C. A dictionary of the flowering plants and ferns

Raw Title	: A dictionary of the flowering plants and ferns; Ed.8
Analyzed Title	: Botany (BF) Pteriodophyta, filicinal(Fern) [1P1] Encyclopedia, world (ACI)
Synthesized Title	: I(BF),42[1P1]"k1(ACI)
CC7	: I,42"k1
CC6	: I42k1
DDC 21	: 587.03

SCR. Chemicals in agriculture

Raw Title : Chemicals in agriculture
Analyzed Title : Agriculture (BF) Chemistry, General chemistry, Chemicals [1P] (Inter-Subject Tool or Application Phase Relation)
Synthesized Title : J(BF)&eE1,a[1P] (I-S Application P.R)
CC7 : J&eE1,a
CC6 : J0bE1
DDC 21 : 630.2540

Francis, Charles A, Ed. Multiple cropping system

Raw Title : Multiple cropping system
Analyzed Title : Agriculture (BF) Plant [1P1] Crop rotation (1MP1)
Synthesized Title : J(BF),0Z[1P1]:58(1MP1)
CC7 : J,0Z;58
CC6 : J:5-7
DDC 21 : 631.55

Benada, J, etc, Ed. Atlas of diseases and pests on beet

Raw Title : Atlas of diseases and pests on beet
Analyzed Title : Agriculture (BF) Beetroot [1P1] Disease, Pest, Parasite [1MP1] Atlas (ACI)
Synthesized Title : J(BF),331[1P1];43[1MP1]"f(ACI)
CC7 : J,331;43"f
CC6 : J331:43f
DDC 21 : 635.119

Carwardine, Mark. The encyclopedia of world wildlife: a survey of animals and their habitats

Raw Title : The encyclopedia of world wildlife: a survey of animals and their habitats
Analyzed Title : Zoology (BF) Animal [1P1] Abode, Habitat [1MP1] Encyclopedia, World (ACI)

Synthesized Title : K(BF),0Z[1P1];571[1MP1]"k1(ACI)
CC7 : K,0Z;571"k1
CC6 : K:571k1
DDC 21 : 591.03

Barton, Miles. Animal rights

Raw Title : Animal rights
Analyzed Title : Zoology (BF) Animal [1P1] Ecology, Conservation [1MP1] Philosophy, Ethics(Inter-Subject General Phase Relation) Conduct towards animals [1P1 to Ethics]
Synthesized Title : K(BF),0Z[1P1];527[1MP1]&aR4(Inter subject General PR),7 [1P1 to Ethics]
CC7 : K,0Z;527&a R4,7
CC6 : K:5270aR47
DDC 21 : 591.7 [OR]179.3

Arrignon, Jacques. Management of freshwaters fisheries

Raw Title : Management of freshwaters fisheries
Analyzed Title : Animal husbandry (BF),Fish (array division),Freshwater [1P1],Management [CEI]
Synthesized Title : KX(BF),33251:x[CEI]
CC7 : KX,33251:x
CC6 : KZ332
DDC 21 : 639.31068

Richardson, M. Care for your tropical fish

Raw Title : Care for your tropical fish
Analyzed Title : Animal husbandry(BS) Tropical animal husbandry(Specials Sp.to BS) Aquarium fish [1P1] Breeding [1MP1]
Synthesized Title : KX(BS)-9U3(Specials Sp. to BS),142[1P1];6[1MP1]

CC7 : KX-9U3,142;6
CC6 : KZ142:6.192
DDC 21 : 639.34

Alexander, J.I; Hill, R.G. Postoperative pain control

Raw Title : Postoperative pain control
Analyzed Title : Medicine (BF) Body [1P1] Disease, Pain [1MP1] Surgery [E] Aftercare [2E]
Synthesized Title : L(BF),1[1P1];417[1MP1]:7[E]:91[2E]
CC7 : L,1;417:7:91
CC6 : L1:417:7:91
DDC 21 : 617.01

Lee, Emanoel C.G, etc, Ed. Surgery of inflammatory bowel disorders

Raw Title : Surgery of inflammatory bowel disorders
Analyzed Title : Medicine (BF)Intestine [1P1]Disease, Inflammation [1MP1] Surgery [E]
Synthesized Title : L(BF),25[1P1];415[1MP1]:7[E]
CC7 : L,25;415:7
CC6 : L25:415:7
DDC 21 : 616.34

Furlan, Anthony J, Ed. The heart and stroke: exploring mutual cerebrovascular and cardiovascular issues

Raw Title : The heart and stroke: exploring mutual cerebrovascular and cardiovascular issues
Analyzed Title : Medicine (BF) Cerebrum [1P1] Heart (Intra-Facet Influence Phase Relation) Disease [1MP1]
Synthesized Title : L(BF),7221[1P1]&r32(Intra-Facet Influence Phase Relation);4[1MP1]
CC7 : L,7221&r32;4
CC6 : L72210r32:4
DDC 21 : 616.1207

Jones, Elise F, etc. Teenage pregnancy in industrialised countries: a study sponsored by the Alan Guttmacher Institute

Raw Title	:	Teenage pregnancy in industrialised countries
Analyzed Title	:	Medicine(BS) Female medicine(Specials Sp.to BS) Adolescent medicine(Specials Sp.to BS) Female genital organ [1P1] Obstetrics, Pregnancy [1MP1] Industrialised countries [S]
Synthesized Title	:	L(BS)-9H (Specials Sp.to BS)-9D (Specials Sp.to BS),55 [1P1];31[1MP1].1-yXX[S]
CC7	:	L-9H-9D,55;31.1-yXX
CC6	:	L9F0u9D,55:31.1(X8(A))
DDC 21	:	618.2

Wilson, C.G. Swimming and diving

Raw Title	:	Swimming and diving
Analyzed Title	:	Water sports (BF)
Synthesized Title	:	LTN (BF)
CC7	:	LTN
CC6	:	MY251
DDC 21	:	797.2

Gogate, Vishnu Mahadeva. Ayurvedic pharmacology and therapeutic uses of medicinal plants

Raw Title	:	Ayurvedic pharmacology and therapeutic uses of medicinal plants
Analyzed Title	:	Ayurvedic Pharmacology (BF)
Synthesized Title	:	LX3-B(BF)
CC7	:	LX3-B
CC6	:	LB0bLZ3
DDC 21	:	615.53

Plunkett, E.R. Handbook of industrial toxicology

Raw Title	: Handbook of industrial toxicology
Analyzed Title	: Toxicology (BF) Industrial medicine (Specials Sp. to BS)
Synthesized Title	: LX34(BF)-9X(Specials Sp.to BF)
CC7	: LX34-9X
CC6	: L9X;4
DDC 21	: 615.902

Briggs, Keith; Stewart, Andrew. Case studies in mental health nursing: problems and approaches

Raw Title	: Case studies in mental health nursing: problems and approaches
Analyzed Title	: Nursing (BF) Psychology(Inter-Subject Bias Phase Relation) Mentally disordered [1P1]
Synthesized Title	: LY1(BF)&bS(I-S Bias P.R),61[1P1]
CC7	: LY1&bS,61
CC6	: L:4:10bS63
DDC 21	: 610.7368

Jarman, Katherine. Freshwater fishing

Raw Title	: Freshwater fishing
Analyzed Title	: Animal husbandry (BF),Fish (array division),Freshwater [1P1]
Synthesized Title	: KX(BF),33251
CC7	: KX,33251
CC6	: KZ332
DDC 21	: 639.31

Eastcott, Michael J. The silent path: a comprehensive introduction to the study of meditation

Raw Title	: The silent path: a comprehensive introduction to the study of meditation
Analyzed Title	: Mysticism (BF) Religion [1P1] Man [1P2]

		Meditation [E]
Synthesized Title	:	MZ(BF),0Z[1P1],14[1P2]:07[E]
CC7	:	MZ,0Z,14:07
CC6	:	MZ:36
DDC 21	:	158.12

Cohen, Ralph, Ed. Studies in eighteenth century British art and aesthetics

Raw Title	:	Studies in eighteenth century British art and aesthetics
Analyzed Title	:	Fine arts (BF, Style in Fine arts) Great Britain,1700-1800(Division by GD and CD) Aesthetics (Inter-Subject General Phase Relation)
Synthesized Title	:	Na(BF, Style in Fine arts)-(56,L)(Division by GD and CD)&aR5(I-S General P.R)
CC7	:	Na-(56,L)&aR5
CC6	:	N56,L0aR5
DDC 21	:	709.03941

Aston, Michael; Bond, James. The landscape of towns

Raw Title	:	The landscape of towns
Analyzed Title	:	Town planning (BF)Town [1P1] Landscape [1P2] Plan [1MP1] England [S] Upto1970s [T]
Synthesized Title	:	ND(BF),2[1P1],3[1P2];3[1MP1].561[S]'N75 [T]
CC7	:	NB,2,3;3.561'N75
CC6	:	NB561,N3,3:3
DDC 21	:	711.40942

Bhagyaleshmy, S. Ragas in carnatic music

Raw Title	:	Ragas in Carnatic Music
Analyzed Title	:	Fine Arts (BF), Music (array division) Carnatic music [1P1], Raga [MP]

Synthesized Title : NR(BF),15[1P1],18[MP]
CC7 : NR,15;18
CC6 : NR,18
DDC 21 : 781.264

Shakespeare, William. The sonnets. London

Raw Title : The sonnets.
Analyzed Title : Literature (BF) English [1P1] Drama [1P2] William Shakespeare (1564) [1P3] Collection (ACI)
Synthesized Title : O(BF),111[1P1],2J64[1P2 and 1P3]"x (ACI)
CC7 : O,111,2J64"x
CC6 : O111,2J64x
DDC 21 : 821.33

Nirenburg, Sergei, Ed. Machine translation: theoretical and methodological issues

Raw Title : Machine translation: theoretical and methodological issues
Analyzed Title : Linguistics (BF) Language [1P1] Translation [1P2] Computer Science (Inter-Subject Tool Phase Relation)
Synthesized Title : P(BF),0Z[1P1],795[1P2]&e9S(I-S Tool P.R)
CC7 : P,0Z,795&e9S
CC6 : P,795;D65
DDC 21 : 418.020285

Baron, Dennis E. Grammer and gender

Raw Title : Grammer and gender
Analyzed Title : Linguistics (BF) English [1P1] Word [1P2] Morphology [1MP1]
Synthesized Title : P(BF),111[1P1],3[1P2];22[1MP1]
CC7 : P,111,3;22

CC6	: P111,3:22
DDC 21	: 428.2

Chapman, Robert L, Ed. New dictionary of American slang

Raw Title	: New dictionary of American slang
Analyzed Title	: Linguistics (BF) American English [1P1] Slang (Sp.to 1P1) Meaning for a given element [1MP1] Dictionary (ACI)
Synthesized Title	: P(BF),11173[1P1]=b (Sp.to 1P1);4 [1MP1]"k(ACI)
CC7	: P,11173=b;4"k
CC6	: P111,9B73:4k
DDC 21	: 427.973

Courtright, Paul B. Ganesa: Lord of obstacles, Lord of beginnings

Raw Title	: Ganesa: Lord of obstacles, Lord of beginnings
Analyzed Title	: Religion (BF) Hinduism Ganapatyism [1P1] Mythology [1MP1]
Synthesized Title	: Q(BF),24[1P1];1[1MP1]
CC7	: Q,24;1
CC6	: Q24:1
DDC 21	: 294.513

Barnett, Suzanne W.; Fairbank, John King, Eds. Christianity in China: early Protestant missionary writings

Raw Title	: Christianity in China: early Protestant missionary writings
Analyzed Title	: Religion (BF) Christianity, Protestant [1P1] Mission [1MP1] China [S] 1819-1890 [T]
Synthesized Title	: Q(BF),63[1P1];65[1MP1].41[S]'M9 ←19[T]
CC7	: Q,63;65.41'M9←19

CC6 : Q63:65.41'M919
DDC 21 : 266.02373051

De Bono, Edward. Six thinking hats

Raw Title : Six thinking hats
Analyzed Title : Philosophy, Logic (BF) Deduction [1P1]
Synthesized Title : R1(BF),2[1P1]
CC7 : R1,2
CC6 : R12
DDC 21 : 162

Gent, John. Yoga seeker

Raw Title : Yoga seeker
Analyzed Title : Yoga Philosophy (BF)
Synthesized Title : R635(BF)
CC7 : R635
CC6 : R635
DDC 21 : 181.45

Ainsworth, Peter B; Pease, Ken. Police work

Raw Title : Police work
Analyzed Title : Social psychology (BF) Individual [1P1] Policeman (Sp.to 1P1) Behaviour [1MP1]
Synthesized Title : SY(BF),11 [1P1]=wMX (Sp.to 1P1);B1 [1MP1]
CC7 : SY,11=wMX;B1
CC6 : S84
DDC 21 : 150.287

Mobley, Maureen. Evaluating curriculum materials

Raw Title : Evaluating curriculum materials
Analyzed Title : Education (BF) Curriculum [1P1] Institution (Sp.to 1P1) Teaching methods with special aids [E] Evaluation (CEI)
Synthesized Title : T(BF),L[1P1]-H(Sp.to 1P1):72[E]:aT(CEI)

CC7 : T,L-H:72:aT

CC6 : T:3:g

DDC 21 : 371.3078

Mason, Patricia; Essen, Juliet. The social, educational and emotional needs of gifted children

Raw Title : The social, educational and emotional needs of gifted children

Analyzed Title : Educational psychology (BF) Learner [1P1] Gifted (Sp.to 1P1) Child (Sp.to 1P1) Needs [1MP1]

Synthesized Title : TUS(BF),1[1P1]-211(Sp.to 1P1)-111 (Sp. to 1P1); 4[1MP1]

CC7 : TUS,1-211-111;4

CC6 : T61-13

DDC 21 : 371.95

Jones, Ann, etc, Ed. The computer revolution in education: new technologies for distance teaching

Raw Title : The computer revolution in education: new technologies for distance teaching

Analyzed Title : Education (BF) Teacher [1P1] Non-formal education (Sp.to 1P1) Educational programme [1MP1] Indirect teaching [E] Educational technology (Sp.to E)

Synthesized Title : T(BF),B [1P1]-1911(Sp. to 1P1);134 [1MP1]:72[E]-512(Sp. to E)

CC7 : T,B-1911;134:72-512

CC6 : T:3,1

DDC 21 : 371.3078

Jones, Jonah. The lakes of North Wales

Raw Title : The lakes of North Wales

Analyzed Title : Geography, Travel (BF) Wales [S] North (Sp. to S) Lakes (Sp. to S)

Synthesized Title : U8(BF),564[S]=9N(Sp. to S)=zf5(Sp. to S)

CC7 : U8,564=9N=zf5

CC6 : U8.562.9S.p6

DDC 21 : 914.2904

Thesiger, Wilfred. Visions of a nomad

Raw Title : Visions of a nomad

Analyzed Title : Geography, Travel (BF) World [S] 1930-1985 [T]

Synthesized Title : U8(BF),1[S]'N9 ← 3[T]

CC7 : U8.1'N9←3

CC6 : U8.1'N9←3

DDC 21 : 910.222

Ramazani, R.K. Revolutionary Iran: challenge and response in the middle east

Raw Title : Revolutionary Iran: challenge and response in the Middle East

Analyzed Title : History (BF) Arabian Peninsula [1P1] Foreign policy towards Iran [1MP1]

Synthesized Title : V(BF),46[1P1];1845[1MP1]

CC7 : V,46;1845

CC6 : V46:1945

DDC 21 : 327.56055

Oman, Sir Charles. A history of the art of war in the xvith century

Raw Title : A history of the art of war in the xvith century

Analyzed Title : History (BF) Europe [1P1] Foreign policy towards countries [1MP1] War (Sp.to 1MP1) 1450-1650 [T]

Synthesized Title : V(BF),5[1P1];180Z[1MP1]=K(Sp.to 1MP1)'K55[T]

CC7	: V,5;180Z=K'K55
CC6	: V5:19 (zM)'K55
DDC 21	: 355.02094

Ross, Stewart. Trade unions and pressure groups

Raw Title	: Trade Unions and Pressure groups.
Analyzed Title	: Political Science (BF) Pressure groups [1P1] Function [1MP1] Great Britain [S]
Synthesized Title	: W(BF),9B[1P1]; 3[1MP1].56[S]
CC7	: W,9B;3.56
CC6	: W:58 (X:97D).56
DDC 21	: 322.430941

Rose, Richard. Ministers and ministries: a functional analysis

Raw Title	: Ministers and ministries: a functional analysis
Analyzed Title	: Public administration (BF) Minister [1P1] Administrative Function [1MP1] Great Britain [S]
Synthesized Title	: WT(BF),47 [1P1];35[1MP1].56[S]
CC7	: WT,47;35.56
CC6	: W,2:3.56
DDC 21	: 348.0250941

Jain, L.C, etc. Grass without roots: rural development under government auspices

Raw Title	: Grass without roots: rural development under Government auspices
Analyzed Title	: Economics (BF) India [S] Rural [Sp. to S]
Synthesized Title	: X(BF).44[S]=0Z(Sp.to S)
CC7	: X.44=0Z
CC6	: X31:1:7.44
DDC 21	: 307.140954

Wasow, Bernard.; Hill, Raymond D, Eds. The insurance industry in economic development

Raw Title	: The Insurance industry in economic development
Analyzed Title	: Social Finance, Insurance (BF)
Synthesized Title	: X8(BF)
CC7	: X8
CC6	: X81
DDC 21	: 332.38

Cullis, John G; Jones, Philip R. Microeconomics and the public economy: a defence of Leviathan

Raw Title	: Microeconomics and the public economy: a defence of Leviathan
Analyzed Title	: Microeconomics (BF) Public finance (Canonical Sp.to BF)
Synthesized Title	: XV(BF)-7(Canonical Sp.to BF)
CC7	: XV-7
CC6	: X7
DDC 21	: 338.5

Schmidt, Christian, Ed. The economics of military expenditures: military expenditures, economic growth and fluctuations

Raw Title	: The economics of military expenditures: military expenditures, economic growth and fluctuations
Analyzed Title	: Industrial Economics (BF) Military equipment industry [1P1] Management [E] Expenditure [2MP1]
Synthesized Title	: XX(BF),(MV)[1P1]:8[E];DP[2MP1]
CC7	: XX,(MV):8;DP
CC6	: X8(MV41):8D
DDC 21	: 338.43623

Palma, Catalina. Women in Chile: yesterday and today

Raw Title	:	Women in Chile: yesterday and today
Analyzed Title	:	Sociology (BF) Community organization [1P1] Female (Sp.to 1P1) Chile [S] 1984 [T]
Synthesized Title	:	Y(BF),ZF[1P1]-21(Sp.to 1P1).774[S]'N84[T]
CC7	:	Y,ZF-21.774'N8
CC6	:	Y15-8.7914'N8
DDC 21	:	305.420983

Alcohol Concern. Alcohol services: a directory for England and Wales

Raw Title	:	Alcohol services: a directory for England and Wales
Analyzed Title	:	Social Work (BF) Individual [1P1] Alcoholism [1MP1] Treatment [E] Directory, England (ACI)
Synthesized Title	:	YX(BF),0Z[1P1];411[1MP1]:6[E]" n561(ACI)
CC7	:	YX,0Z;411:6"n561
CC6	:	Y:411:6n561
DDC 21	:	362.292802542

Grenville, J.A.S. The major international treaties, 1914-1945:a history and guide with texts

Raw Title	:	The major international treaties, 1914-1945:a history and guide with texts
Analyzed Title	:	Law (BF) International law [1P1] Treaty [1P2] History (ACI) 1914-1945 [T]
Synthesized Title	:	Z(BF),1[1P1],3[1P2]"v(ACI)'N45 ←14[T]
CC7	:	Z,1,3"v'N45←14
CC6	:	Z1,3v'N5
DDC 21	:	341.026

Lew, Julian D.M, Ed. Contemporary problems in international arbitration

Raw Title	:	Contemporary problems in international arbitration
Analyzed Title	:	Law (BF) International law [1P1] Cause of action [1P2] Arbitration [1P3]
Synthesized Title	:	Z(BF),1[1P1],7[1P2],16[1P3]
CC7	:	Z,1,7,16
CC6	:	Z1,7,16
DDC 21	:	343.087

Computer Science and Telecommunication Board. The digital dilemma: intellectual property in the information age

Raw Title	:	The Digital Dilemma: Intellectual Property in the Information Age
Analyzed Title	:	Law (BF),Intellectual Property [1P1],Communication Science (inter-subject influence phase relation)
Synthesized Title	:	Z(BF),267[1P1]&g1
CC7	:	Z,267&g1
CC6	:	Z,267
DDC 21	:	346.048

Narayanan, P. Trademark cases: including cases on trade names and passing off

Raw Title	:	Trademark cases: including cases on trade names and passing off.
Analyzed Title	:	Law (BF) Great Britain [1P1] Trademark [1P2]
Synthesized Title	:	Z(BF),56[1P1],2675[1P2]
CC7	:	Z,56,2675
CC6	:	Z56,2675
DDC 21	:	346.04880941

Jones, Michael A. A text book on torts

Raw Title	: A text book on torts
Analyzed Title	: Law (BF) Great Britain [1P1] Tort [1P2]
Synthesized Title	: Z(BF),56[1P1],4[1P2]
CC7	: Z,56,4
CC6	: Z56,4
DDC 21	: 346.030941

PART 8

CATALOGUING

CHAPTER 81

INTRODUCTION

810 Function of Catalogue

Note: The examples of entries in this part are numbered serially for convenience of reference.

The function of a catalogue is to provide to readers answers to questions such as the following:

1 Is there a book in the library by such and such an author ?

11 What are all the books in the library by him ?

2 Is there a book in the library with such and such a title — that is, name ?

3 Is there a book in the library with such and such a collaborator — that is, editor, translator, reviser, compiler, commentator, etc ?

31 What are all the books in the library with him as collaborator ?

4 Is there a book in the library in such and such a publisher's series ?

41 What are all the books in the library in that publisher's series ?

5 Is there a book in the library on such and such a subject ?

51 What are all the books in the library on that subject and on its subdivisions and on subjects of which it is a subdivision?

811 Author Entry

A catalogue has author entries to answer question 1. An Author Entry has the name of the author at its very beginning:

Example

1 RANGANATHAN (Shiyali Ramamrita) (1892).

Library manual. Ed 2. 22 N60

8111 CONSOLIDATED AUTHOR ENTRY

A catalogue has consolidated author entries to answer question 11. A Consolidated Author Entry has the name of the author at its beginning. It gives after it all the books of the author in the library.

Example

2 RANGANATHAN (Shiyali Ramamrita) (1892).

Classified catalogue code. Ed 4.	2:55N	N58
Colon classification. Ed 6.	2:51N3	N60
Five laws of library science. Ed 2.	2	N57
Library manual. Ed 2.	22	N60
Reference service. Ed 2.	2:7	N61

812 Title Entry

A catalogue has title entries to answer question 2. A Title Entry has the title of the book at its very beginning.

Example

3 HERMES.
By Jones. Ev1.N3 N28

813 Collaborator Entry

A catalogue has collaborator entries to answer question 3. A Collaborator Entry has the name of the collaborator at its very beginning.

Example

4 CROOKES (William) (1832), *Tr* and *Ed*.
Wagner: Chemical technology. F N04

814 Series Entry

A catalogue has series entries to answer question 4. A Series Entry has the name of the publisher's series at its very beginning.

8141 CONSOLIDATED SERIES ENTRY

A catalogue has consolidated series entries to answer question 41. A Consolidated Series Entry is a series entry giving in a serial sequence all the books of the series available in the library.

Example

5 RANGANATHAN SERIES IN LIBRARY SCIENCE.

1 Kaula, *Ed*: Library movement in India.	2.2.N5	N58
2 Ranganathan: Classified catalogue code. Ed 4.	2:55N	N58
3 Ranganathan: Library administration. Ed 2.	2:8	N59

815 Subject Entry

A catalogue has subject entries to answer question 5. A Subject Entry has the name of the subject at its very beginning. See also sec 8153.

8151 Consolidated Subject Entry

A catalogue has consolidated subject entries to answer question 51. A Consolidated Subject Entry is a subject entry giving in rough alphabetical sequence all the books in the subject available in the library.

Example

6 BOTANY.
Coulter: Text-book of botany. 2 V. I N10.1-.2
Sabesan: Intermediate botany. I N37
Warburg: Planzenwelt. 3 B. I 113N13.1-.3

8152 Subject Analytical Entry

If a subject is treated only in a part of a book, it is brought to the notice of readers by a Subject Analytical Entry. It too answers question 5. It specifies the part, the chapter, the section, on the pages of the book, containing the subject. See also sec 8154

Example

7 REFERENCE SERVICE.
Ranganathan: Library manual. Part 3. 22 N60

8153 Call Number Entry

The very beginning of an entry in a catalogue may have the call number of a book instead of the name of its subject. It too answers question 5. It is called Call Number Entry. This is an alternative to subject entry.

Example

8 22 N60
RANGANATHAN (Shiyali Ramamrita) (1892).
Library manual for Library Authorities, librarians, and honorary library workers. Ed 2.
(Ranganathan series in library science, 6).
(Madras Library Association, publication series, 25).
135,791.

8154 Cross Reference Entry

If a subject is treated only in a part of a book, it is brought to the notice of readers by a Cross Reference Entry. It too answers question 5. It specifies the part, the chapter, the section, or the pages of the book, containing the subject. The class number of the subject occurs at the very beginning of such an entry. This is an alternative to subject analytical entry.

Example

9 2:7
See also
22 N60
Ranganathan
Library manual. Part 3.

816 Types of Catalogue

There are two important types of catalogue. They are:

1 Classified catalogue; and
2 Dictionary catalogue.

Their essential difference is in respect of subject entries. In the classified catalogue, all the subject entries, including subject-analytical entries, are arranged together by their respective class numbers. This enables the classified catalogue to answer question 51 quite easily. In the dictionary catalogue, the subject entries, including subject-analytical entries, are scattered alphabetically by the names of the subjects. Another difference is in respect of the main entry — that is, the entry giving the largest amount of information about the book and forming the chief source of all the other brief added entries. In the classified catalogue, the call number entry is made the main entry. In the dictionary catalogue, the author entry is made the main entry.

Examples

1 The entry 8 in section 8153 is the main entry of this book for classified catalogue.

2 The following is its main entry for dictionary catalogue.

10 RANGANATHAN (Shiyali Ramamrita) (1892).
Library manual for Library Authorities, librarians and honorary library workers. Ed 2.
(Ranganathan series in library science, 5).
(Madras Library Association, publication series, 25). 22 N60.
135,791.

8161 *See also* Entry

A reader, looking for books on a particular subject, looks up the name of the subject entries. Usually, hardly any reader is able to name his precise subject. He generally mentions a subject of greater extension — that is, a broad subject having his precise subject as a subdivision. For example, suppose the precise subject sought by a reader is "Drinking vessel in use among gypsies". The reader may say, "I wish to have a book on 'Gypsies' ". He may even mention "Ethnology" or simply "Sociology". Some may perhaps be a little more precise and mention "Equipment of gypsies". To help readers in all such contingencies, the dictionary catalogue should give direction from each such broad subject to his precise subject. Such an entry is called a *See also* Entry. In the particular case mentioned above, the following *See also* entries may be necessary.

Examples

11 SOCIOLOGY.
See also
DRINKING UTENSIL, GYPSY.

12 ETHNOLOGY.
See also
DRINKING UTENSIL, GYPSY.

13 GYPSY.
See also
DRINKING UTENSIL, GYPSY.

14 EQUIPMENT, GYPSY.
See also
DRINKING UTENSIL, GYPSY.

15 UTENSIL, GYPSY.
See also
DRINKING UTENSIL, GYPSY.

Such *see also* entries enable the dictionary catalogue to answer question 51 in an involved way.

8162 CLASS INDEX ENTRY

In the case of the Classified Catalogue, the reader will not know the number either of his precise subject or of any of the six broader subjects mentioned in the entries of section 8161. He should therefore be helped by an entry to find the class number of each of the subjects mentioned by him. Such an entry is called a Class Index Entry. The following class index entries will therefore be necessary, in the case under consideration.

Examples

16 SOCIOLOGY. *see* Y.
17 ETHNOLOGY. *see* Y7.
18 GYPSY. *see* Y738.
19 EQUIPMENT, GYPSY. *see* Y738:8.
20 UTENSIL, GYPSY. *see* Y738:82.
21 DRINKING UTENSIL, GYPSY. *see* Y738:825.

Note: For brevity, "*see*" is used as the directing element. The full directing element prescribed is "For books in this class and its subclasses, see the Classified Part of the catalogue under the "Class Number".

817 Recommendation

The Classified Catalogue is recommended for adoption. Charles Ammi Cutter, the pioneer in catalogue, wrote, "It is true that by following up all the references of a dictionary catalogue under Theology, for example, a man may construct for himself a list of the theological literature in the library; but to do this requires time and mental effort, and it is characteristic of the desultory reader that he is averse to mental effort. What is wanted by him and by the busy man when now and then he has the same object, is to find the titles from which he could select titles brought together within the compass of a few pages" [90]. All this implies that Cutter preferred the classified catalogue, because it answers question 51 in a better way than the dictionary catalogue. But he could not adopt it in the 1870's, when he wrote this, because there was then no elaborate scheme of classification, with which books could be closely classified and individualized. Now such schemes of classification are available. Therefore, the world trend is now towards the classified catalogue. The British National Bibliography and the Indian National Bibliography have adopted this type of catalogue. It is too late in the day to go back to the dictionary catalogue or for any new library to adopt that type of catalogue.

We have been told of the fox that lost its tail. There are such fox-like librarians who persist in recommending the dictionary catalogue to the libraries being newly formed in India. They are to be pitied; their advice is not to be followed.

818 Catalogue Code

A catalogue is full of details. There are many alternative choices possible in respect of many of these details. To catalogue with the aid of a badly drafted or patchy catalogue code will soon make the catalogue a hotch-potch. The only safeguard against this is to adopt a rigorously drafted catalogue code. The only complete and rigorous code for classified catalogue existing today is the Classified Catalogue Code. The other code in vogue is the ALA code. It has no rules for subject entries. It has rules only for author and title entries. Moreover 9 of its rules are faulty and 37 rules are redundant [91]. This has now been realized by its promoters. It is therefore undergoing drastic revision. Further, it is not of much help in rendering Indian names. On the other hand, the Classified Catalogue Code gives useful instructions on this subject. According to Sayers, it is "by far the largest contribution on the subject" [92]. Speaking about it, an American cataloguer says "Of particular interest . . . are the sections dealing with the structure and rendering of personal names, particularly those of South and South East Asia" [93]. Thus on grounds of merit, the adoption of the Classified Catalogue Code is recommended. Its being of Indian origin is a secondary reason for its adoption.

CHAPTER 82

STRUCTURE OF ENTRIES

820 Terminology

This chapter deals with the structure of an entry in a card, according to the Classified Catalogue Code. The following terms will be of use in what follows:

8201 Kinds of Entry

1 **Entry**. Ultimate unit-record in a catalogue.

11 **Specific Entry**. Entry mentioning a specific book.

12 **General Entry**. Entry not mentioning any specific book.

13 **Consolidated Entry**. Two or more entries consolidated into a single entry.

14 **Number Entry**. Entry beginning with a call number or a class number.

15 **Word Entry.** Entry beginning with a word, or in rare cases, with a symbol given in the author statement of a document as a substitute for name of author.

16 **Main Entry.** Specific entry giving maximum information about the whole of the book catalogued. All the other entries — specific or general — relating to the document, are normally derived from the main entry.

17 **Added Entry**. Entry other than main entry.

8202 Section of an Entry

2 **Section of an Entry**. That which is prescribed to be a separate paragraph in an entry in a card catalogue.

21 **Leading Section**. Section 1 of an entry.

22 **Heading Section.**

1 Leading Section of a word entry.

2 Section 2 of a call number entry of a book, or of a class number entry of a periodical publication — i e, of a main Entry in a classified catalogue.

3 Section 3 of a *see also* subject entry.

4 Section 3 of a cross reference index entry.

23 **Title Section.** Section of a main entry, giving the title of the document catalogued, along with the names of collaborators and of edition if any.

232 **Locus Section.** Section giving the locus in a cross reference entry of a classified catalogue.

24 **Note Section.** Section of a main entry giving the name of the series, if any, to which the book belongs.

25 **Accession Number Section.** Last section in a main entry, giving the accession number of the book.

26 **Tracing Section.** Back of a main entry card, denoting **all** the added entries of the book.

27 **Second Section.** Section in a book index entry giving the specification of the concerned book(s).

271 **Directing Section.** Section in an added entry directing attention to a book, or a class number, or an alternative name.

28 **Index Number Section.**

1 Section in a book index entry, giving the call number of the book.

2 Section in a class index entry, giving the class number of the class.

821 Main Entry

Call number entry. Specific subject entry. Subject entry. Specific entry.

22 *Leading Section*	Y738:825 N59
Heading	Schmidt (Gustav) (1905).
Title section	How gypsies drink, a descriptive account of their drinking vessels, *tr* by Krishna Pillai Gopala Pillai, from ed 3 of the German. Ed 2.
Note section	(Indian anthropological series, ed by Kumbakonam Krishna Ayyar, 12).
Accession number section	135,793.

8211 Cross Reference Entry

Class number entry. Subject analytical. Specific subject entry. Subject entry. Specific entry. Added entry.

23 *Leading section* Y7v1'N5

Directing section *See also*
Y738:825 N59

Location section Schmidt.
How gypsies drink, *tr* by Gopala Pillai, ed 2, p 250-300.

The class number in the leading section represents "History of the study of ethnology in the world brought up to 1950's." The location section is made of three sections.

822 Author Entry

Specific entry, Added entry.

24 *Heading* SCHMIDT (Gustav) (1958)
Second section How gypsies drink.
Index number section Y738:825 N59

8221 TRANSLATOR ENTRY

Collaborator entry. Specific entry. Added entry.

25 *Heading* GOPALA PILLAI (Krishna Pillai) (1912), *Tr.*
Second section Schmidt: How gypsies drink.
Index number section Y738:825 N59

824 Series Entry

Specific entry. Added entry.

26 *Heading* INDIAN ANTHROPOLOGICAL SERIES.
Second section 12 Schmidt: How gypsies drink, tr by Gopala Pillai, ed 2.
Index number section Y738:825 N59

8241 EDITOR OF SERIES ENTRY

Cross reference index entry. General entry.

27

Referred from heading	KRISHNA AYYAR (Kumbekonam) (1892), *Ed.*
Directing section	*See also*
Referred to heading	INDIAN ANTHROPOLOGICAL SERIES.

825 Class Index Entry

Subject entry. General entry.

28 *Heading*	DRINKING VESSEL.
Directing section	For books in this class and its subclasses see the Classified Part of this catalogue under the Class Number
Index number section	Y738:825

826 Library Hand

Writing should be in detached upright impersonal hand. This is called Library Hand. This is necessary because, with each one writing in his own hand not conforming to this standard, will make the catalogue ugly. For, the catalogue cards will be written by successive cataloguers. But all the cards will be kept together permanently.

827 Style of writing

Similarly it is necessary to conform to one fixed standard in respect of space between words, space between class number and book number, formation of paragraphs, indention of paragraphs, and writing of numbers other than call number. To facilitate this, the standard catalogue card is 125 × 75 mm. It is ruled horizontally to take the writing. It has two vertical rules — the first vertical at a distance of 10 mm from the left shorter edge and the second vertical at a further distance of 5 mm from the first. The following items are to begin at the vertical:

1 Leading section;
2 Heading of every kind;
3 Continuation lines of all sections; and
4 Accession number section.

Any section, other than the index number section and those specified for the first vertical, is to begin at the second vertical. The index number section is to be written in the line in which the title section or the series section, as the case may be, ends if there is sufficient space in it or in the next line. It is to begin as far to the right as possible in its line, so as to end just near the end of that line.

8271 Capitals, Italics, and Numerals

All the letters, except those of a conjunction if any, in any heading of any kind are to be in capitals. The first letter after a colon is to be in capital. Otherwise, the usual convention of prose is to be followed. The title portion in any entry is to be written as if it were a sentence in prose — that is, no word in the title except the first is to be begun with a capital letter, unless it is a proper noun. A descriptive term, such as *Ed, Tr, Comm,* occurring in a heading, is to begin with a capital notwithstanding its following a comma. The term is to be underlined. In print, it will be in italics. All numbers other than class number and book number are to be written in Indo-Arabic numerals. The following collection symbols may be used:

1 Pamphlet. Underline book number.

2 Over-sized book; Overline book number.

3 Book of poor build, such as a book with many plates: Underline and overline book number.

4 Book to be kept in the reading room for ready reference: Add "R R" above the Class Number.

5 Book to be kept temporarily in the topical collection: Put in the first vacant line of its date-label the date fixed for its release from the topical sequence and encircle it.

8272 Punctuation Mark

Punctuation marks are to be as in ordinary prose, subject to the following modifications:

1 A comma is to separate two consecutive blocks in a heading. See examples 11 to 15 in section 8161, 19 to 21 in section 8162, 1-7 in section 8332.

2 A comma is to separate a Descriptive Element in a block in

a heading from what it separates. See examples 25 of section 8221 and 27 of 8241.

3 Circular brackets are to enclose each individualizing secondary element in a block in a heading or the heading as a whole, as the case may be. See examples 1, 2 and 4 of section 811; 5 of section 8141; 8 of section 8153; 10 of section 8156; 22 of section 821; 24 of section 822; 25 of section 8221; and 27 of 8241.

828 Arrangement of Entries

8281 Classified Part

The entries in the classified part of the catalogue are to be arranged by their respective class numbers. Of the entries with the same class number, those with book numbers are to precede those without book numbers. The former are to be arranged by their respective book numbers. The latter are to be arranged among themselves by the book numbers in the third section and the words in the fourth section.

8282 Alphabetical Part

The entries in the alphabetical part of the catalogue are to be arranged alphabetically as in a dictionary. There are some conventions to be followed. Only the letters actually written in the entry are to be taken into consideration. That is, contractions are not to be arranged as if they were expanded. In particular, as an example, Scotch names beginning with "Mac" should come together. Those beginning with "Mc" should come together in their own place. Again, "New York" is to precede "Newark". This is called "Nothing before something" rule. For more complicated cases, the original Classified Catalogue Code should be consulted.

CHAPTER 83

RENDERING OF NAME IN HEADING

830 Introduction

The following is a list of the kind of names likely to occur in headings of entries. The later sections of this chapter indicate the way of rendering them in a heading:

1 Name-of-person;
2 Geographical name;
3 Name of government;
4 Name of institution;
5 Name of conference;
6 Name of book — that is, title; and
7 Name of series — that is, publisher's series.

Here the following definitions will be of use:

1 **Entry Element.** The word or word group prescribed to be written first in a heading, main heading, or subheading.

2 **Entry Word.** The first word of an entry element.

3 **Secondary Element.** The word or word group occurring in a name but not selected as entry element and therefore to be written after it.

A secondary element has the status of an individualizing element. Further, while taking a name-of-person from the title-page any word denoting academic degree, civil or military honours, and all honorific words are to be ignored. The words left over in the name-of-person may be called the **Reduced Name.**

831 Name-of-Person

8311 Simple Name

An oversimplified rule is "Make the last word in a name-of-person the entry word. Make all the other words the secondary element." This will work well in:

1 Most modern names of the West;

2 A modern name of Assam, Bengal, Gujarat, Kashmir, Maharashtra, Orissa, and Sindh; and

3 A modern name of South India, not ending with an attached word — such as Ayyangar, Ayyar, Chettiar, Mudaliar, Pillai, etc — indicating sub-community. In the first two cases, the last word denotes **Family Name;** and the earlier words denote **Given Names** — that is, name or names given during the naming ceremony or later. In Marathi and Gujarati, the second of the earlier words is father's given name. In the third case, the last word denotes the Given Name; and the earlier words may denote father's name, or family name, or name of locality.

8312 South Indian Name Ending with Attachment Word

In a South Indian name with an attached word, such as those indicated in section 8311 — the entry element is to consist of the word-group made of the Given Name preceding the attached word followed by the attached word itself. The other words form the secondary element. For example, see examples 25 of section 8221 and 27 of section 8241.

8313 Hindi and Punjabi Name

In a Hindi or Punjabi name-of-person not having a family name in imitation of the West, the original single coalesced (*Samasa*) word denoting the given name is split into two or more words. All the components of the split word should be taken together as a word-group for use as entry element. For example, Labhu Ram, Manohar Lal, and Rama Prasad.

8314 Complicated Cases

The original Classified Catalogue Code should be used for complicated cases with double and treble family names, whose whole word-group should be used as entry element. So also, for Muslim names and for lists of irremovable attachment at the end of South Indian names.

8315 Resolution of Homonym

Historically, the secondary element was used, in a heading made of a name-of-person, chiefly to resolve homonyms. In spite of it, homonyms may crop up. Such homonyms are to be resolved by adding the year of birth of the person as a further individualizing element. It should be enclosed in circular brackets. It is now considered desirable to add the year of birth in all possible cases to avoid the formation of homonyms in future.

832 Geographical Name

The name of a geographical entity is to be written in the favoured language of the library, if it has a name in that language. It is to be written in the language of its own locality, if it does not have a name in the favoured language of the library.

8321 Homonym: Areas outside One Another

If two or more geographical areas have the same name and lie in different countries, the individualizing element for resolving the homonym is to be the name of the country in which it lies, except that it may be omitted if it is the country of the library. If two or more geographical areas have the same name and lie outside one another within the same country, the individualizing element for resolving the homonym is to be the name of the largest geographical area, among the areas of the constituent states, districts, taluks, etc, containing the respective geographical areas and sufficient to individualize them.

Examples

1 Sattanur (Kumbakonam).
Sattanur (Tanjavur).

Here Kumbakonam and Tanjavur are Taluks.

2 Tiruvalangadu (Chingleput).
Tiruvalangadu (Tanjavur).

Here Chingleput and Tanjavur are Districts.

3 Salem.
Salem (Ohio).
Salem (Virginia).

The first Salem is in India. Ohio and Virginia are constituent states of USA.

8322 Homonym: Area within Area

If two or more geographical areas have the same name and lie one within another in succession, the individualizing element for resolving the homonym is to be the word state, district, taluk, city, town, village, etc, as the case may be, except that it can be omitted if it is the name of the largest of the above mentioned areas among those needed for resolving the homonym.

Examples

1 MYSORE.
MYSORE (District).
MYSORE (Taluk).
MYSORE (City).

Here the first denotes the State of Mysore.

2 TANJAVUR.
TANJAVUR (Taluk).
TANJAVUR (Town).

Here the first denotes the district of Tanjavur.

KUMBAKONAM.
KUMBAKONAM (Town).

Here the first denotes the Kumbakonam Taluk.

833 Name of Government

8330 DEFINITION

The term "Government" is used to denote a corporate body with

1 Full sovereign power, as the Government of India, or Government of Britain, or Government of USA;

2 Limited sovereign power as the Governments of the States of Madras, Bengal, or New York;

3 Without sovereign power, but a local body established for the regulation, promotion, and/or provision of specific public services in an area, such as Mysore District Board, Mysore Taluk Board, or Mysore City Municipality; and

4 Any constitutional or administratively created organ of any of the above.

8331 NAME OF WHOLE GOVERNMENT

When used as the corporate author of a book, the name of the government is to be the name of its territory.

Examples

1 INDIA is the rendering of "Government of India".

2 MYSORE is the rendering of the "Government of the constituent state Mysore".

3 MYSORE (District) is the rendering of the "District Board of Mysore District".

4 MYSORE (Taluk) is the rendering of the "Local Body or the Taluk Board of the Mysore Taluk".

5 MYSORE (City) is the rendering of the "Local Body or the Municipal Council of the City of Mysore".

8332 CONSTITUTIONAL ORGAN

In the case of an organ of a government, the first heading is to be the name of the whole government. Then should come the name of the organ as subheading:

Examples

1 INDIA, PRESIDENT.
2 INDIA, CABINET.
3 INDIA, LOK SABHA.
4 INDIA, SUPREME COURT.
5 MADRAS, HIGH COURT.
6 MADRAS (City), MAYOR.
7 MADRAS (City), COUNCIL.

8333 ADMINISTRATIVE DEPARTMENT OF GOVERNMENT

In the case of an administrative department of a government, the first heading is to be the name of the whole government. Then should come the name of the department as subheading. In the subheading, the word or word-group denoting the sphere of work is to be the entry element. It should be reduced to the noun form in the nominative case. The other words in the name of the department are to be made a secondary element and added within circular brackets. The place of the entry element should be indicated by a dash within the brackets cantaining the secondary element.

Examples

1 INDIA, FINANCE (Ministry of —).

2 MADRAS, INSTRUCTION (Department of Public —).
3 BOMBAY, AGRICULTURE (—Department)
assuming that it is called Agricultural Department.

8334 TEMPORARY ORGAN

In the case of a temporary organ of a government, the year of its formation is to be added as an individualizing element.

Examples

1 INDIA, BANKING (Indian Central — Enquiry Committee) (1929).
2 MADRAS, PUBLIC LIBRARIES (Review Committee on —) (1960).
3 MADRAS, LEGISLATIVE ASSEMBLY, PUBLIC LIBRARIES BILL (Select Committee on —) (1948).

834 Name of Institution

8340 DEFINITION

The term "Institution" is used to denote an independent or autonomous corporate body, other than a government, whether:

1 created by a government;
2 constituted under a statute; or
3 formed voluntarily — formally or informally.

The term denotes also an Organ of an Institution.

8341 NAME OF WHOLE INSTITUTION

The name to be used in rendering the name of an institution is to be the one in the shortest form found in the:

1 title-page; or
2 half-title page; or
3 any other part of the book.

The initial article and every honorific word not forming an inseparable part of the name, if any, are to be omitted. Whenever necessary, individualizing element is to be added.

Examples

1 ANDHRA UNIVERSITY.

2 Asiatic Society of Bengal,
and not Royal Asiatic Society of Bengal.

3 Royal Society of London,
as the word "Royal" is inseparable from the name.

4 Srinivasa Sastry Entertainment Committee,
and not Rt. Honorable Srinivasa Sastry Entertainment Committee.

5 State Bank of India (Delhi).

6 State Bank of India (Madras) (City).

7 University Grants Commission (India).

8342 Name of Organ of Institution

In the case of an organ of an institution, the first heading is to be the name of the whole institution. Then should come the name of the organ as subheading. The latter should be rendered as in the case of an organ of a government.

835 Name of a Conference

8350 Definition

The term "Conference" is used to denote a meeting for deliberation, or formulation or expression of opinion or sentiment,

1 not convened by government(s) and made up of its (their) own personnel;

2 not convened by and made up only of the members of a single institution or to form an institution; but

3 convened and conducted either spontaneously by a number of persons or institutions to consider matters of common interest; or

4 convened by a body with no function or existence beyond the conference convened and held by it.

The term denotes also an Organ of a Conference.

8351 Individualization

The rendering of the name of a conference is to be on the analogy of that for institution. And the name of the place or/and the year of the conference is/are to be added as individualizing element(s).

Examples

1 Basant Memorial Meeting (1933).

2 CONFERENCE OF ORIENTALISTS (Simla) (1911).
3 GENEVA SUMMIT CONFERENCE (1956).

836 Title of a Book

8361 INITIAL ARTICLE AND HONORIFIC

The initial article and honorific, if any, are to be omitted in rendering the title of a book either in a heading or in any other section.

8362 PUFF

Puff, if any, in the title of a book is to be omitted. In the main entry, in the title section, its place should be indicated by "...". In an added entry, in the second section, such an indication is not necessary; the title may be in a shortened form, without taking away intelligibility.

8363 IN THE HEADING

When the title occurs in a heading, the first two words are to be deemed to form the entry element.

837 Name of Series

In rendering the name of a series, in the note section or in the heading, the initial article and honorific words, if any, are to be omitted. And the remaining words are to be written in the sequence in which they occur in the book. If the name of the series is not an individualizing one — for example, English series, Publication series, Translation series — its name is to be preceded by the name of an individualizing entity with which it is associated, say as publisher, sponsor, university. The name of the entity used as the individualizing entity is to be rendered as prescribed for the entities of its kind.

Examples

1 Wiley farm series.
2 Madras Library Association, publication series.
3 Bombay, Agriculture (Department of —), Bulletin.

The style of writing will be as shown above in the note section of the main entry. If the name of the series occurs in the heading of an entry, caps and small caps will be used in the usual style.

CHAPTER 84

WHO IS THE AUTHOR ?

840 Introduction

The name of the author is to be taken from the title-page. It is usually indicated there. If it is not indicated, the book is to be taken to be anonymous. For most of the books, the author is a single person. For some, it may be two or more persons. In both these cases, it is the person or persons, who create the thought content of the book and express it. Such a book of personal authorship will give no difficulty, unless there are collaborators. Some books are produced on the responsibility of a corporate body — a government, an institution, or a conference — or two or more corporate bodies. They are responsible for the thought content and for the expression. Such a book is of corporate authorship. Some difficulty may arise in books of this kind. The difficulty arises when the title-page of a book of corporate authorship gives the name of a person also. The following sections give a summary of the convention used to solve such difficulties. For a full discussion of the problem, Chapter "14 Conflict in Authorship" of the *Classified catalogue code* ed 4, should be read.

841 Person *vs* Person

Ser Numb	*Type of Work*	*Author*
1	Ana, table-talk	Talker
2	Dialogue, conversation, debate	Participants
3	Interview	Person(s) interviewed
4	Narration (real and not fictitious)	Narrator
5	Mediumistic communication	Medium(s) and not the disembodied soul(s)
6	Correspondence	Correspondent(s) unless it is all of one person only with several others in which case only that one person

8411 Dependent Work of Kind 1

The author of the original work should be taken as the author of the following kinds of dependent works. The other associated person is to be taken only as collaborator:

1 Abridgment
2 Adaptation
3 Paraphrase
4 Revision
5 Selection
6 Translation

8412 Dependent Work of Kind 2

The author of the dependent work itself should be taken as the author of the following kinds of dependent work:

1 Commentary
2 Concordance
3 Continuation
4 Dramatization
5 Imitation
6 Index
7 Libretto
8 Music-setting
91 Novelization
92 Parody
93 Sequel
94 Supplement
95 Versification
96 Version in the same or another language, which has sufficient new qualities in thought and/or expression to deem it an independent work on its own right

842 Person *vs* Corporate Body

8421 If the title-page mentions the name(s) of person(s) only and does not mention or indicate the name of any corporate body other than the one belonging to the publishing trade mentioned in the imprint, the work is of personal authorship.

8422 If the title-page does not mention the name of any person but mentions or indicates the name of a corporate body other than a body belonging to the publishing trade mentioned in the imprint, the work is of corporate authorship.

8423 Even if the title page mentions a person, if it indicates the name of a corporate body other than the publisher, the work is of corporate authorship, if it is of a deliberative, legislative, directive, judicial, administrative, or routine character limited by the purpose or function or outlook of the corporate body. But the mere fact that the book is published, financed, aided, approved, sponsored, or authorized by a corporate body is not sufficient reason to deem it to be of corporate authorship.

8424 On the other hand, if the primary purpose of the book is the extension of the boundary of the field of knowledge, or its intensification, and the responsibility for the thought-content and expression of it, rests on the person and not on the office held by him in the corporate body, it is of personal authorship. The mere mention of the personal name of an official of the corporate body in the title-page is not sufficient reason to deem it to be of personal authorship.

843 Government *vs* Institution

8431 GROUP 1

Each of the following kinds of institutions is to be taken as author of its works, as if it were independent of the parent body, if any exists, be it government or institution:

Abbey
Bank
Board of Trade
Cathedral
Cemetery
Chamber of Commerce
Church (place of worship)
College
Convent
Endowment
Exchange (Money)
Firm of Enterprise
Foundation
Guild
Masonic body
Monastery
Mosque
Park
Political party
Post office
Produce exchange
Religious Order
School
Stock-exchange
Telegraph office
Telephone exchange
Temple
University

8432 GROUP 2

Each of the following institutions are to be taken as author of its work as if it were independent of the parent body, provided it has a distinctive name:

Botanical garden
Chapel
Experimental station
Exhibition
Hospital
Laboratory
Library
Museum
Observatory
Zoological garden

Note: If any of the above institutions has no distinctive name, it should be treated as an organ of its parent body.

8433 Group 3

Any formal or informal group of the members of a parent body, formed for recreative, ameliorative, or any other economical or social purposes other than forming a distinctive purpose of the parent body, should be treated as an organ of the parent body, even if it has a distinctive name.

CHAPTER 85

HEADING OF MAIN ENTRY

850 Introduction

The structure — that is the sections, their sequence, and their make-up — of a main entry have been shown by examples in section 821. The rendering of the heading and of the later sections has been described in Chapter 83. This chapter deals only with the choice of heading for the main entry of the book.

851 Choice of Heading

The heading is to consist of the earliest of the following, which the book admits and Chapter 84 prescribes as the author:

1 Name of personal author;
2 Names of joint personal authors;
3 Name of corporate author;
4 Names of joint corporate authors;
5 Pseudonym;
6 Name of collaborator;
7 Names of joint collaborators; and
8 Title of the book.

852 Two Joint Authors

If the title-page contains the names of two and only two joint authors, both the names are to be used as the heading with the conjunction "and" connecting them.

Example

1 SREENIVASAN (G A) (1894) and KRISHNAMACHARI (C) (1894).
2 AMERICAN LIBRARY ASSOCIATION and LIBRARY ASSOCIATION (Great Britain).
3 INDIAN STANDARDS INSTITUTION, DOCUMENTATION (—Section) and INSDOC, TECHNICAL (—Committee).

853 Three or More Joint Authors

If the title-page contains the names of three or more joint authors, the name of the first mentioned author alone is to be used as the heading and the word "etc" is to be added thereafter.

Example

RANGANATHAN (Shiyali Ramamrita) (1892) etc.
is the heading for the *Union catalogue of learned periodicals of South Asia* (1953) which has 20 other joint authors.

854 Pseudonym

A pseudonym is a false or fictitious name used by an author in the title-page of the book. If the title-page gives only a pseudonym, the pseudonym is to be used as the heading and it is to be followed by the descriptive element "*Pseud*" If the title-page gives the real name of the author also in a subordinated manner, it is to be added in circular brackets after the descriptive element. The real name is to be preceded by the symbol "*i e*". A comma is to be placed before the bracket begins.

Examples

LIBRA, *Pseud.*
TWAIN (Mark), *Pseud.*
TWAIN (Mark), *Pseud,* (*i e* Samuel Langhore Clement).

855 Collaborator Heading

If the title-page does not give the name of personal author(s) or indicate corporate authorship or give a pseudonym, but contains the name of a collaborator, that name is to be used as the heading; and a descriptive element is to be added thereafter indicating the role of the collaborator.

856 Title-heading

If a book is a general biographical dictionary or an encyclopaedia belonging to the class generalia, or science general, or useful arts, or social sciences, or is a volume of a periodical, or if the heading cannot be chosen in accordance with the prescriptions in sections 851 to 855, the title, is to be used as the heading.

CHAPTER 86

HEADING OF BOOK INDEX ENTRY

860 Introduction

The structure — that is section(s) etc — of a book index entry has been shown by examples in sections 822, 8221 and 824. The rendering of the heading and of the later sections has been prescribed in Chapter 83. This chapter deals only with the choice of the headings for which book index entries are to be given for a book.

861 Choice of Book Index Entry

A book index entry is to be given using as heading each of such of the following, as the main entry of the book admits of.

1 Derived from Heading

11 Heading, provided it is not, as such, eligible to be used as the heading of a class index entry appropriate to the book;

12 Each permutation of the names in the heading, if it is one of two joint authors or two collaborators;

13 Name of each of the third and later authors, if there are three or more joint authors (optional).

2 Derived from Title Section

21 Name of each collaborator mentioned in the Title portion; and

22 Title of the book,

1 If it is fanciful; or

2 If it contains a proper noun; or

3 If it is treated in usage as a proper noun, provided that it is not, as such, eligible to be used as the heading of a class index entry of the book.

3 Derived from Note Section

31 Name of the series occurring in each independent series note.

CHAPTER 87

HEADING OF CROSS REFERENCE INDEX ENTRY

870 Introduction

The structure — that is the section(s) etc — of a cross reference index entry has been shown by examples in section 8241. The rendering of the referred-from-heading has been described in Chapter 83. The referred-to-heading is to be the same as in the main entry or book index entry to which it relates. This chapter deals only with the types of cross reference index entry.

8701 Types of Cross Reference Index Entry

A cross reference index entry may be one of the four types:

1 Alternative name entry;
2 Variant-form-of-word entry;
3 Pseudonym-real-name entry; and
4 Editor-of-series entry.

8702 Avoidance of Duplication of Entry

Care is to be taken not to write a cross reference index entry suggested by a book, if an identically similar entry is already found in the catalogue.

871 Alternative Name Entry

There is to be an alternative name entry using as referred-from-heading each of all the possible alternative names by which any person, any corporate body, any geographical entity, any series, or any book, respectively whose name has been used as the heading of the main entry or a book index entry, is known or is likely to be known.

Example

29 Ananda Matteyya.
see
Bennett (Allan).

872 Variant-form-of-word Entry

There is to be a variant-form-of-word entry using as referred-from-heading each of all possible variant forms in which the word(s) in the name of a person or a corporate body or a geographical entity or a book, occurring in the heading of a main entry or a book index entry, or an alternative name index entry, has(have) occurred or is(are) likely to occur.

Example

30 BANERJEE
see also
BANGOPADHYAYA.

31 BANGOPADHYAYA
see also
BANERJEE.

873 Pseudonym-real-name Entry

There is to be a pseudonym-real-name entry in the case of every person whose pseudonym alone or pseudonym as well as real name appears in the main entry concerned. The referred-to-heading is to be the pseudonym.

Example

32 RUSSEL (George) (1867).
see
A E, *Pseud.*

874 Editor-of-series Entry

There is to be an editor-of-series entry using as referred-from-heading the name(s) of the editor(s), if any, occurring in the series note in any main entry in the catalogue. In the case of joint editors, an editor-of-series entry is to be made for each of the permuted sequences of the names. The referred-to-heading is to be name of the series.

Example

33 EGERTON (Clement) ( ), *Ed.*
See
BROADWAY ORIENTAL LIBRARY.

34 GETMAN (A K) (1887) and LADD (C E) (1888), *Ed.*
See
WILEY FARM SERIES.

35 LADD (C E) (1888) and GETMAN (A K) (1887), *Ed.*
See
WILEY FARM SERIES.

36 CAPPS (Edward) (1886), etc, *Ed.*
See
LOEB CLASSICAL LIBRARY.

CHAPTER 88

HEADING OF CLASS INDEX ENTRY

880 Introduction

The sections of index entry have been shown by illustration in section 825. The choice and rendering of the headings of class index entries is regulated by the Chain Procedure. It is a method using the class number of the book for the purpose. It is illustrated here by throwing into a chain the class number of the book whose main entry is given as example 22 in section 821. For every book, the class index heading should also be derived from the class numbers in all its cross references entries. Care should be taken that the same cross reference entry is not made in the catalogue more than once.

881 Chain for the Class Number in Example 22

Y = Sociology
↓ (Sought heading)
Y7 = Ethnology
↓ (Sought heading)
Y73 = Ethnic groups
↓ (Sought heading)
Y738 = Gypsy
↓ (Sought heading)
Y738:3 = Equipment of gypsies
↓ (Sought heading)
Y738:32 = Utensils of gypsies
↓ (Sougth heading)
Y738:325 = Drinking vessels of gypsies
(Sought heading)

882 Chain for the Class Number in Example 23

Y = Sociology
↓ (Sought heading) (But already written)
Y7 = Ethnology
↓ (Sought heading) (But already written)
Y7*v* = History of Ethnology
↓ (Sought heading)
Y7*v*1 = History of ethnology in the world
↓ (Sought heading)
Y7*v*1'N5 = History of ethnology in the world brought up to 1950's
(Unsought heading)

ANNEXURE 1

Conversion Table

In case the translators of this book into the Indian languages wish to use Indian script for Class Numbers, it is desirable that all the languages should adopt the same or the equivalent symbols to represent a Class. To facilitate this, a conversion table is given in this section to convert a Class Number from Roman script into Devanagari script. The phonetic equivalent of any letter in any other language will be obvious. The "alphabet with anusvara" is used to represent lower case letters of the Roman script. In a Dravidian language, the equivalent of "anusvara" will have to come after, instead of on the top of, the host letter. We would recommend that the Indo-Arabic numeral may be retained without being converted into Devanagari or Dravidian numerals.

इ	A	*a*	इं
उ	AZ		
ए	B	*b*	एं
क	BZ		
कि	C	*c*	किं
कु	D	*d*	कुं
के	E	*e*	कें
कै	F	*f*	कैं
च	G	*g*	चं
चि	H	*h*	चिं
चु	HX		
ट	I	*i*	टं
टि	J	*j*	टिं
टु	JX		
टे	K	*k*	टुं
टै	KX		
त	L	*l*	तं
ति	LX		
तु	M	*m*	तुं
न	M(ZZY)		
नि	M(ZZZ)		
नु	Δ		
ने	N	*n*	नें
प	NZ		
पि	O	*o*	पिं
पु	P	*p*	पुं
म	Q	*q*	मं
मि	R	*r*	मिं
मु	S	*s*	मुं
र	SZ		
रि	T	*t*	रिं
रु	U	*u*	रुं
ल	V	*v*	लिं
लि	W	*w*	लुं
लु	WX		
ले	X	*x*	लें
व	XX		
वि	Y	*y*	वं
वु	YZ		
वे	Z	*z*	वें

ANNEXURE 2

Glossary of Library Terms

English — Sanskrit

This glossary gives Sanskrit equivalents of Library-terms to facilitate the formation of cognate terms in the several Indian languages and the rendering of this book into those languages.

Accession	परिग्रहण
— number	—संख्या
Act	विधि
Adaptation	प्रकारान्तर
Adaptor	—कार
Added entry	अतिरिक्त-संलेख
Additional	अतिरिक्त
Administration	संचालन
Alphabetical sequence	वर्णक्रम
Alphabetization	वर्णक्रमण
Alternative	अवान्तर
— title	—आख्या
Arrangement	व्यवस्थापन
Array	पंक्ति
Artificial composite book	कृत्रिम समासित-ग्रन्थ
Assistant	सहायक
Author	ग्रन्थकार
Author-analytical	—विश्लेषक-संलेख
Author-catalogue	—सूची
Auxiliary title	उपाख्या
Bay guide	खात-दर्शक
Bespoken book	प्रतिश्रुत-ग्रन्थ
Bibliography	वाङ्मय-सूची
Binding	संपुटन
— collection	—कक्षा
Bipartite	द्विभागिक
Book card	पुस्तक-पत्रक
— index entry	—निर्देशी-संलेख

ANNEXURE 2

Book number	पुस्तक-चिह्न
— selection	पुस्तक-वरण
— ticket	—चिटिका
Borrower	विसेव्य
Branch library	शाखा-ग्रन्थालय
Business library	कार्यभार-ग्रन्थालय
Call number	क्रामक-संख्या
Canon	उपसूत्र
Canonical sequence	संप्रदाय-क्रम
Card	पत्रक
— catalogue	—सूची
Catalogue	सूची
Cataloguer	सूचीकार
Cataloguing	सूचीकरण
Caution money	प्रातिभाव्य-धन
Chain	परंपरा
— procedure	—रीति
Changed title	परिवृत्ताख्या
Characteristic	भेदक
Charged tray	आरोपित-पात्रक
Charging	आरोपण
— tray	—पात्रक
Chronological sequence	कालक्रम
Circulation	संचारण
City central library	नगर-केन्द्र-ग्रन्थालय
Class	वर्ग
— index entry	—निर्देशी-संलेख
— number	—संख्या
Classic	चिरगहन-ग्रन्थ
Classification	वर्गीकरण
Classificationist	वर्गाचार्य
Classified catalogue	अनुवर्ग-सूची
— sequence	—क्रम
Classifier	वर्गकार
Code	कल्प
Co-extensiveness	समव्यापकत्व
Collaborator	सहकार
Collection	कक्षा

Collection symbol	कक्षा-संख्या
College library	महाविद्यालय-ग्रन्थालय
Colon	द्विबिन्दु
— Classification	—वर्गीकरण
Colophon	पुष्पिका
Commentator	भाष्यकार
Compilation	समवाय
Compiler	संग्राहक
Composite book	समासित-ग्रन्थ
Compound name	—नाम
Connecting symbol	योजक-चिह्न
Contribution	अंशग्रन्थ
Contributor	अंशकार
index entry	—निर्देशी-संलेख
Co-ordinate	समपंक्ति
Corporate author	समष्टि-ग्रन्थकार
— body	समष्टि
Cross reference	अन्तर्विषयी
— — entry	—संलेख
— — index entry	नामान्तर-निर्देशी-संलेख
Date guide	तिथिदर्शक
— label	—पत्र
Dater	तिथ्यङ्कक
Decimal classification	दशमलव-वर्गीकरण
Delivery station	समर्पण-प्रतिष्ठान
Derived composite term	यौगिक-समासित-पद
Dictionary	अनुवर्ण
— catalogue	—सूची
Digit	अङ्क
Director	निर्देशक
Directory	निर्देशिका
Discharging	अकरोपण
— tray	—पात्रक
— work	—कार्य
Donation number	दान-संख्या
Due date	देयतिथि
Duplicate ticket	प्रति-चिटिका

ANNEXURE 2

Editing	संपादन
Edition	आवृत्ति
Editor	सम्पादक
Encyclopaedia	विश्वकोश
Entrance	प्रवेश
Entry (Catalogue)	संलेख
Epitomizer	संक्षेपक
Evolutionary sequence	विकास-क्रम
Extract	भागोद्ग्रह
Exchange list	विनिमय-सूची
Exit	निर्गम
Facet	मुख
Facet-formula	—परिसूत्र
Fascicule	अवदान
Filiation	ज्ञातेयता
Filiatory	ज्ञाति
— sequence	—क्रम
First vertical	प्रथमोर्ध्व-रेखा
Five Laws of Library Science	ग्रन्थालय-शास्त्र-पंचसूत्री
Focus	लक्ष्य
Formula	परिसूत्र
Function	धर्म
Fundamental	मौलिक
— constituent term	—घटक-पद
Furniture	उपस्कर
Gangway guide	अन्तर्मार्ग-दर्शक
Generalia class	सर्व-वर्ग
Gate register	द्वारपञ्जिका
Geographical facet	प्रदेश-मुख
— sequence	—क्रम
Guarantee	प्रतिभावित
Guarantor	प्रतिभू
Guide	दर्शक
— card	—पत्रक
Half-title	लघु-आख्या
Heading	शीर्षक

Helpful sequence	अनुकूल-क्रम
Horizontal line	सम-रेखा
Impression	अङ्कन
Imprint	मुद्रणांक
Inclusive notation	समाविशाङ्कन
Index	निर्देशी
— entry	—संलेख
Initionym	अग्राक्षर-नाम
Issue	निर्गम
— (of periodicals)	अवदान
— counter	निर्गम-स्थान
Job	क्रिया
—, Immediate	सद्यःक्रिया
Joint author	सहग्रन्थकार
— editor	सहसम्पादक
Later title	पराख्या
Leading line	अग्र
— section	अग्रानुच्छेद
Librarian	ग्रन्थालयी
Library	ग्रन्थालय
— hand	—लिपि
Loan	उद्धरण
Long-range reference	व्याप्त-अनुलय-सेवा
Main class	मुख्य-वर्ग
— entry	—संलेख
Maintenance section	प्रदशक-गण
Member	विसेव्य
Membership card	—चिटिका
Multi-faceted	बहुमुख-
Multifocal	बहुलक्ष्य
Multivolumed	बहुसंपुटक
National Central Library	राष्ट्रीय-केन्द्र-ग्रन्थालय
Notation	अङ्कन
Note	टिप्पण

Number	संख्या
— (of a periodical)	अवदान
Octave principle	अष्टकरीति
Off-print	उन्मुद्रण
Open access	आसङ्ग
— notation	मुक्ताङ्कन
Ordering	आदेशन
Ordinal number	क्रम-संख्या
Ordinary composite book	सहज-समासित-ग्रन्थ
Organization	संघटन
Overdue	अतिदेय
Pamphlet	पुस्तिका
Parallel movement	समगति
Parody	अनुकार
Part	भाग
Penultimate	उपान्त्य
Periodical	सावदान
Periodical publication	सामयिक
Personal author	व्यक्ति-ग्रन्थकार
Personnel	कर्तृगण
Phase	संश्लेष
— relation	—सम्बन्ध
Phased	संश्लिष्ट
Planning	आयोजन
Principle of Parallel Movement	समगति-न्याय
Problem facet	प्रमेय-मुख
Procedure	रीति
Pseudonym	कैतव-नाम
Public library	सर्वजन-ग्रन्थालय
Public Libraries Act	सर्वजन-ग्रन्थालय-विधि
Rack	ग्रन्थाधार
Reader	सेव्य
—, Inside	आसेव्य
Reader, Outside	विसेव्य
Reader's ticket	—चिटिका
Ready reference service	प्रस्तुत-अनुलय-सेवा

Recto	पत्रमुख
Reference librarian	अनुलयी
— service	अनुलय-सेवा
Regional school library	विद्यालय-मण्डल-ग्रन्थालय
Regulation	नियम
Reprint	उन्मुद्रण
Reprinted	पुनर्मुद्रित
Research library	गवेषणा-ग्रन्थालय
Reserved collection	निहित-कक्षा
Return	प्रत्यावर्तन
— counter	—स्थान
— date	—तिथि
Reviser	संशोधक
Room	शाला
Routine	परिपाटी
Rule	धारा
Rural central library	ग्रामीण-केन्द्र-ग्रन्थालय
Scheme	पद्धति
School library	विद्यालय-ग्रन्थालय
Second vertical	द्वितीयोर्ध्वरेखा
Serial	निरवदान
— number	मालिकसंख्या
Series	माला
— note	—टिप्पण
Set	संघांत
Schedule	तालिका
Shelf	फलक
— arrangement	ग्रन्थव्यवस्थापन
— guide	फलक-दर्शक
— register	ग्रन्थ-पञ्जिका
— section	प्रदर्शक-गण
— work	प्रदर्शन-कार्य
Short title	लघु आख्या
Simple book	साधारण-ग्रन्थ
Single-volumed	एकसंपुटक
Sorting	विमिश्रण
— tray	—पात्रक
Special cross reference entry	विशेष-अन्तर्विषयी-संलेख

Specific subject	विशिष्ट-विषय
Stack	चयन
— room	—शाला
Staff	कर्तृगण
Standard	मानक
— card	मानित-पत्रक
Standing vendor	स्थायी-विक्रेता
State central library	राज्य-केन्द्र-ग्रन्थालय
Statistics register	गणन-पञ्जिका
Subheading	उपशीर्षक
Subject analytical	विषय-विश्लेषक-संलेख
— matter	प्रतिपाद्य-विषय
Subordinate	परंपरित
Substance facet	पदार्थमुख
Successive	क्रमागत
Supply	पूर्ति
Symbol	प्रतिरूप
System	प्रणाली
Tab	पत्रक-दर्शक
Table (of entries)	सारिणी
Tag	ग्रन्थ-दर्शक
Technical work	निरूपण-कार्य
Temporary collection	अस्थायी-कक्षा
Theory	सिद्धान्त
Three-phased	द्विसंश्लिष्ट
Tier guide	भूमिदर्शक
Title	आख्या
Title-page	आख्या-पत्र
— Back of the	— —पृष्ठ
Train	श्रेणी
Translator	भाषान्तरकार
Travelling library	जङ्गम:ग्रन्थालय
Tray	पात्रक
Two-phased	एकसंश्लिष्ट
Unifocal	एकलक्ष्यक
Unipartite	एकभागिक
University library	विश्वविद्यालय-ग्रन्थालय

Vendor	विक्रेता
Verso	पत्रपृष्ठ
Vertical file	ऊर्ध्वलम्ब-अनुयोग
Volume	संपुट
Who's who	नामवृत्त
Wicket gate	यान्त्रिकद्वार
Work	ग्रन्थ

ANNEXURE 3

BIBLIOGRAPHY

Note: 1 The reference after the serial number is to the number of the section in this book, where the reference occurs.

2 Except where otherwise stated, the author of the book or article is S R Ranganathan.

1. Sec 02. From the publisher to the reader: Work flow in university and college libraries. 1958 (Mimeographed by the University Grants Commission of India).
2. Sec 03. Five laws of library science. Ed 1, 1931. Ed 2, 1957.
3. „ Preface to library science. 1948.
4. „ Colon classification. Ed 1, 1933. Ed 5, 1957.
5. „ Prolegomena to library classification. Ed 1, 1937. Ed 2, 1957.
6. „ Library classification: Fundamentals and procedure. 1944.
7. „ Elements of library classification. 1945.
8. „ Classification of Marathi literature. 1945.
9. „ Classification of Telegu literature. 1947.
10. „ Philosophy of library classification. 1951.
11. „ Classification and communication. 1951.
12. „ Depth classification (a symposium). 1953.
13. „ Classification of management. 1956.
14. „ Classification terminology: A glossary. 1958.
15. „ Classified catalogue code. Ed 1, 1934. Ed 4, 1958.
16. „ Theory of library catalogue. 1938.
17. „ Dictionary catalogue code. Ed 1, 1945. Ed 2, 1952.
18. „ Library catalogue: Fundamentals and procedure. 1950.
19. „ Anuvarga-suchi-kalpa. 1952.
20. „ Headings and canons: Comparative study of five catalogue codes. 1955.
21. „ Library administration. Ed 1, 1935. Ed 2, 1959.
22. „ Reference service and bibliography (with C Sundaram). 1940.
23. „ Bibliography of reference books and bibliographies (with K M Sivaraman). 1941.

24. Sec 03. Library book selection. 1952.
25. „ Social bibliography: Physical bibliography for librarians, authors, and publishers. 1952.
26. „ Social education literature. 1952.
27. Sec 04. Abgila (quarterly). 1949-1953 (The Annals part alone continued as 28)
28. „ Annals of library science (quarterly). 1954.
29. „ Classification and international documentation. 1948.
30. „ Classification, coding, and machinery for search. 1950.
31. „ Public library provision and documentation problems (a symposium). 1951.
32. Sec 05. School and college libraries. 1942.
33. „ Organisation of libraries. Ed 1, 1946. Ed 2, 1956.
34. Sec 061. Library legislation: A handbook to Madras Library Act. 1953.
35. Sec 062. Model Library Act. 1931.
36. „ Model Public Library Bill. 1941.
37. „ Post-war reconstruction of libraries in India. 1944.
38. „ National library system: A plan for India. 1946.
39. „ Library development plan with a draft library bill for Bombay. 1947.
40. „ Library development plan with a draft library bill for United Provinces. 1949.
41. „ Library development plan for India with draft library bills for the Union and the constituent States. 1950.
42. „ Library personality and library bill: West Bengal. 1958.
43. Sec 073. Library development plan for India. 1950. Chap 5.
44. Sec 078. Library terminology (with M L Nagar). (Annals of library science, 1, 1950, 43-48, 70-72, 94-96, 150-152.)
45. Sec 108. Five laws of library science.
46. Sec 111. TAGORE (Rabindra Nath). What makes a library big ? (Library movement by diverse hands. 1929. Essay 1. Published by the Madras Library Association.)
47. Sec 118. Social education literature. 1952.

48. Sec 124. Literature for neo-literates (Proceedings of a Seminar). 1954.

49. Sec 145. Library administration. Sec 144 and 145.

50. Sec 146. Headings and canons. Sec 93.

51. Sec 155. Library administration. Sec 1145.

52. Sec 213. First All Asia Educational Conference, papers offered to the Library Service Section. 1930. 429.

53. Sec 214. AMERICAN Library Association, Library Extension Board. Library extension, a study of public library conditions and needs. 1926. 102.

54. Sec 224. MCCOLVIN (Lionel Roy): Library extension work and publicity. 1927. 179-180.

55. Sec 225. Bulletin, American Library Association. 24, 1930, 459.

56. Sec 242. Annual report, Madras Library Association. 5. 1933. Sec 16.11 and annexure 13.

57. Sec 2441. MCCOLVIN (Lionel Roy). Library extension and publicity. 1927. 142.

58. Sec 254. Annual report, Madras Library Association. 31, 1959. Sec 5.3.61.

59. Sec 257. *Ibid*. Annexure 5.

60. Sec 311. RIDER (Fremont). Compact book storage. 1949.

61. Sec 312. Adelphi. 16. Nov 1939. 44-46.

62. Sec 312. TOWNSEND (FRANK). Earth. 1935. 83.

63. ,, Reference service and bibliography.

64. Sec 333. TAGORE (Rabindra Nath). The scavenger.

65. Sec 352. Reference service and bibliography. Chap 13, 23, 33 and 34.

66. Sec 361. JAST (L Stanley). Libraries and living. 1932. 154.

67. Sec 3762. BROCKINGTON (A Allen). Mysticism and poetry: On a basis of experience. 1934. 26-28.

68. Sec 384. Highways and by ways of reference books (with K M Sivaraman). (Memoirs, Madras Library Association, 1941, 131-141.)

69. Sec 385. DATE (Y R). Marathi encyclopaedia. (Memoirs, Madras Library Association, 1941, 122-126.)

70. Sec 632. Library tour 1958, Europe and America: Impressions and reflections. 1950. Sec 344.

71. Sec 641. Annual report, Madras Library Association. 31. 1959. Annexure 5.
72. Sec 647. BLOSS (Meredith). Libraries without books? (ALA bulletin, 53, 1959, 201).
73. Sec 663. Library tour 1958, Europe and America: Impressions and reflections. 1950. Sec 33.
74. Sec 683. Library legislation: Handbook to Madras Library Act, 1953. Sec 31:44.
75. Sec 685. Library personality and library bill: West Bengal, 1950. Sec 3.
76. Sec 712. KYLE (Barbara). Drafting general classification. (Review of documentation, 26, 1959, 17,18.)
77. „ PALMER (Bernard Ira) and Wells (Arthur James). Fundamentals of library classification. 1951. 109.
78. Sec 713. BLISS (Henry Evelyn). Organisation of knowledge in libraries. Ed 2, 1939. 299.
79. Sec 7131. PHILLIPS (Howard W). Primer of book classification. 1933. 122-126.
80. Sec 7134. SAYERS (W C Berwick). (Years work in librarianship. 6, 1933. 133.)
81. Sec 7136. Prolegomena to library classification. Ed 2, 1957. Sec 1875.
82. Sec 7137. PARKHI (R S), *Tr*. Dvibindu vargikarana paddhathi. 1957.
83. „ Granthalaya prakriya (with M L Nagar). 1951. Chap 5.
84. Sec 7141. BLISS (Henry Evelyn). Organisation of knowledge in libraries. Ed 2, 1939. 228-229.
85. „ Library Association record, ser 3, 3, 1933, 249.
86. Sec 715. Library Association record, ser 4, 1, 1934, 98.
87. „ FOSKETT (D J). Modern trends in classification. (International Congress of Libraries and Documentation Centres, Brussels, 1955. 2B. Communications. 99.)
88. „ CLASSIFICATION RESEARCH GROUP (London). Need for a faceted classification as the basis of all methods of information retrievably. [Proceedings of the Study Conference on Classification for Information Retrieval, Dorking, England. 1957. Appendix 2. Also published as Unesco (IAC Doc

Ter PAS) document 320/5515, 26 May 1955].

89. Sec 770. Postulational approach to faceted classification. (Depth classification 29) (Annals of library science. 5. 1958. 33-51) and Elements of library classification. Ed 3. 1961. chap N.

90. Sec 817. QUINN (Henry A). Library cataloguing. 23-24.

91. Sec 818. Heading and canons. 1955. Sec 4113, 4123, 4313, 432.

92. " SAYERS (W C Berwick). Manual of classification for librarians and bibliographers. Ed 3. 1955. 336.

93. " SPALDING (C Summer) in the Library information bulletin of the Library of Congress, 18, 1959, 268.

INDEX

Note: 1. The index number is the number of the part, chapter, or section of the occurrence of the item indexed.

2. The following contractions are used:
def = defined *illust* = illustrated *irt* = in relation to